D1447194

DUDLEY MURPHY, HOLLYWOOD WILD CARD

This book was published with assistance from the

Margaret S. Harding Memorial Endowment,

which honors the first director of the
University of Minnesota Press.

DUDLEY MURPHY,
HOLLYWOOD WILD CARD

Susan Delson

UNIVERSITY OF MINNESOTA PRESS

MINNEAPOLIS • LONDON

Published by the University of Minnesota Press
111 Third Avenue South, Suite 290
Minneapolis, MN 55401-2520
http://www.upress.umn.edu

Library of Congress Cataloging-in-Publication Data

Delson, Susan.
Dudley Murphy, Hollywood wild card / Susan Delson.
p. cm.
Filmography of Dudley Murphy: p.
Includes bibliographical references and index.
ISBN-13: 978-0-8166-4654-8 (hc/j : alk. paper)
ISBN-10: 0-8166-4654-6 (hc/j : alk. paper) 1. Murphy, Dudley, 1897–1968.
2. Motion picture producers and directors—United States—Biography. I. Title.
PN1998.3.M873.D45 2006
791.4302′33092—dc22
[B]
2006011665

Printed in the United States of America on acid-free paper

The University of Minnesota is an equal-opportunity educator and employer.

14 13 12 11 10 09 08 07 06   10 9 8 7 6 5 4 3 2 1

FOR *Jeff*

CONTENTS

AT THE EDGE
OF THE FRAME

In January 1966, two years before he died, Dudley Murphy sat down to recollect his life. Most likely he spoke his thoughts into a tape recorder; the resulting manuscript has a conversational air and not much structure. Typos and misspellings imply a transcriber with little knowledge of film history, art, or French—all of which, as it happens, are essential to his story.

It's a life that reads like a picaresque novel interspersed with movies. "I feel I have been so fortunate to have been in what I call the creative centers of the world at the right time," he wrote.[1] And he was. He moved effortlessly from Greenwich Village bohemia to avant-garde Paris, the Harlem Renaissance, Hollywood, and beyond. Tall, blond, and charming, he was a cheerfully wide-ranging philanderer with little thought for the consequences. For him, scrapes and scandals were normal background noise, from courtroom dramas to love-crazed divorcées. Looking back on his life, *mad* and *gay* (in the giddy, nonsexual sense of the term) were among his favorite adjectives.

As a filmmaker, Murphy was something of a provocateur—erratic, messy, even irritating, but an envelope pusher nonetheless. Impulsive and extemporaneous, he alternated between industry insider and outsider, playing both roles with zeal if not always finesse. At a time when the classical Hollywood film form was rapidly solidifying, he determinedly pursued a looser, more evocative style. As mainstream moviemaking was straitened by an increasingly narrative approach, Murphy envisioned a different kind of cinema—turning out, among other things, the equivalent of modern music videos in an obscure technology that lasted barely three years. Swerving in and out of the studio system, he was an early independent, searching out alternatives not only to the system but to Hollywood itself, attempting to set up production centers in New York, London, and Mexico City.

Even for a provocateur, though, his track record is disconcertingly uneven. Active from the 1920s through the 1940s, Murphy was the guiding intelligence behind some of the key films in early twentieth-century cinema and some of the worst clunkers the screen has ever seen. With artist Fernand Léger and others, he made *Ballet mécanique,* one of the seminal works of avant-garde cinema, then followed with the lamentable *Alex the Great.* He was responsible for blues great Bessie Smith's sole appearance on film and the dismal *Confessions of a Co-ed.* His filmography is studded with intriguing projects: he directed Paul Robeson in *The Emperor Jones,* had a hand in shaping Tod Browning's *Dracula,* and, over David O. Selznick's objections, gave Bing Crosby one of his first appearances on-screen. He adapted unconventional Broadway productions to film and made melodramas in Mexico. Collaborating with William Faulkner, he tried, unsuccessfully, to bring one of the author's most challenging novels to the screen. In between, he turned out forgettable Hollywood fodder. Throughout, he struggled to express a filmic vision that ran utterly against the grain of the industry in which, against improbable odds, he hoped for stellar success.

Formulated at the height of the silent era, Murphy's aesthetic was visually oriented and musically inspired. In the face of an industry style that valued story and character above all, his approach foregrounded visual wit and the pleasures of spectatorship, from kaleidoscopic imagery to visual rhymes and analogies. For him, music wasn't merely accompaniment but an organizing principle. It was a type of filmmaking that intelligently synthesized the best of what silent and sound film had to offer, and it was emphatically not what Hollywood was looking for. Insofar as he could, he resisted the drive toward narrative-dominated film that overtook the studios after sound. He was by no means the only one to do so; many of the industry's most gifted filmmakers resisted the shift with all the skills at their disposal. Few, however, fought it as both independents and studio directors or continued skirmishing for quite as long. Murphy's relationship to the film industry was uncomfortable at best, and his fit into film history has been little better. We don't know what to make of him or of an output so startlingly diverse, so uneven and discontinuous.

This is precisely what makes him interesting. By its nature, Murphy's career calls into question the basic oppositions that have shaped our understanding of cinema and its history: avant-garde versus mass entertainment, art versus business, highbrow versus low. Disordered as it is, his output reveals a sensibility that's instructively at odds with classical Hollywood film form; there's something to be gleaned from all that chaos. From the beginning of his career to the end, Murphy wanted to make films that could stand as both works of art and popular commercial hits. In his relative success at the outset—with early works such as *Soul of the Cypress* and *Danse Macabre*—and the increasing difficulties he faced as his career progressed, we can trace not only Murphy's own history but also, from a highly focused perspective, the evolution of the film industry. In the years that he was active, film became an avant-garde art form, the Hollywood studio system developed and consolidated, vaudeville surrendered to the movies, and sound film irrevocably succeeded silent. To one extent or another, he played a part in these events.

But the broader significance of Murphy's career lies beyond the edge of the film frame, where cinema overlaps with other areas of early twentieth-century culture. At a time when the American film industry was rigidly parochial in its worldview, Murphy pushed the boundaries, looking beyond mainstream culture for his subjects and directing some of the earliest commercial films to feature black actors in leading roles. His vision extended beyond the conventions of the industry in terms of who deserved the camera's attention as well as how films were made, distributed, and shown. He had distinct ideas of what the medium could and should do with respect to formal experimentation, technological innovation, and cultivating the tastes of moviegoing audiences. His career is of interest both for the films he managed to make and for the tantalizing projects that were never realized, from individual films to cooperative production ventures.

Was Murphy a "good" filmmaker? This traditional question is perhaps less illuminating, and less useful, than a more open-ended inquiry into his work. A close reading of Murphy's career—his accomplishments and failures, innovative ideas and half-baked schemes—offers insights into the development of film in the early twentieth century, as well as how we've come to think about it, and how that thinking has determined whose contributions count. By refusing to dismiss him, we implicitly call into question the assumptions that have relegated him to obscurity. In the canon of film history, Murphy is easily classed as an also-ran, but that reflexive judgment does a disservice to film history, if not to Murphy himself. In searching out the larger cultural logic of his disjointed career, we arrive at a broader understanding of not only film history but how it's reckoned, not only cinema but the modernity that nurtured it.

Murphy himself is of some help in the process, though not as much as one might expect. For someone whose recollections filled eighty-odd pages of typewritten manuscript, he remains a surprisingly elusive figure. He seldom reflected on his own filmmaking to a degree that would satisfy a scholar and rarely addressed questions that cry out for elaboration: exactly how *Ballet mécanique* was made, for instance, or why he was so drawn to depicting African Americans on-screen. Even his randiest anecdotes carry a whiff of genteel reticence. Guided by his memoir, the life story that unfolds here is pieced together from many sources, ranging from personal correspondence to long-forgotten gossip columns; what unfolds along with it is a dazzling slice of cultural history.

Murphy was born and bred in the Boston area and made most of his important films in New York. But he belonged, in the truest sense, to Los Angeles, with an Angeleno's knack for self-invention, reinvention, and spin. Through him, we see the nineteenth century giving way to the twentieth and modernity remaking American culture, starting in L.A. Murphy's struggle to establish himself as a filmmaker may be equally understood as a struggle to master the basics of a new cultural and economic structure—one for which mass-media entertainment, public relations, and the cult of celebrity were essential building blocks. The son of artists, he saw film as one art form among many and himself as a creative individual in cultural milieux that extended from Los Angeles to New York and Paris. At one time or another, he collaborated with Ezra Pound, Man Ray, Duke Ellington, architect Richard Neutra, and a good percentage of the Algonquin Round Table. He talked montage theory with Sergei Eisenstein and got drunk with James Joyce. Charlie Chaplin turned up at his parties; Dashiell Hammett was a poker-game regular. Fats Waller purportedly worked out arrangements at the piano in Murphy's New York penthouse, and at Murphy's instigation what became the only surviving North American mural by Mexican artist David Alfaro Siqueiros was painted in the yard of his Los Angeles home. In a low-key, informal way, Murphy was a catalyst, and his life story is a careening ride, as mad and gay as he could make it, through the cultural landscape of the early twentieth century. He never pulled off the brilliant coup that would have rocketed him into the Hollywood stratosphere, but the fates were kind, and in the end he landed on his feet, lightly. At every turn, film, art, and life inter-twined furiously. He wouldn't have had it any other way.

On the title page of his memoir Murphy wrote, by hand, two inscrip-tions. The first quotes the crewman Stubb in Herman Melville's *Moby Dick:* "I know not all that may be coming, but be [it] what it will, I'll go to it laughing." The second is his own: "Have one on the house." If one is an epitaph, the other is an invitation. By all means, belly up to the bar. It's a good story.

CHAPTER I

ROOTED IN ART

In the early years of Hollywood, when Murphy began his career, the path into the film business was often meandering and unpredictable. For him, the route led through electrical engineering, military aviation, and the mysticism that was already percolating through Southern California. But it began, and was most firmly rooted, in art. Dudley Bowles Murphy was born in 1897 in Winchester, Massachusetts, on the northwestern edge of greater Boston. On his father's side, he came from old New England and Irish stock. His mother's family hailed from the South.

Both parents were artists. They met in Paris in the 1890s while studying at the Académie Julian, a private art school that counted Henri Matisse and Pierre Bonnard among its students. Murphy's father, Hermann Dudley Murphy (1867–1945), achieved a certain renown as a member of the Boston School, a group of impressionist-influenced painters active through the 1930s.

For American artists of the 1890s, European training was virtually obligatory, and the Académie Julian was a popular Paris destination. Originally founded in 1868 to prepare students for admission to the fiercely competitive École des Beaux-Arts, by the late 1880s the Académie had acquired a reputation as a center for impressionism and modernism in general. It was one of the few such institutions to admit women, putting them on an equal footing with, if largely separate from, the men.

Murphy's mother, Caroline H. Bowles Murphy (1868–1923), thrived in this emancipated environment. In his memoir, Murphy described her as "a free thinker, having friends like Emma Goldman."[1] If Bowles Murphy was radical in her thinking, she came by it naturally. Her southern-born father, John Bowles (1832–1900), had been an ardent abolitionist in Lawrence, Kansas, in the 1850s, and during the Civil War served as a lieutenant colonel in an African-American unit, the First Kansas Volunteer Infantry Regiment (Colored). As Murphy recalled, he later became a scout for wagon trains en route to California.[2] In 1892, Bowles wrote *The Stormy Petrel,* a melodramatic adventure novel based on his Kansas experiences. Among the papers he left at his death were the text for a talk, "The Standard of Success in Business," given in the 1890s at a spiritual retreat hotel in Maine, and an unfinished story about a rocket expedition to Mars.

Hermann's antecedents were, by contrast, more prosaic. On his mother's side he descended from a bedrock New England family, the Ladds of New Hampshire. His father, Daniel Murphy, no more than a generation removed from Ireland, was a self-made man who achieved solid success as a shoe manufacturer in Stoneham, a few miles east of Winchester.

In the early 1900s, American art was just beginning to shake off the overwhelming influence of Europe, and artists were fighting for recognition, not only for themselves, but also for American styles and subjects. Throughout the Northeast, cities were coping with rapid industrialization, waves of immigration, and exploding populations, and artists were quick to respond to these trends. In Philadelphia and New York, for instance, an informal movement of urban painters later dubbed "the Ashcan School" looked to portray city life in all its boisterous vitality. Renouncing the academic pretensions of American art at the time, painters such as Robert Henri, George Luks, and John Sloan chose as their subjects working-class street scenes, rough-and-tumble boxing matches, and other gritty urban themes. In New York, photographer Alfred Stieglitz's modernist 291 Gallery introduced American audiences to the work of such artists as Henri Matisse and Auguste Rodin.

The battle for modern art, however, was not waged in Boston. In the 1880s, local artists and collectors had been among the first in America to embrace the bold new art of impressionism. But at the turn of the century, Boston was on its way to becoming an artistic backwater, and by 1910, its adventurous streak had petered out completely. Well into the 1920s and 1930s, the city's deep conservatism and unswerving loyalty to such favorite artists as John Singer Sargent and Claude Monet—early Monet, that is— had a stifling effect on artistic growth. The strongest local artists, such as Childe Hassam and Maurice Prendergast, shot off to New York at the earliest opportunity, and even its most progressive collectors showed little interest in acquiring anything really new. Most Boston School artists came from the same tight-knit, privileged background. Sharing similar views and values, they were an insular community, comfortably cushioned by status and wealth. "Although familiar with other parts of the United States and Europe," observed art historian Trevor Fairbrother, "they believed that Boston had everything they could ever wish for, and preferred to paint at home."[3]

This, then, was the artistic community to which the Murphys returned from Paris in the late 1890s. Married in 1895, they were comfortably settled in Winchester by the time Dudley was born in 1897.

Many Boston School painters, such as Frank Benson and William Paxton, drew inspiration from the French impressionists. Others revered the local favorite, John Singer Sargent. Unlike his colleagues, Hermann Dudley Murphy was most strongly influenced by James McNeill Whistler. Whistler's art emphasized subtle tonal relationships and a sense of harmony akin to music; terms like *symphony, harmony,* and *nocturne* appear in many of his painting titles. Following Whistler's lead, Hermann painted evocative, near-abstract seascapes in a subtle, muted palette. In Fairbrother's estimation, he was one of the most innovative landscape artists working in Boston at the time.

Like Whistler, Hermann was influenced by the Arts and Crafts movement, and he and Caroline were among the founding members of the Winchester Arts and Crafts Society. Originating in Britain in the second half of the nineteenth century, the movement was an artistic response to advancing industrialization and machine-made goods. Quickly spreading to continental Europe and the United States, it emphasized handmade craftsmanship, uncluttered design, and unity between architecture and the fine and decorative arts. Like Whistler and other artists influenced by the movement, Hermann considered the frame to be an integral aspect of his artistic statement, and he designed and made the frames for many of his paintings.

As an artist, Hermann enjoyed a comfortable, conservative career. He presented solo exhibitions in Boston, New York, Detroit, St. Louis, and other cities and was awarded prizes at many international expositions— prominent venues for art at that time—including the 1901 Pan-American Exposition, the 1904 Louisiana Purchase Exposition, in St. Louis, and the 1915 Panama-Pacific International Exposition, in San Francisco. (He also exhibited work in the New York Armory Show of 1913 but was eclipsed, with most other artists, by the fracas over Marcel Duchamp's *Nude Descending a Staircase,* which made its American debut there.) By 1902, Hermann had joined the faculty of Harvard's School of Architecture, where he taught drawing until 1937. Over time, his art was acquired by the Museum of Fine Arts, Boston, the Art Institute of Chicago, the Fine Arts Museums of San Francisco, and other institutions. Today, his work is still handled by a small number of private galleries and occasionally turns up at auction.

Despite his own privileged upbringing, Hermann inherited his father's enterprising nature. In addition to teaching at Harvard and pursuing his art, Hermann's interest in integrating frames and paintings led him to establish a frame-making workshop in partnership with Maurice Prendergast's brother, Charles Prendergast.[4] Set up in the basement of Hermann's newly built home and studio complex on Highland Avenue, it was called the Carrig-Rohane Shop, after Hermann's Celtic name for the house. Business flourished, and the firm was soon making hand-carved frames for Childe Hassam, William Merritt Chase, and other prominent artists.[5] Though Hermann sold his share in the company in 1917, his influence on American framing greatly surpassed his impact on American art.[6]

An undated self-portrait depicts Hermann as a lean, lanky man with red hair and beard, gazing intently at the viewer. At six-foot-six, he topped his grown son by a good two inches. A champion sailing canoeist, he was a passionate outdoorsman his entire life. Murphy inherited his father's fair coloring and fine-boned, long-legged physique. Murphy's older children, Michael and Poco, called their stiff, glowering grandfather Big Man (though never to his face). Murphy called him Pops. Through much of his career, Murphy publicly emphasized the link to his father, often to establish his own credentials as a creator of "artistic" films. As an ongoing source of financial support and a powerful if contested influence, Hermann was a significant figure in Murphy's life until his death in 1945.

Though Murphy's childhood at Carrig-Rohane was filled with art and artists, it was in other ways conventional. He attended the Milton Academy, a traditional prep school with a solid reputation. Nurturing a passion for the wireless, he became a shortwave radio enthusiast—"one of the early hams," as he put it.[7] In later life, his strongest childhood memories were of the constant friction between his parents, the conservative Hermann and free-spirited Caroline. While Dudley was still a teenager, a recently widowed girlfriend of Hermann's youth, Nellie Littlehale Umbstaetter (1867–1941), reappeared on the scene, effectively ending the Murphys' marriage in 1915. "Mother was very upset over the event of her divorce," wrote Murphy, "and practically died of a broken heart."[8] That year, Caroline moved with Dudley and his younger sister, Caroline Bowles Murphy (known as Carlene), to Southern California. In 1916, Hermann and Nellie Umbstaetter were married.

The departure of Caroline and the children mirrored a deeper split in the family. In the eyes of the conservative, traditional "East Coast Murphys," the "West Coast Murphys" quickly acquired a reputation for unorthodox, impulsive behavior bordering on recklessness. Still stinging from Hermann's desertion, the West Coast Murphys—notably Dudley—came to view all things rigid, straitlaced, and hidebound as "stuffy Bostonian." Yet Hermann's influence on Dudley was undeniable. And though Murphy went to considerable lengths to obliterate it, the Bostonian in him never entirely disappeared.

ON THE BRINK OF THE BOOM

In 1915, moving across the country to California was still a lengthy and onerous journey. Yet, Murphy's mother couldn't have chosen a better place for a fresh start. If Boston had lost its adventurous spirit, Southern California was the polar opposite, and the Murphys were among thousands who poured into the area that year.

Throughout the second half of the nineteenth century, Los Angeles had been a sleepy regional center, running a distant second to booming San Francisco. But by 1901, two different railroad companies had linked Los Angeles to the rest of the country, a deepwater port had been dredged, and a network of trolley cars connected fifty communities in four counties. In late 1913 the Los Angeles Aqueduct opened, guaranteeing an abundant, predictable water supply, and in 1914, the opening of the Panama Canal increased the city's stature as a shipping port. Eastern film companies had already discovered the advantages of Southern California weather and scenery, and the first studios were starting to take shape in local horse barns and open lots. Between 1909 and 1915, Los Angeles more than doubled in size, annexing not only Hollywood and Wilmington–San Pedro but also the entire San Fernando Valley, in what historian Kevin Starr called "the Louisiana Purchase of Los Angeles history."[9] The city had laboriously positioned itself for dramatic economic growth. In 1915, its efforts began to bear fruit. By the 1920s, it would be booming.

At the time, the population was overwhelmingly American-born and white. Between 1890 and 1920, when Los Angeles mushroomed from 50,000 to 577,000, its percentage of nonwhite population actually decreased, from 6.3 percent to 5.2.[10] In 1920, with the census topping half a million, African-American Angelenos numbered 15,579, not quite 3 percent of the population. Figures for Asian- and Mexican-born populations were comparably low.[11] In the years before the Civil War, California had enacted a fugitive slave law, and Los Angeles had always been what historian Carey McWilliams called "a 'bad town' for Negroes."[12] For many flocking to the region in the 1910s and 1920s, Southern California represented a refuge of whiteness—Anglo-Saxon, Protestant whiteness—in a time of widespread social and economic flux. "It is of this racial movement—it is of this supreme migration and consummation of Aryan energy—that Hollywood is at once the symbol and the acme," wrote novelist and screenwriter Perley Poore Sheehan in 1924. "These people of Hollywood are the Aryan last and best."[13]

Caroline and the children settled in Pasadena. Other parts of the metropolitan area were being inundated with small-town midwesterners: "'leading citizens' from Wichita; honorary pallbearers from Emmetsburg; Good Templars from Sedalia; honest spinsters from Grundy Center," as one disgruntled former *Los Angeles Times* editor put it.[14] But Pasadena in 1915 was a haven for affluent, well-educated easterners who, though they savored the region's Spanish, Mexican, and Native American traditions, spoke English—a refined, upper-class English at that.

Murphy turned eighteen the summer he moved West. His childhood enthusiasm for wireless radio had grown into an interest in electrical engineering, and shortly after arriving, he enrolled at Troop College in Pasadena (soon to become Cal Tech). He also made himself at home among the young Pasadena social set—friends to whose families he would turn, five years later, for financial backing for his first films.

It may have been a sprawling, half-formed city, but even in 1915, Greater Los Angeles wasn't entirely a cultural wasteland. In many ways, the art scene that greeted Murphy's mother wasn't all that different from the one she'd left behind in Boston. The landscape, ocean, and dazzling California light made impressionism an easy stylistic choice for local artists, linking them not to the gritty realism and radical modernity of New York but to the refined American impressionism of the Boston School. Southern California artists such as John Hubbard Rich and Donna Schuster trained with Boston School painter Edmund Tarbell at the Museum of Fine Arts, Boston. Schuster and other California painters also studied with American impressionist William Merritt Chase, both in Europe and in nearby Carmel, where Chase taught in the summer of 1914.[15]

As in Boston, the mainstream art community had little use for new schools of thought. Virtually from its beginnings in 1909, the influential California Art Club threw its weight behind representational art, impressionism in particular, eschewing anything that even hinted at modernism.[16] Following the Duchamp ruckus at the 1913 New York Armory Show, local sculptor Julia Bracken Wendt was quoted in the *Los Angeles Examiner* denouncing "the work of the decadent schools of the so-called futurists and cubists . . . let them exhibit such work in a dime museum and not in an art museum."[17]

Though reactionary, this comment points to one difference between the art worlds of Boston and Southern California in the 1910s: the active and vocal participation of women, not only in the California Art Club, but in its more forward-looking counterparts. As Murphy progressed through his freshman year at Troop, his mother, now known as Caroline Bowles, found like-minded colleagues. Among them were artists Helena Dunlap, Henrietta Shore, and Meta Cressey, three of the founding directors of the Modern Art Society, which was established in 1916. All three had studied with Ashcan School painter Robert Henri, whose art encompassed the type of urban subjects that Boston School painters rejected out of hand. While William Merritt Chase conducted his classes at Carmel, Henri had spent the summer of 1914 painting and teaching at La Jolla, and his vibrant portraits—which pointedly featured ethnically diverse subjects—had created a stir in local progressive art circles.

Settling into Southern California life, Bowles once again became part of an artistic circle. Although the Modern Art Society dissolved in 1918 after presenting two exhibitions, in 1919 Shore reorganized her colleagues into the California Progressive Group. That year, they presented an exhibition of their work, including Bowles's paintings, at the Lafayette Tea Room on South Grand Avenue.

Bowles pursued other interests as well. She enjoyed taking Carlene, a promising dancer, to Denishawn, the Los Angeles studio and school founded in 1914 by modern dance pioneers Ruth St. Denis and Ted Shawn. She was a devotee of sociology pioneer Lester Ward and organized a sociology club that regularly welcomed University of California professors to lecture on social issues. Like the Murphys, the muckraking novelist Upton Sinclair, then at the height of his renown, moved to Pasadena in 1915, and he and Caroline soon became part of the same social set.[18]

Meanwhile, Murphy completed his year at Troop in the spring of 1916. But he wasn't happy there and, against his father's advice, transferred to the Massachusetts Institute of Technology for the fall semester. Newly remarried, Hermann was not inclined to spend much time with his college-student son but kept a watchful eye on his progress. What he saw couldn't have been encouraging. Hermann disapproved of Murphy's sweetheart (and for that matter, her mother, whom he'd known in Paris), and his academic performance was far from promising. Instead of focusing on his studies, Murphy gravitated toward people in the arts. Foundering in mathematics, his interest in engineering waning, he enlisted in the aviation division of the navy in May 1917, a few weeks after the United States entered World War I and just before year-end exams at MIT. He hadn't yet turned twenty.

As a pilot, Murphy trained at the naval air facility at Squantum Point, in Quincy, Massachusetts, where he fell in with a crowd of up-and-coming young men like himself. "There were about twenty of us learning to fly," he recalled. "My friends in this group were Bill Gaston, who was from Harvard and an old Boston family; Hank Flower, who subsequently became a vice president of J. Walter Thompson; Chauncey Galoop [*sic*] (which is a fascinating name), who always amused us because in determining the direction of the wind, he would wet his finger and hold it up. But it was always in the propeller stream, so consequently he would take off in whatever direction his plane was pointing."[19] Finishing his training in Newport News, Virginia, Murphy soon shipped out to a British air base at Killingholme, in Lincolnshire. He served out the war at a succession of British and Scottish air bases, as a naval ensign flying bombing missions over the North Sea.

Wartime service brought out Murphy's daredevil streak. According to his memoir, he was credited with sinking at least one enemy submarine. He was also confined to barracks in Hull, England, for riding a motorcycle through a plate-glass window. His engineering aptitude found scope in flying whatever aircraft he could get his hands on. Between bombing runs, he thought nothing of hedge-hopping around the British countryside in an ancient single-seater Morris Farnham, "very much like sitting in the middle of a bird cage, completely surrounded by wires,"[20] or "landing a sea plane in a potato field without even scratching a potato," as Hermann described one of his exploits.[21]

Barnstorming over the North Atlantic was a far cry from trench warfare at Ypres or Verdun, and Murphy finished the war unscarred by the experiences that ravaged so many World War I veterans. Instead, he came away with a lifelong taste for piloting small aircraft and the sort of appetites that would soon set the 1920s reeling. Several pages of his memoir were devoted to post-Armistice exploits in France and in Monaco, where he swapped clothes with an obliging civilian—casinos then barring men in uniform—and headed off for a night of gambling. With a screenwriter's flair, he cast himself as the leading man in an exaggerated episode of romantic fancy. "I had read about roulette, so with my last 20 francs, I made a bet," he wrote. "As the ball was spinning, a very beautiful girl spoke to me. I turned around and talked to her. In the meantime, my number apparently had won and they had paid off, but as she was more fascinating than the board, I delayed in picking up my money and the croupier announced 'rien va plus' and I could not withdraw my winnings. But my Leprechaun was sitting on my shoulder: the number repeated and in the space of a few minutes, I now had more money than [my traveling companion] Don had with his savings for two years. Grabbing my winnings and the beautiful girl, I went back to the café, paid the civilian handsomely for his clothes and was off."[22]

Murphy's final post-Armistice caper almost cost him his military reputation. Awaiting transport from Brest, France, back to the States, he contrived to deliver a parcel of documents to the SS *Leviathan,* crammed to capacity with returning troops, just before it set sail for New York. His launch returned to port without him, and at one stroke he became an AWOL and a stowaway. Only his father's frantic exploitation of personal connections, including a United States senator and the Massachusetts governor, averted a dishonorable discharge. In early 1919, Murphy was finally demobilized to New York City. Obliged to declare a destination, he opted first for Hermann's new home in Lexington, Massachusetts. Ultimately, though, he chose Los Angeles, arriving at his mother's house with enough navy travel money left to buy a car, even then a necessity in Southern California.[23]

THE CAPITAL OF SELF-INVENTION

For Murphy, Los Angeles was an easy choice over Boston. In the three years since he'd left for MIT, Southern California had continued to grow, culturally as well as economically, and in 1919 was already starting to boom. Home to hundreds of small airfields, it was rapidly becoming a center for the emerging aviation industry, and the discovery of oil a few years later would cause derricks to sprout all over town. The film industry was firmly established; that year, some 80 percent of the world's movies came out of Southern California.[24] In 1915, Los Angeles could boast one car for every eight residents, against a national average of one to forty-three; by 1924, membership in the Automobile Club of Southern California had jumped to one hundred thousand. Literally and figuratively, the Southland was a region on the move.

More significantly for Murphy, it was a region whose culture was still in formation and receptive to an astounding array of influences. Greater Los Angeles in the early 1920s was a haven for religious countercultures and self-proclaimed prophets of every persuasion, and the burgeoning cultural landscape encompassed not only the refined tastes of the conservative oligarchy but a nascent bohemian community and the over-the-top sensibilities of an increasingly successful film industry. "Here, after all, was an overnight society in search of its history, which it would both discover and manufacture," wrote Kevin Starr.[25] Highbrow and low, seedy and sublime, the genuine and the genuinely fake were all part of the churning, tumultuous mix.

The city's cultural ferment seemed to burst out in every direction. In 1919, the year that Murphy returned from the war, Frank Lloyd Wright had already completed the first of twenty-five houses he'd eventually build in California, while his son, architect and urban planner Lloyd Wright, was quickly becoming a fixture on the cultural scene.[26] The newly established Philharmonic Orchestra of Los Angeles gave its debut performance that October. By 1920, more than twenty film companies called Hollywood home, and budding moguls Irving Thalberg and Jack Warner already headed production departments. In 1921, a version of Duchamp's notorious *Nude Descending a Staircase* came to Southern California with art collectors Walter and Louise Arensberg. And 1923 saw Aimee Semple McPherson, a Canadian-born, divorced single mother, preaching her own canny, captivating brand of Protestant revivalism in a new $1.5 million, forty-three-hundred-seat temple and over the airwaves of radio station KFSG (K Four Square Gospel).

As Los Angeles leaped into the 1920s, its clamorous cultural life teemed with possibilities that other cities couldn't begin to approximate. In *Southern California Country: An Island on the Land,* writer, editor, and California historian Carey McWilliams evoked a sense of the dizzying, off-kilter vitality of Los Angeles in the early 1920s, as Murphy might have experienced it:

In front of the hotel newsboys were shouting the headlines of the hour: an awful trunk-murder had just been committed; the district attorney had been indicted for bribery; Aimee Semple McPherson had once again stood the town on its ear by some spectacular caper; a University of Southern California football star had been caught robbing a bank; a love-mart had been discovered in the Los Feliz Hills; a motion-picture producer had just wired the Egyptian government a fancy offer for permission to illuminate the pyramids to advertise a forthcoming production; and, in the intervals between these revelations, there was news about another prophet, fresh from the desert, who had predicted the doom of the city, a prediction for which I was morbidly grateful. . . . Then it suddenly occurred to me that, in all the world, there neither was nor would there ever be another place like this City of Angels. Here the American people were erupting, like lava from a volcano; here, indeed, was the place for me—a ringside seat at the circus.[27]

Movies and Spiritual Matters: Getting Started in L.A.

Fresh from the war, not quite twenty-one and eager to prove himself, Murphy had no idea where to begin. He knew he had no further interest in electrical engineering but was at a loss as to what to pursue instead. His mother urged him into psychoanalysis with her friend Mary Wilshire (wife of Los Angeles real-estate magnate Gaylord Wilshire), who'd trained under Carl Jung. But analysis proved of little help.

A chance encounter with a fellow pilot from the war gave Murphy his new direction. Now an assistant casting director at Paramount, the friend advised Murphy that he could find ten-dollar-a-day work as a movie extra, the only requirement being a tuxedo. Murphy was game and was soon hired as an extra on Cecil B. DeMille's *Male and Female* (1919), a Gloria Swanson feature shooting on the Paramount lot. It was an enticing taste of film production, and it gave him his goal: to break into the industry, one way or another.

But in a town so flooded with job seekers that the chamber of commerce was forced to publish ads telling people *not* to come, even work as a film extra wasn't easy to come by.[28] Murphy took a job selling subscriptions to the *Los Angeles Evening Express,* where he quickly talked his way into a position as assistant drama critic, a career jump that attests to his energy and persuasiveness. Around this time, he also made the acquaintance of

Paul Jordan Smith, a former clergyman who had married into a family of wealthy Southern California landowners. A Virginian proud of his pre-revolutionary lineage, Jordan Smith was forced from the pulpit by a sexual scandal involving the woman he eventually married. Cushioned by his new wife's wealth, he happily settled into a genteel literary life as a writer, sometime university lecturer, and book collector.

With such interests Jordan Smith was, surprisingly, in the right place. By the early 1920s, Central Los Angeles was home to a rich and varied community of bookstores, such as Dawson's and the Abbey, which served as informal clubs, coffee houses, and local publishers. As the decade progressed, Jordan Smith's book collecting drew him into the literary circle coalescing around poet and bookseller Jake Zeitlin. Among its members were Carey McWilliams, Lloyd Wright, and Phil Townsend Hanna, editor of *Touring Topics,* the surprisingly influential magazine of the Automobile Club of Southern California.[29] Years later, Jordan Smith found his calling as literary editor of the *Los Angeles Times.* But to Murphy, a college dropout with little background in literature, he was already a fascinating character when they first met around 1920—a wry, bookish, but worldly gentleman of leisure who encouraged Murphy's interest in literature.

His encounters with Jordan Smith only increased Murphy's impatience over his own career. Writing about movies for a daily paper was not the same as working on them, and after managing to land a few more bit parts (notably as a young gigolo in a naval uniform), Murphy began to imagine his future behind the camera instead of before it. He had no qualms about drawing on family ties or capitalizing on the artistic aura lent by his parents' reputations and his own bohemian connections. He applied for a position in the art department at Goldwyn Pictures under Hugo Ballin, an old friend of Hermann's from their Paris days. Ballin was an accomplished artist as well as a film director and art director; after retiring from film in the late 1920s, he went on to paint acclaimed murals in several landmark buildings around Los Angeles, including the Griffith Observatory. At the time, though, he had a full slate of films to design. "I guess he felt that I had taste," Murphy recalled, "so I was given a job in the drafting department."[30] But he didn't stay long, quickly jumping to a position as set dresser under another Goldwyn art director, Cedric Gibbons.[31]

Despite his artistic upbringing, Murphy had never been an artist himself, and though it offered his easiest entrée into the industry, art direction was not his métier. After a short stint under Gibbons, he left for the art department at Fox, where he worked on at least one film before being fired. Undeterred, he bounced over to Universal, where he advanced to assistant art director.

One of Murphy's Pasadena friends, Mal St. Clair, had broken into the movie business at Mack Sennett's studio, where he started as a Keystone Kop before graduating to gag writer and director.[32] Murphy's recollections of his friend's workplace offer a glimpse of the informal, improvisational nature of silent film production at the time, especially comedy. "In those days," he wrote, "most of the studios were open so that they could use sunlight for their light source. At the Sennett studio, there was a tower like a lighthouse in the middle of the lot. The gag-men would sit in the tower and watch the various directors working in the sets which surrounded the tower. When a director ran out of ideas, he would climb the steps to the tower and by that time, the gag-men would have thought of what he should do next. They would discuss it and the director would return to the set."[33]

Psychoanalysis with Mary Wilshire may not have given Murphy the answers he was looking for, but he soon found spiritual sustenance in Theosophy. A blend of Eastern and Western philosophies, Theosophy proclaimed the gradual evolution of human beings toward a state of truth and spiritual unity. Founded in New York in 1875 by Madame Helena P. Blavatsky, the Theosophical Society was (and is) an international movement, which has counted among its followers such artists as Wassily Kandinsky, Piet Mondrian, and the young Jackson Pollock.[34]

For the arts community in 1920s Southern California, Theosophy was perhaps the most influential spiritual movement in a spectrum that included Hinduism, Buddhism, Vedantism, and other Eastern philosophies. Los Angeles artists had little use for the mass-market revivalism of radio preachers like Aimee Semple McPherson, but Theosophy's pronounced aesthetic focus made it particularly appealing to visual artists and designers. One Theosophical treatise, "Key to the Meanings of Colors," for instance, defined equivalencies between specific colors and emotional states, while other projects sought to correlate color and music.[35]

This aspect of Theosophical theory may have been of particular interest to Murphy; it appears to have been of interest to his mother, who compiled her own list of color-mood correlations. (She described blue, for instance, as "no desire, negative, ethereality; total lethargy, non expertise," while yellow-green was "like a vapid laughter; a wearing out pleasure with a strain of sadness.")[36] Murphy may have first learned of Theosophy through Bowles, who wrote at least one wartime letter to him from Krotona, the Theosophical colony established in 1912 in the Hollywood hills.

At its height, Krotona was home to hundreds of followers and welcomed many more to its classes, lectures, and spiritual worship, feeding them in a vegetarian cafeteria and offering the attractions of a tranquil lotus pond and well-stocked library. "The architecture is Moorish," Bowles wrote, "and this picturesque effect of snow white temples and little palaces on the terraced hillsides is most lovely!"[37]

Immersing himself in Theosophy, Murphy for a brief time took up residence at Krotona. But sociability occasionally won out over spirituality, and he attended gatherings at the Studio Club, a Hollywood residence hall for single women breaking into the movies. There he met Chase Herendeen, the dancer and aspiring actress who became his first wife.[38]

The youngest child of a prominent family in Geneva, New York, Herendeen had been sent West when her mother, a discontented and determined woman, divorced Chase's father to marry the family chauffeur. The new relationship was volatile from the start, and tossing an attractive teenage daughter into the mix would have wreaked considerable havoc. Chase was hastily packed off to relatives in Southern California. She was soon on her own and, like thousands of others, hoping to break into the industry.

To Murphy, Chase was a "beautiful, sylph-like creature" with whom he shared "a gay and spiritual love at first sight. . . . We drove to Laguna," he wrote, "where we slept on the beach and swam in the moonlight and early morning like children, without worrying about bathing suits. We had such joy in being together that she moved out of the Studio Club into a hilltop house that I had rented on the top of Cahuenga Pass. . . . It had a lovely terrace, where we slept. . . . Though we slept together, we had no intercourse."[39]

Steeped in the mystical idealism of Theosophy, Murphy was blithely, and rather remarkably, content with his chaste love. Others, however, saw it differently. A visit from Murphy's mother prompted a trip to City Hall for a marriage license; though the couple found marriage "a very corny thing to do," they compensated with an unorthodox wedding ceremony, courtesy of the former reverend Paul Jordan Smith. "May you wear the garments of matrimony as lightly as if they were a secret sin," Murphy recalled him pronouncing over them.[40]

Secret or not, sin was apparently not on the agenda. According to Murphy, even after benefit of legal sanction the relationship remained celibate. Chase was young—possibly as young as fifteen at the time of her marriage—and emotionally immature.[41] In his memoir, Murphy offers no explanation for their chaste behavior, nor does he seem to regard it as unusual.[42] But in 1920s Hollywood, and in a life as filled with sexual encounters as Murphy's, it is singular indeed.

Whether physical or platonic, domestic pleasures couldn't compete indefinitely with the allure of Hollywood. Breaking into the industry through art, with ties to the Los Angeles cultural community and its spiritual counterculture, Murphy easily understood cinema as a creative art as well as a moneymaking business. To him, the film industry was a community of adventurous, artistic innovators. "The whole atmosphere of Hollywood was bohemian and it was becoming a creative center in this new art form," he wrote.[43] "People were in the movies because they loved it and because of the glamour and not solely because of the money. Writers would sell their stories by telling them to some director at a bar. The director would buy the story for $100 and proceed to make the picture."[44]

It was this sense of improvisation, creative opportunity, and money to be made that attracted Murphy. No longer content with minor positions at major studios, he believed he would advance more swiftly by making movies of his own. And in 1920, with little more than a year of film experience behind him, he did.

CHAPTER 2

GREEK GODDESSES FOR
THE MOVIEGOING PUBLIC

Murphy began his filmmaking career as many filmmakers do: raising money. From families of the young Pasadena elite that he'd gotten to know during his year at Troop, and from Sarah Bixby Smith, the wealthy wife of his friend Paul Jordan Smith, he raised two thousand dollars, a considerable sum for the time. With it, he bankrolled four short films, the first projects of his proposed Scenic Production Company.[1]

The concept behind the films was simple but savvy: to exploit the splendors of the California coast as settings for lyrical, experimental films that were short on plot, long on beauty shots, and inspired by classical music. Influenced by his studies in Theosophy, Murphy envisioned films that would, as William Moritz put it, "combine the best of music, dance, and visual arts into a *Gesamtkunstwerk*"—a total artwork.[2] At the same time, he was hoping for a smash hit in the movie theaters.

These expectations weren't as contradictory as they might seem. Though decades of film criticism have positioned avant-garde filmmaking and Hollywood studio production as worlds apart, recent scholarship has questioned that polarity, positing a closer relationship between these approaches in their early development. This perspective is informed by a renewed interest in early American cinema and a broadened definition of avant-garde practice—one that moves beyond what Jan-Christopher Horak called "the valorization of the independent filmmaker" to encompass "all those discursive practices outside the institutional mode of representation, including avant-garde, documentary, and amateur."[3]

Murphy embarked on his filmmaking at the height of the silent era, a time when mainstream moviemaking, "the institutional mode of representation," was rapidly evolving. At the time, commercial and experimental cinema were intertwined to a surprising degree, corroborating Murphy's perception of Hollywood as a creative center. "The first popular American avant-garde films were created not by independents, but by individuals from within Hollywood who would continue working there," wrote Brian Taves. "Not only did their avant-garde pictures have a basis in commercial filmmaking, but they would apply their experimental techniques during their subsequent [more mainstream] careers."[4] This was certainly Murphy's intention. "My goal since I first got a job as an extra had been to be a director of feature movies," he wrote, and he saw making short experimental films as a valid step toward achieving that objective.[5]

In the early 1920s, most movie theaters regularly screened short films—episodes of serials, "scenics," comic narratives, and the like—as part of programs that in large theaters usually included live musical presentations, dances, and other performances. Here, for example, is the program for the end of July 1921 at a major New York City theater.

> The Second Hungarian Rhapsody is the overture at the Strand this week. The Topical Review is the second number and is followed by "The Fox," one of the Adventures of Bill and Bob series. Carlo Ferretti, baritone, sings "O Sole Mio." The feature is "Nobody," a Roland West Prod. with Jewel Carmen. Lottice Howell, soprano, sings "Moonlight-Starlight" and the comedy is Larry Semon in "The Fall Guy."[6]

Like feature films, popular shorts usually circulated among theaters nationwide. Reviews in daily newspapers and film industry trade publications occasionally made reference to them, and a positive mention could easily translate into additional bookings.

As a maker of experimental films, even ones intended for movie palaces, Murphy was not alone in his interest in interpreting music on film. Given that virtually all film screenings of the period were presented with some sort of musical accompaniment, from full orchestra to lone piano, this was perhaps to be expected. In any case, the visual expression of music on film was a recurring motif in avant-garde filmmaking during the late silent era, inspiring works as diverse as Hans Richter's *Rhythmus 21* (1921), Oskar Fischinger's abstract animations, and the "city symphony" films of the late 1920s.[7]

Since returning to Southern California, Murphy had visited Carmel with his mother and sister and taken the famed seventeen-mile scenic drive at Point Lobos. With Claude Debussy's *Prelude to the Afternoon of a Faun* as the musical inspiration, Murphy wrote a scenario for his first film, *Soul of the Cypress* (1920). "Chase was to be the spirit of the cypress," Murphy wrote, "and a young composer whom I had met at the Theosophical Society at Krotona was the lonely musician who enticed her with his flute to emerge from one of the weird, gnarled cypresses in Point Lobos. She danced for him and he fell in love with her, but being immortal, he could not touch her and in trying to catch her, she disappears back into the tree."[8] Enticed by the beauty of the dryad—the "soul of the cypress"—the young man throws himself into the sea, so that he, too, might become immortal, uniting the couple for eternity.

In creating this scenario, Murphy may have been influenced by the work of Anne W. Brigman, a Pictorialist photographer based in San Francisco (later in Southern California). Many of Brigman's images depict female nudes merging with and drawing power from nature: mountains, water, and, above all, trees. Her 1905 image *The Dryad* features a nude woman crouched in a pine tree, arm outstretched. *Heart of the Storm* (1912) depicts two women posed dramatically in the split trunk of a cypress tree. Other images, such as *The Soul of the Blasted Pine* (1908) and *The Dying Cedar* (1906), similarly merge female figures and trees in striking images, reflecting both Brigman's protofeminist convictions and her self-declared pagan relationship to nature. Active from 1901 into the 1940s, Brigman was a key figure in California photography in the early twentieth century.[9] Throughout the 1910s and 1920s, her work was shown in San Francisco and Southern California, and Murphy would have easily encountered it in exhibitions and publications.

Running approximately ten minutes, *Soul of the Cypress* is a laudable debut film. The shoreside cliffs of Point Lobos provide a stunning backdrop, and Murphy's intertitles, with their references to "California's romantic coast" and the musician's "mortal touch," capture the poetic spirit of the enterprise. He capably employs filmmaking conventions of the day, using superimpositions to depict the dryad emerging from and returning to the tree and tinting selected scenes in different colors—a common practice since the earliest days of filmmaking, still widely used in the 1920s.[10] Though the camera work randomly violates the 180-degree rule, making a hash of the cinematic space, the piece maintains its coherence and a certain charm.[11] It adroitly plays into the public's perception of

Southern California at the time, as a distant, scenic land of romance and grandeur.

With dragging feet and hand-to-forehead anguish, the stiff, angular musician turns in a performance worthy of *The Cabinet of Dr. Caligari,* making him an altogether satisfying foil for his light-footed temptress. Murphy's wife, Chase, is a fetching dryad. Cavorting around the cliffsides, she moves with a dancer's grace, and her costume (a short, diaphanous robe of vaguely Grecian design) reveals every curve in motion and the occasional flash of nipple and hint of pubic hair. Cloaked in an ennobling mantle of art and classical myth, *Soul of the Cypress* presents a vision of female sexuality at once cultured and titillating: part Isadora Duncan, part Folies Bergères.

In later years, Herendeen fondly recalled making the film: shooting a few scenes, then jumping into the back seat of the car with Murphy for a quick cuddle.[12] Affectionate though it was, the marriage remained celibate. It's unclear whether the choice was Herendeen's, Murphy's, or by mutual agreement; but the specter of the film's thwarted musician suggests that Murphy's "gay, spiritual" affair had its frustrations.

Soon after shooting on *Soul of the Cypress* was completed, the Murphys were visited by a close friend of Herendeen's, a fellow dancer named Katharine Hawley. A tall, stunningly beautiful woman, Hawley had been a student of Isadora Duncan's sister, Elizabeth Duncan, and was training, like Murphy's sister, Carlene, with Ruth St. Denis at Denishawn.

Once again Murphy was love-struck. "Katharine was like a Greek goddess and lived in a completely imaginary spiritual world," he wrote. "Simply to look at her made my heart glow with joy."[13] That spring, Chase was sent on an extended visit to her family in upstate New York (and to Murphy's surprised but chivalrous father in Massachusetts) while he plunged into a sexual relationship with Hawley. The situation left him completely torn. "I wanted to be true to both of them," Murphy recalled.[14] Despite his passionate involvement with Hawley, he maintained an intense emotional connection to Herendeen, albeit at a distance, and made films with them both. "This pattern of devotion to beauty and girls in connection with my work perhaps started a pattern of behavior that has followed me through life," he wrote.[15]

Hawley is the star of *Aphrodite* (1920), in which she portrays the goddess of love emerging from the sea to dance through the Southern California landscape. No print of the film is known to exist, but Murphy's photographs of the filming survive, several annotated on the reverse. In these images, Hawley appears in a filmy Grecian gown, her hair dressed in classical curls. If Herendeen in *Soul of the Cypress* is a sprightly wood nymph, Hawley in *Aphrodite* is every inch the stately but sexy goddess.

Shot in the hazy, backlit style of Pictorialism, the photographs suggest Murphy's increasingly assured visual style and a cinematic terrain stitched from diverse locations. According to Murphy's notes, Aphrodite came ashore at Laguna, danced across a field in Santa Monica, walked through a glade in L.A.'s Elysian Park, and contemplated a small ornamental pond on the Pasadena property of Gaylord and Mary Wilshire. A good portion of the movie appears to have been filmed at Murphy's spiritual stomping ground, Krotona. A number of photographs bear that notation, and the picturesque "snow white temples and little palaces" that Caroline Bowles described to her son in 1918 appear in the background.

Although *Aphrodite* was presumably paired with a classical music composition, Murphy makes no mention of it, nor does he identify the music for his third film, *Anywhere out of the World* (1920), inspired by the Baudelaire poem of that title. Here, Herendeen is the performer again, but this time even diaphanous veils may have been dispensed with: Murphy noted in his memoir that she portrayed "a beautiful nude nymph bathing in the crystal waters and pools of Palm Canyon in Palm Springs."[16]

In his memoir, Murphy makes no mention of the fourth production. But in letters of this period, he referred to it as "my Japanese film," and one newspaper account described it as "the adventures of a Japanese girl and her lover and father."[17] It's unclear whether Herendeen, Hawley, or another actress took the lead role. As with *Anywhere out of the World,* no print is known to survive.

A HIT IN NEW YORK

With four films shot, Murphy began looking for a distributor. He approached Sol Lesser, a Los Angeles film exhibitor and distributor who was beginning to produce as well.[18] Murphy wrote that Lesser "offered to buy the films outright with a profit of $1,000 to Murphy"—a handsome 50 percent return on his investment—"and a contract to make more."[19] Looking back decades later, Murphy regretted not taking Lesser up on the deal. Instead he chose to take the rough-edited films to New York. Hollywood had become the center of the American film industry, but New York remained the cultural capital. A successful opening there would put him on the film-industry map as no Los Angeles screening could. Too, Herendeen was still back East, and Murphy, yet in the throes of his double romance, wanted to be with her again.

Early August 1920 found him in Rochester, New York, with Chase, her mother, and her mother's husband. By the end of the month he was in Boston, screening the films for "a small company of invited guests" at the Boston Motion Picture Supply Company. One senses Murphy's father pulling a few strings on his behalf; though a private screening, the event attracted encouraging write-ups in at least two Boston newspapers. Describing the films' plots as "too simple as narratives to interest the crowd," the *Boston Evening Transcript* warmly praised "the landscape part of the show," considering it "enough in itself to justify all the effort involved in Mr. Murphy's experiment."[20] Lauding the cinematography, visual style, and beautiful use of color tinting, the *Boston Post* called the films "a distinct achievement" and ran an alluring image of Hawley in *Aphrodite*.[21]

With press notices in hand, Murphy arrived in New York in September 1920. He had two goals: theatrical bookings for the films and financial backing for additional productions. The following month, he signed a contract with the Community Motion Picture Bureau for the financing of his four films and the production of twelve to eighteen more, "of the general character of the four above named."[22] Under the agreement, Murphy retained the rights to the films he'd already made and the lion's share of the profits on them, along with a salary of five hundred dollars a month. For a fledgling filmmaker, even a well-reviewed one, it was a handsome deal.

Still, it's not surprising that in hindsight Murphy regretted passing up Sol Lesser's earlier offer. By December, a scant two months after the contract signing, the arrangement had fallen apart. As Murphy put it, the company, "a church organization . . . gypped me in a fine Presbyterian manner, so that I was not able to return the investment to my [original California] backers."[23] He sued, and in June 1921 was awarded twenty-five hundred dollars in back payments.[24] In December 1921, Community took Murphy back to court, looking to recover three thousand dollars in a countersuit alleging breach of contract.

It was a rowdy legal dustup, with Community charging that Murphy "refused to accept the plaintiff's suggestions, that he made wasteful and unauthorized expenditures, rendered a poor quality of service, brought a number of suits against the plaintiff . . . and took possession of the films in question."[25] This last charge was a fine piece of litigational legerdemain,

as the films in question were the ones that Murphy had made before signing with the company, to which the contract granted him title. As a legal
strategy, it was on a par with Community's suing Murphy, in essence, for
having sued them first.

No further reports of the case appeared in the industry press. It was
likely settled out of court and not entirely to Murphy's satisfaction. Correspondence with his father indicates that despite a nine-hundred-dollar
judgment in his favor, Murphy ended up owing close to three hundred dollars on a bond to Community, a sum reluctantly paid out in mid-1922 by
a grumbling Hermann, who was legally obligated as Murphy's guarantor.[26]

It wasn't the first time his father had come to Murphy's financial rescue,
nor would it be the last. Murphy's ideas about money and its uses bore
little relation to Hermann's, and few men were more different in character and temperament. Steeped in the values of nineteenth-century New
England, Hermann saw his son's behavior as impulsive, irresponsible, and
spendthrift. Murphy in turn viewed Hermann as stingy, rigidly conservative, and hopelessly out of step with modern times. Murphy wanted what
modernity promised: speed, style, and the chance to make his mark on
the strength of his ideas and personal charisma, not hard work and right
living. Content with a dignified if somewhat provincial life in Boston,
Hermann had little use for the public spotlight, while Murphy actively
courted the fame that the burgeoning mass media—movies, magazines,
and soon radio—could confer. Yet as Murphy struggled to find his footing,
Hermann repeatedly extended support in whatever way he could, while
paradoxically attempting to impart to his son a sense of responsibility, fiscal
and otherwise. An undated letter to Murphy poignantly summarizes Hermann's profound sense of connection and frustration during these years.
"My Dearest Dudley Boy," he wrote, "I have felt so sad over our parting
to-day that I couldn't stand it any longer and have come down to just say
good night to you and try and tell you that there never was a father prouder
of his son's successes than yours—and if you really believe that I am not
proud of you, you are as mistaken as you are when you think that your
father or my father were miserly. If I *nag* you about your shortcomings it's
because I am so ambitious for you that I want you to be *fine* in *every* way."[27]

But in a world that had just undergone a horrendous bloodletting and
was embarking on a decade-long bender, a fine character was not necessarily the sine qua non that it once was, and Murphy bridled at Hermann's
attempts to curb his excesses. Still, his father's support was in many ways
essential to him, and Murphy bore with Hermann's strictures as best he

could. "From now on I shall be businesslike and have my affairs and money organized," he wrote to Hermann. "Whoopie!"[28]

Having legally separated himself from the Community Motion Picture Bureau with the June 1921 ruling in his favor, Murphy lost no time in putting his films into circulation. He screened them for composer and conductor Hugo Riesenfeld, the managing director of two major Broadway theaters, the Rialto and the Rivoli. Riesenfeld booked *Soul of the Cypress* on the week-long program that ran at the Rivoli in mid-July. There, it opened for the feature film *The Conquest of Canaan,* sharing the bill with an orchestral rendition of Rimsky-Korsakoff's *Scheherazade,* a duet of "I Hear a Thrush at Eve," and a Pathé comic short called *At the Ringside.* A small notice in an industry trade paper announced the film's opening, noting that it was "photographed under the direction of Dudley Bowles Murphy, son of Herman [*sic*] Dudley Murphy, the artist, of Boston."[29]

Trimmed to roughly half the twenty-minute length of its Boston screening the previous summer, *Soul of the Cypress* more than fulfilled Murphy's hopes for a successful New York run. Not only was the Rivoli booking followed by a week at the Rialto—a rare occurrence on the Broadway movie circuit—but the film attracted critical attention in both the city and industry press. The *New York Times* called it "an unusually interesting scenic picture" and, though complaining about the lack of plot, wrote that "its separate scenes are striking photographic works, distinctively composed and expressive."[30] A few months later, the work's "lyric quality" was commended once again in the *Times'* roundup of notable films for 1921.[31] The *New York Globe* declared that the film "points the way to a new field of motion picture theater entertainment,"[32] while a lengthier write-up in the trade paper *Wid's Daily*—"The Bradstreet of Filmdom, the Recognized Authority"—qualified as a rave. "The photography in this film stands out as some of the very best work yet accomplished in this line," wrote *Wid's.* "A great deal of attention is given to composition and tone, and some of the lighting effects are most beautiful. . . . If you are looking for a scenic that will please a very discriminating audience and make a high class filler, see 'The Soul of the Cypress.'" Two weeks on Broadway for a scenic "is indicative of its quality and attractiveness," the reviewer noted, then switched gears for a little industry soap-boxing. "Perhaps the biggest thing about this single reel production is that it breaks away completely from the stuff that has been repeated so often, and makes a decided step forward both in an artistic sense, and in pictorial qualities. The public seems to want and appreciate good pictures, and the day is fast approaching when the producer will realize that in cheapening the product he is risking failure rather than greater popularity."[33]

Although *Wid's* and the *New York Times* both praised the film's cinematography, Murphy did not shoot *Soul of the Cypress* himself. The *New York Times* index lists him as the cinematographer on the film, but in his memoir he recalled that the cameraman was John Eyreman, "a talented young still photographer who had done some movie work"—an interesting admission, given that no mention was made of Eyreman's involvement at the time.[34]

However, Murphy's own interest in technology soon resurfaced. Some two weeks after its review of *Soul of the Cypress, Wid's Daily* announced that the young filmmaker was spending the summer of 1921 "doing some research work in the Department of Physics of Dartmouth College. He is working in connection with A. Ames of Boston in the Wilder Laboratory, and will make a special effort to develop a moving picture camera lense [*sic*] that would record the same impression as that normally received by the retina of the eye."[35] "A. Ames" was Adelbert Ames, Jr., a former lawyer and artist who, drawn to the physics and physiology of visual perception through his painting, went on to found the Dartmouth Eye Institute. Murphy came to the position in part through Hermann, who knew Ames and was eager to see his feckless son in just this type of situation: a steady job with a scientific bent.[36] At the time Murphy joined him, Ames was researching physiological optics and the mechanics of sight. As William Moritz has noted, it's quite plausible that Murphy's work that summer led to the beveled lenses that he later used in *Ballet mécanique* and *Black and Tan*.[37]

A PORNOGRAPHIC DETOUR TO THE LIBRARY OF CONGRESS

Before moving on from *Soul of the Cypress,* it's worth a moment to examine the circumstances surrounding the discovery of the print at the Library of Congress. As film scholars have expanded their examination of early American cinema, Murphy's early work has attracted increased attention. This has proved a somewhat frustrating proposition. It's unclear how many films Murphy made during this period. Of these early films, only *Danse Macabre* (1922) and *Soul of the Cypress* are known to survive, the latter having been rediscovered only recently. The George Eastman House in Rochester, New York, holds a print of *Danse Macabre*. Over the past thirty years, the Library of Congress received two nitrate prints of *Soul of the Cypress.*

The first of these two prints was acquired through the American Film Institute in 1976, as part of a film collection assembled by a San Francisco film projectionist, George T. Post. Film preservationist David Shepard, then on the American Film Institute staff, made the acquisition. In 1988, Shepard donated a second print through his company, Blackhawk Films.[38]

Made of flammable nitrate film stock, the Post print was badly deteriorated when the Library of Congress received it. It was quickly copied to a duplicate "safety" negative on nonflammable stock. A black-and-white reference print was made for screening purposes, and the original was destroyed.[39] For years, the film languished in the library's vaults, perhaps because of the three words at the bottom of its original record card: "contains pornographic footage."

Chase's diaphanous gown notwithstanding, the Post print of *Soul of the Cypress* and the Blackhawk print as well do indeed contain footage of a graphic nature. The origins of these reappropriated prints are unknown, but the footage grafted onto *Soul of the Cypress* was not randomly chosen.[40] It reverberates with Murphy's film in intriguing ways, making wry use of his cinematic language and mise-en-scène.

As *Soul of the Cypress* closes with a sunset shot of the dreamily musing dryad, the narrative is abruptly ruptured by a title card: "Explain This!" The film then cuts to a shot of a lithe young woman, naked save for a pair of dainty stockings, reclining on a blanket *en plein air.* Her partner appears in the frame; she looks to the camera and then to him. A title card, "We'll have time—if we hurry," is followed by a lengthy shot of the woman, her pubis squarely centered in the frame, offering herself to the camera. As the two zestfully couple on the blanket, the camera frame remains steady, with none of the close-ups that have become standard for the genre. Instead, two shots of exploding fireworks follow; the couple separate as the woman continues to fondle her partner's penis. Cut to an old-fashioned schoolboy, possibly lifted from an early silent film, his gaze directed more or less toward the couple and his expression incredulous. A title card reads, "What—again?" followed by a return to the couple. Another title announces, "Turning back the pages of memory," then a shot of the sun setting in a grove of trees. More titles draw the film to its conclusion: "Educational Pictures: The Spice of the Program" and "FINIS: An Ensign Picture." A smiling Spanish dancer flirtatiously lowers a fan from her face, and the final title reads, "The End of The Soul of the Cypress."[41]

Given Murphy's sexual openness and his sly sense of humor, it's tempting to attribute to him not only *Soul of the Cypress* but its unrepressed doppelgänger. It's feasible; according to specialists at the Library of Congress, the edge codes on the film stock for the pornographic footage date from 1919, roughly the same time period in which Murphy's film was shot. The open-air setting of the pornographic footage vaguely resembles the setting of *Soul of the Cypress,* but then, so did much of Southern California. There has been some speculation that Chase is the woman in the pornographic footage, but it isn't so; family photographs clearly indicate that Herendeen's eyes are blue, while her inadvertent costar's are a limpid brown.

Murphy's own memoir argues against his participation in the pornographic filming in that he makes no mention of it. Given his genteel candor in discussing sexual matters, it's unlikely that such a project would have gone entirely unremarked. Too, *Soul of the Cypress* was his first film and first commercial success; it's unlikely that he would have deliberately treated it in this manner. If the pornographic footage was in fact shot at roughly the same time as *Soul of the Cypress,* it's also unlikely that Murphy, then immersed in Theosophy and matters of the spirit, would have committed such scenes to film—especially with Herendeen, his skittish, celibate soulmate, as the woman in question.

As noted, the first end title of the pornographic sequence credits it to Educational Pictures. There was a production company called Educational Pictures in Hollywood at the time (and "The Spice of the Program" was, in fact, its slogan). It specialized in short subjects and was run by a flamboyant, glad-handing film-industry fixture named Earle Hammons. In 1922, Hammons bought the old Principal Pictures studio on Santa Monica Boulevard from producer Sol Lesser. Though a photograph taken on the studio lot depicts the same Aladdin's lamp logo that appears on the Educational Pictures title card in the pornographic sequence, the company was not necessarily in the blue-film business. According to Eric Schaefer, author of *"Bold! Daring! Shocking! True!" A History of Exploitation Films, 1919–1959,* Educational Pictures was a legitimate, low-end producer of short subjects. By contrast, hardcore pornographic film production was an entirely anonymous, highly illegal business. During this period, pornography producers would never have affixed their own logos or other identifying marks to the films for fear of giving police and prosecutors a means of identifying them.[42]

Film curator Bruce Posner, who included the Post version of *Soul of the Cypress* in his 2001 film series Unseen Cinema (with a note about "interpolated footage"), thinks the print is most likely a "square-up reel"—

a short assemblage of racy scenes, shown at the end of screenings in towns where tight police controls dictated that any "hot" footage in the evening's big film be clipped out.[43] If an audience became angry that they hadn't gotten what they thought they'd paid for, the projectionist would show a reel that would, assuming no police were around, "square the beef" with the audience. Schaefer, on the other hand, thinks it likely that the pornographic footage in the Post print was intended as a stag film. As such, it would have been shown privately, "in smoky fraternity houses or the basement of the American Legion Hall."[44] In either case, Murphy's "unusually interesting scenic picture," the success that launched his career, would have been little more than a blind: artistic drapery for the real action, which required no such embellishment.

Somewhat fussy, outdated, and at a real disadvantage when shorn of the music that inspired it, *Soul of the Cypress* nevertheless shares a certain libidinous impulse with its wilder companion footage. The male gaze so strongly implicated in the pornographic segment is also at work in Murphy's film. Though the treatment differs, at heart both films are about more or less the same thing. And in an uncanny way, they form an intriguing whole. With earthy abandon and ironic good humor, the pornographic footage throws into high relief the artistic pretensions and teasing, circumlocutory nature of *Soul of the Cypress*. At the same time, Murphy's film imparts to the pornographic footage a grace it wouldn't otherwise possess. The move from one filmic element to the next is undeniably jarring, but together the two segments articulate what Murphy, as an aspiring mainstream director and a young man engrossed in an intense but oddly celibate love affair, could not express on film himself.

As David James has pointed out, the Post version of *Soul of the Cypress* is "doubly minor."[45] Originally serving as a mere prelude to the main attraction on a movie program, it was then coupled with illicit footage and banished, figuratively speaking, to the basement of the American Legion Hall. Reappropriated for pornographic purposes, *Soul of the Cypress* is the first of Murphy's films to have been substantially reedited after completion. It isn't, however, the last. *Ballet mécanique* is perhaps the most reedited film in the history of early avant-garde cinema, with several distinct variants in existence, and *The Emperor Jones* suffered significant cuts and deletions in the effort to accommodate censors, southern theater owners, and African-American audiences. Vanished or irretrievably deteriorated prints are among the most common means by which early filmmakers have dropped out of the critical discourse, and several of Murphy's films have disappeared in these ways. But the pornographic reappropriation of *Soul of the Cypress* is something else entirely, pointing to a theme that emerges at certain critical points in Murphy's career: the loss of creative control over projects after completion.

This is due, in part, to Murphy's erratic approach to film distribution. After his relationship with the Community Motion Picture Company soured in late 1920, he worked swiftly to put his films into circulation, eventually using them as the basis of his next venture. But his concept of film distribution was limited. He approached it as an artist, not a businessman. To him, it was a small-scale, intensely personal activity, based on friendships with key exhibitors, not national networks of distributors and theater chains. This naive, somewhat cavalier approach to the distribution of his films, particularly the independent productions, at times cost him dearly.

"ARTISTIC EFFORTS OF COMMERCIAL VALUE": VISUAL SYMPHONY PRODUCTIONS

In the same July 1921 issue of *Wid's* that announced the Rivoli's *Soul of the Cypress* booking was a front-page story that might well have caught Murphy's eye. Under the headline "Show Synchronized Film," the story reported a new development in film exhibition: "For the first time in France a moving picture show was given this afternoon in which every action was synchronized absolutely with the music." The mechanics of the apparatus were simple: "A musician or other person [possibly a projectionist] works a sort of small keyboard with sliding keys, by means of which he follows the conductor in accelerating or slackening the movement [of the film] in sympathy with the music."[46] Connected to the film projector, the keyboard acted as a rheostat, speeding or slowing the film to coincide better with the music performed by a live theater orchestra. Two months later, another brief article in *Wid's* noted the successful trial of the "Visiophone" apparatus in a large screening at the Théâtre des Champs Elysées in Paris. Accustomed as we are to synchronous sound media, it's hard to imagine the breakthrough that such an invention represented. Ingeniously if laboriously, it solved one of the major problems plaguing silent film exhibition: keeping live musical performances in sync with projected film.

Murphy was quick to capitalize on the possibilities that such a system afforded his musically inspired films. In December 1921, the same month that the Community Motion Picture Bureau filed its countersuit against him, he announced the formation of Visual Symphony Productions, Inc. The new company would produce short films based, like *Soul of the Cypress,* on well-known works of classical music. Intended for use in place of orchestral overtures or as special musical numbers in movie-program prologues, the films' running times were designed to coincide with the running times of their musical accompaniments; like the French equipment, the apparatus would permit theater staff to adjust synchronization during performances. Catering to the needs of small exhibitors as well as large, the company could supply musical arrangements for everything from solo piano to full orchestra, as well as "player rolls for piano, orchestrion and organ."[47] At the time of the announcement, the first production, inspired by Camille Saint-Saëns's symphonic poem *Danse macabre,* was already underway with Murphy as director.[48]

In his memoir, Murphy referred to an unnamed partner in Visual Symphony Productions, "a restauranteur, who was intrigued with show business."[49] But trade publications identified him as Claude Macgowan, an industry professional who had headed Universal's financial and accounting department for several years.[50] In the trade press, Macgowan shrewdly outlined the advantages of his new product—"that rare combination, an artistic production elaborately produced, which will save the exhibitors hundreds of thousands of dollars"—and described Murphy's artistic training as starting "under the tutelage of his father, the celebrated Boston portrait painter."[51] With Macgowan's business acumen behind the company and Murphy's vaunted artistic sensibility at the fore, Visual Symphony Productions and its products were an appealing film industry package.

Set to Saint-Saëns's music, the film (variously known as *Dance of Death, Death and the Maiden,* and most commonly *Danse Macabre*) was adapted from a stage ballet by Adolph Bolm, a well-known dancer and choreographer who had appeared with Diaghilev's Ballets Russes before establishing his own company in the United States.[52] Loosely based on Edgar Allan Poe's "The Masque of the Red Death," *Danse Macabre* recounts the tale of a young couple hoping to escape the plague. They flee to an abandoned castle, where Death overtakes them—a plot that's also reminiscent of Fritz Lang's film *Der müde Tod (Destiny),* released the year before.[53] Bolm danced the role of the young man, opposite Ruth Page, a promising young ballerina from Chicago. The project's other collaborator was photographer Francis Bruguière, who designed the shadowy, expressionistic lighting.[54]

The film opens with an animation sequence, which had been created by a commercial production house that claimed it could turn out titles in twenty-four hours.[55] Composed of human figures and skeletons, the cleverly animated title only gradually assumes legibility as the figures take their positions. The skeleton forming the letter *C* in MACABRE, for instance, picks up a skeleton infant and holds it aloft to form the curving top of the letter, while a nearby skeleton and human figure lean together to form an *A*. The title gives way to an animated scene in which the lovers flee while a church-tower clock strikes midnight. The clock face dissolves into the hollow-eyed face of Death, who starts tuning up a violin. Once the couple arrives at the castle, live actors take over. Filmed in ghostly superimpositions, the character actor Olin Howland, wearing an oversized skull mask, portrays Death.[56] As in his previous work, Murphy used tinted film stocks in *Danse Macabre* to heighten the film's expressivity. And in his animated close-up, the eerie, glowing eyes of Death were hand-colored, frame by frame—a more costly effect usually limited to a brief sequence or two.[57]

Speedily shot in a New York studio, the tightly controlled style of *Danse Macabre* bears little resemblance to the spontaneous improvisation of *Soul of the Cypress*. The production seems to have been dominated by its strong-willed choreographer star. In the opening credits, Murphy as director is listed after Bolm, who is credited with the film's conception. During its New York run, a few newspaper ads and articles presented it as entirely Bolm's work, making no mention of Murphy: "Saint Saëns' 'Danse Macabre' visualized by Adolph Bolm," for example, or "a film characterization of Saint-Saens' music, made by Adolf [*sic*] Bolm."[58] In any case, the *New York Times* gave it an enthusiastic review, singling out Murphy's direction and calling it "an entertaining and encouraging little film. . . . It is to be hoped that those who made this satisfying and significant film will go on to fulfill the cinematographic promise it holds out."[59]

In filmic terms, *Danse Macabre* is a straightforward narrative with some effective artistic touches. Even scholars such as Moritz and Horak, who situate Murphy in the forefront of America's early cinematic avant-garde, have some difficulty classifying *Danse Macabre* as an avant-garde film.[60] It is, however, a good example of the ground that Murphy sought to occupy: both "class" and "mass," as *Variety* would have put it. For Murphy and for the film industry, it mattered little whether *Danse Macabre* was avant-garde or not. The film confirmed his growing reputation as a director with an artistic eye and solid instincts for popular tastes, capable of turning out appealing "high class filler" for the moviegoing public.

The timing couldn't have been better. For film exhibitors struggling with the unwieldy live presentations of a typical movie palace, Murphy's "visual symphonies" were a godsend. Debuting at a point when, as one trade paper put it, "exhibitors everywhere are wearying of the expensive burden of prologues, presentations and pseudo vaudeville as program openers," these short films had obvious advantages. "An examination of their qualities proves them to be ideal attraction substitutes and as such are bound to save exhibitors large sums of money now spent on something which many believe has no place in a picture theatre." The article went on to praise Murphy as "that type of director whose ideals, vision and trained and discriminating artistic sense are combined with a practical bent, which makes his artistic efforts of commercial value."[61] For most movie exhibitors, "a practical bent" meant pretty faces, well-framed leg shots, and perhaps a few striking special effects—all of which Murphy's films had in quantity.

Like the French synchronization systems reported in *Wid's* the previous summer, Murphy and Macgowan's Visual Symphony productions promised to link film projection speed to the tempo of a live musical performance. It's unclear whether the company utilized one of the French systems or if Murphy created an apparatus of his own. In a *Motion Picture News* article, Macgowan attributed the Visual Symphony system solely to his partner. "Mr. Murphy's sympathetic knowledge of the twin arts—motion pictures and music—led to the endless experiments in synchronization which solved the entire problem of our interpretations," he stated. "To him must go full credit for originating this new art form."[62] Murphy's memoir noted only that *Danse Macabre* "was synchronized exactly to the movements of the dancers," to which he added the handwritten words *bar for bar,* observing that "this was a distinct innovation and created quite a sensation."[63]

To promote their company, Murphy and Macgowan released to the trade papers a lengthy slate of upcoming productions, including titles and accompanying music. It's unclear how many of these were actually produced or how the films paired up with the musical compositions, which ranged from Rimsky-Korsakoff's *Scheherazade* and Tchaikovsky's *Nutcracker* to Gilbert and Sullivan's *Pirates of Penzance.* It's probable that Murphy's first four films—*Soul of the Cypress, Aphrodite, Anywhere out of the World,* and the "Japanese film" (referred to in the Community Motion Picture Bureau contract as *The Way of Love*)—were rereleased and perhaps retitled as more accurately synchronized Visual Symphony productions. This appears to be the case with *The Way of Love,* which premiered in late

January 1922 as *The Romance of the White Chrysanthemum*. In a letter to his father, Murphy wrote with offhand pride, "My Japanese picture is running this week at the Rialto theatre here in N.Y., and my name is stuck on a card out in front of the theatre."[64]

The only Visual Symphony film known to have been produced in 1922 is *Danse Macabre*, which premiered at the Rialto in July of that year, opening for the feature film *The Mysteries of India*. The rest of the films on Visual Symphony's ambitious production slate were variously figured at twelve or twenty-four titles in the first year. They were apparently never made, and the undertaking seems to have folded with *Danse Macabre*. The reason, apparently, was the usual problem for independent producers: lack of backers. In the same letter to Hermann in which he described the theatrical engagement for *The Romance of the White Chrysanthemum*, Murphy wrote of *Danse Macabre*: "The picture is just about as far along now as I can get it until I sell a few more shares. It surely is a vital point in the company's and in my career for we have people all waiting to see our visual symphony—we have had the publicity and notices about it and now we are held up! But I *will!* make it go—so don't worry. But for comfort the motto is to work for somebody else and not yourself and let them do the worrying!"[65]

In his memoir, Murphy didn't address the outcome of Visual Symphony Productions. Instead, he moved directly from *Danse Macabre* to his next project, a film for producer Pat Powers.[66] Nor did he mention Macgowan beyond the one vague reference to his restauranteur partner. If Visual Symphony Productions dissolved, Murphy might well have lost distribution rights to the completed films, one possible explanation for the pornographic fate of *Soul of the Cypress*.

BUSINESS AND PLEASURE

On his arrival in New York in 1920, Murphy settled into a bohemian life in Greenwich Village. "With my work and minor recognition as an avant-garde (for the time) picture maker," he recalled, "I began to meet other artists." As his business arrangements fluctuated, his personal life became more complicated as well. In late 1920 he thought he was making some headway in his irresolvable romantic conflict, though the choice of imagery in his memoir told a different story. "By this time," he wrote, "I had felt that Chase was my true love and I had left Katharine in California and felt that if I could cut off my feeling for her which was more physical, that I could eliminate one leg of the triangle and concentrate on Chase."[67] But with Chase living in Rochester that fall and back in Los Angeles by the end of the year, Murphy was seeing neither of them.

In December 1920, Murphy telegraphed Chase in Los Angeles to halt their divorce proceedings, claiming that he was over Katharine and "heart-free." Herendeen, however, was dubious. Attempting to resolve his dilemma once and for all, Murphy came up with a solution that would appear logical only to a robust young man of twenty-three. His account of the episode was rendered in an appropriately Hemingwayesque style. "I felt that if I had an affair with some other girl that I could kill the feeling that I had for Katharine," he wrote. "I met a sexy young girl at a little café on 8th Street, called 3 Steps Down. . . . I remember taking this sexy girl up to my room on 12th Street . . . I finally had a sort of half-assed affair with her. A few days later I realized I had caught a dose of clap. In other words, I had, in trying to kill the thing I loved, more than succeeded."[68]

Attended only by a homeopathic physician recommended by his own homeopath in Boston, Murphy grew steadily worse. "At this time, Chase arrived in New York and came to visit me," he wrote. "I told her of my misfortune, and why I had done it, in trying to eliminate Katharine from my heart so that I might love her alone. She was not able to take this situation and left me to my misfortune."[69] Though they continued to correspond and occasionally meet, Murphy and Herendeen never reconciled, and their divorce became final some two years later.

Meanwhile, Murphy's health declined further. Having returned to the East from California, his sister, Carlene, arrived to assess the situation. She wasted no time in packing him off to the hospital by ambulance. By then the disease had affected his eyes. Finally receiving adequate medical care, Murphy began to recover. Understandably, he tried to keep his illness from his father. "I wonder why I hear nothing from you or about you!" Hermann wrote in spring of 1921. "Carlene's last letter didn't say a word about you and the one before that said you were at the hospital for cripples being 'baked'!"[70] Eventually Hermann did find out and was as furious as Murphy had feared. "Had your illness been of a different sort I should feel differently about your lack of earning capacity," he wrote. "I have always *hated* New York. Since your trouble I *loathe* it, and I will not in any way assist you to stay there."[71]

One of Murphy's Theosophy mentors came to his rescue, offering spiritual and material support. In mid-1921, he arranged for Murphy to spend a recuperative weekend at the home of wealthy Theosophist Walter Kirk-patrick Brice, whose Huntington, Long Island, estate drew an artistic crowd. At the time, Brice was supporting the work of Thomas Wilfred, a Danish-born Theosophist and the originator of the clavilux color organ.

In the first decades of the twentieth century, avant-garde filmmakers weren't the only ones experimenting with visual equivalents to music. The clavilux was one of several inventions intended to correlate visual effects with music or express it in visual terms. These ranged from early experiments with color-organ projections by British artist Alexander Wallace Rimington to Charles Dockum's MobilColor Projectors of the 1930s and 1940s.[72] Given the Theosophical interest in correlating color with emotional and spiritual states, the concept of a color instrument would have held particular interest for a follower such as Wilfred.

Unlike some of these instruments, the clavilux did not play audible music. Its effects were entirely based on color, form, and movement. Utilizing a keyboard linked to a light projector, it produced what Wilfred called *lumia:* fluid, gradually shifting colored shapes projected in a darkened space—a visual equivalent to musical compositions.[73] In his grandest schemes he envisioned a number of claviluxes playing together in a kind of color-instrument orchestra, but the effect of a single clavilux was apparently stunning in its own right. One viewer described moments in a performance that were "as beautiful as anything I have ever seen or heard, the passion of the mind said purely in another medium, pure and incredible color, the sense of the life of light itself. They [the lumia] gave me the sense of endless and infinite possibilities. . . . And apart from all that, the color remained impalpable, dwelling in air, free of any vehicle, never seen like this before."[74]

Occurring while he was still recovering from his illness, Murphy's encounter with Wilfred's instrument made a similarly vivid impression. "These forms had a three-dimensional effect and seemed to float in space," he wrote. "I was taken into this room and the dark glasses which I had to wear were removed and the first thing that I had seen for weeks was this fantastic spectacle of color gradually emerging from a gray nebulous background. It was one of the most ecstatic experiences of my life."[75] Over the next several years, Murphy's own experiments with visual musicality took him in a direction quite different from Wilfred and his clavilux, but the ecstatic sense of pleasure in visual spectacle that he experienced that day became an important element of his filmmaking sensibility.[76]

Recuperation at Brice's estate offered other pleasures, including the artists and affluent dilettantes who gravitated there. One may have been

Francis Bruguière, the photographer who in early 1922 would design the moody, expressionistic lighting for *Danse Macabre*. On assignment from *Theater Arts Magazine*, Bruguière photographed the clavilux in perform-ance during 1921. Though shot in black and white, Bruguière's images evoked the subtle, layered translucence of the shifting lumia. Accompa-nying an article about the clavilux, they appeared in the January 1922 issue of *Theater Arts Magazine*, just as production began on *Danse Macabre*.[77]

A wealthy painter named Gerome Brush was among the crowd who frequented Brice's gatherings. He asked Murphy to work on an experimen-tal puppet animation with him, inviting him to move into the Bay Shore house that he shared with several friends. Murphy's correspondence indi-cates that he did move to Bay Shore, but not until several months later, probably in the spring of 1922. In the interval, he pursued his suit against the Community Motion Picture Bureau, worked with Adelbert Ames at Dartmouth, tried unsuccessfully to raise funds for a musically inspired short film based on the Sixty-fifth Psalm, endured the countersuit by Commu-nity, launched Visual Symphony Productions, and made *Danse Macabre*. It was no doubt a relief to head back to Long Island.

As the only experienced filmmaker among Brush's crowd, Murphy was, as he put it, "able to be of considerable help." He characterized the asso-ciation with Brush as "nice . . . but not too productive."[78] Brush's affluent friends, however, were intrigued with moviemaking and were more than willing to make a feature-length film with Murphy. Among their families and associates, the Long Islanders raised enough money to purchase the rights to a *Saturday Evening Post* story by J. P. Marquand, "Only a Few of Us Left."[79]

Looking back, Murphy described it as "a snobbish-type story with the theme of the old guard of the Long Island horsey set opposed to the *nou-veau riche*." It may have been the wrong coast, but Murphy was suddenly a feature film director, and the Long Island elite were completely caught up in the project. "Through Malcolm Stevenson, I had met Tommy Hitchcock, the number one polo player of the famous Meadow Brook polo team, so we got permission to use the Hitchcock estate as a location," Murphy recalled.[80] "We persuaded Sir Ashley Sparks, who had an impos-ing house on Long Island, to lend us his for the newly rich girl's house. Rosalind Fuller, who was Francis Bruguière's girl and a minor actress, played the girl and a very good looking young actor, who posed for Arrow collar ads, named Reed Howes, played the male lead. Our extras were all top Long Island society names, including Hitchcock and other members of the polo team. The film had a truly authentic quality and caught the spirit of Marquand's story."[81] A brief item in the "Picture Plays and People" column of the *New York Times* in July 1922 made note of the film in production, "completed under the direction of Dudley Murphy, the director of 'Danse Macabre.' No part of the picture, it is said, was made in a studio, all of its scenes having been shot in the homes and on the estates of people living on Long Island."[82]

Christened *High Speed Lee*, the film was by no means avant-garde, nor did Murphy intend it to be. It was a Hollywood calling card, as polished a piece of mainstream filmmaking as he could muster. A review in a British film exhibitors' daily gave the film reasonably high marks, calling it a "bright, useful offering" and touting "the star's manly performance, the horsemanship, diving and steeplechase climax." In brief, the review claimed, *High Speed Lee* was a "pleasing and well-acted story of a youth's interests being divided between sport and business. Pretty love story."[83]

High Speed Lee might well have won for Murphy the industry attention he was after had anyone in New York or Hollywood actually seen it. Again, distribution proved to be a stumbling block, one that he was all too willing to disregard. As Murphy was editing the film, Francis Bruguière inadvertently precipitated the next crisis in his love life. "I happened to be at Bruguière's studio one afternoon," he wrote. "He told me that he was scheduled that day to take some pictures of whom he considered one of the most beautiful girls in the world. Suddenly the door opened and there was Katharine. I had not seen her for over a year and like a thunderclap, all my feelings were reborn."[84]

The feelings were mutual, but Katharine was scheduled to leave for Germany in two days' time, resuming her study at Elizabeth Duncan's school of dance in Potsdam. As in 1920, when he'd followed Herendeen to New York from California, Murphy's career pivoted on a personal relationship. "Here again, my love life and my work were in conflict. I wanted to go with her but I had to complete the film, so I made a plan to follow her as soon as possible," he wrote. "But in my desire to see Katharine, I left before any sale of our film had been concluded, leaving it in the hands of my young associates."[85]

From an industry perspective, the climate for independent distribution in the early 1920s was tough and getting tougher. In 1923, the year after *High Speed Lee* was made, *Variety* bluntly called for a better deal for independents, claiming that "over 50 per cent. of the productions slated to be thrown on the open market this season have either been held up or turned over to national distributing organizations at the latter's terms."[86] Murphy's associates on *High Speed Lee* may have been well-connected socially, but they had little film experience, and it took them several months to get the film into even modest distribution. The Arrow Film Company finally released it in March 1923. It was not reviewed by either *Variety* or the *New York Times,* an indication of its limited commercial distribution here in the United States.[87] By that time, however, Murphy's attention had already shifted elsewhere.

ON TO EUROPE

Murphy left *High Speed Lee* as soon as editing was completed, departing for Europe in September 1922. He immediately joined Katharine Hawley in Potsdam. By day, he took the train into Berlin, wandering the city and spending time at UFA (Universum Film Aktien Gesellschaft), the country's largest film studio. Nights were lost in "connubial bliss."[88]

With American dollars, Murphy was able to live spectacularly well on very little. In the tumultuous years after World War I, Germany was ravaged by runaway inflation, black marketeering, hunger riots, and political and economic chaos. "I remember buying beautiful Zeiss lenses and cameras for $3 and $4," he recalled. "I gave a dinner party at Kempinski's— a fashionable Berlin restaurant—in a private room, to which I invited about ten guests. We had caviar, champagne, and a fabulous dinner with a private orchestra and the whole bill was $35."[89]

In this chaotic climate, the arts perversely flourished, nourished by an economic and social breakdown that all but demanded risk-taking and disregard for tradition. Escapist films were in high demand, and despite ruinous inflation, the German film industry was producing a healthy number of them. In fact, the plummeting deutsche mark worked in the industry's favor, since production costs could be recouped even more quickly once films were sold abroad.[90] Directors such as Fritz Lang, Ernst Lubitsch, and F. W. Murnau were still at work in Germany, turning out such international hits as *Dr. Mabuse the Gambler* (Lang, 1922) and *Nosferatu the Vampire* (Murnau, 1922). Spending time at UFA, Murphy became friends with Lubitsch's assistant, Henry Blanke, and had opportunities to observe Lubitsch at work over several weeks.[91]

Murphy's mother and sister had been in Europe since the previous November, giving Carlene the grand tour while stretching a slender income.

Dogged by illness and an exceptionally cold winter, the women had wandered through Italy, Sicily, and as far south as North Africa. With Murphy in Potsdam, they made for Berlin. There, Murphy wrote, Carlene fell in with Constantin Stanislavsky's Moscow Art Theatre. The Russians were quite taken with her; at almost six feet tall, with long strawberry-blond hair, she was quite the Valkyrie. Despite speaking no Russian and very little French, she became part of the entourage, taking small parts in their productions. She eventually accompanied the troupe to the United States, performing in New York and Boston. According to family lore, she met her husband, Harvard engineering student Alexander Samoiloff, in a crowd scene in one of the company's Boston productions.

While Carlene pursued her theatrical career, Murphy dawdled in Potsdam. Even at ridiculously favorable rates of exchange, though, his money eventually ran out. The mark's suicidal plunge offered little impetus to work in Germany, so by early 1923 Murphy reluctantly left Hawley and went to London, where he connected with an artist and cartoonist named Will Dyson. Like Gerome Brush on Long Island, Dyson had an interest in filmmaking. According to Murphy, the two collaborated on an experimental film. Nothing is known of it, and apparently no prints exist.

From London, Murphy quickly moved on to Paris. He zeroed in on Montparnasse, a Left Bank district that had become a magnet for artists. In its narrow streets, the postwar backwash that was roiling Berlin took a different guise, transforming the old neighborhood into a frenzied laboratory of creativity, sexual tumult, and an exuberant mix of caste and class. A shifting international assemblage of artists, musicians, writers, gallery owners, moneyed dilettantes, and wayward tourists jammed the cafés, bars, after-hours boîtes, and scandalous artists' balls. It was, in short, everything Murphy could have hoped for, and he threw himself into it with gusto.

Soon after his arrival, Murphy was invited to the Italian island of Capri by Lady Rothermere, a wealthy British arts patron who'd recently bankrolled T. S. Eliot's literary magazine, *The Criterion*. The expatriate social scene was uninhibited, to say the least. "I went to a very intriguing party given by Count [Jacques Adelsward de] Fersen," Murphy recalled. "He had a beautiful villa with marble terraces and fountains. As the guests arrived, they were ushered into a dressing room where they were required to take off all their clothes . . . then we walked to the salon over a path of rose petals laid on the marble floors of the terrace. He had fortunately selected a group of people, all of whom were attractive, so that this party was a memorable one." Occasionally the count's festivities spun out of control, even by local standards. "After one of his parties," Murphy wrote, "a young lady was found dead near his house and he was told by the mayor of Capri that this was a rather serious thing and if it happened again he would have to leave the island."[92]

Darker moments notwithstanding, Murphy relished "the mad, gay days of Capri" and the wild, bacchanalian nights. But he also longed for his "Grecian goddess" Katharine to join him in what he considered "her native habitat."[93] He was taken by the natural beauty of the island and its grottoes, which struck him as profoundly mythological. Hawley soon arrived, inspiring another visual symphony-style short film, *The Syren* (1923), set to the song "O Sole Mio." Perhaps Lady Rothermere sponsored the project; in any event, it was shot, edited, and released far more rapidly than Murphy's previous productions. By late July, a leggy shot of Hawley in the title role appeared in the London *Daily Mirror*, promoting the film as a one-reel "featuret" produced by Murphy for his new enterprise, D. M. Films. An unidentified press clipping in Murphy's collection, apparently from a British film industry paper of the same period, reported that Murphy was in London to distribute the film and promote his new venture. The write-up also included four images from the production, one of a shaggy-legged, Pan-like creature blowing on his pipes and three of Katharine dancing in the grottoes. Little more is known of the film; in his memoir, Murphy mentions it only in passing, and no prints are known to exist.

During the sojourn on Capri, Hawley became pregnant. After an arduous overland trip to Amalfi she suffered a miscarriage, delivering a markedly premature, stillborn son. It was a traumatic experience for them both. A few weeks later, Hawley's mother came to join them. A concerned and wary parent from upstate New York was hardly a stellar addition to the besotted Capri scene. The three of them returned to Paris, where they rented a studio on the Boulevard Raspail near the Café du Dôme, in the heart of Montparnasse. Under pressure from Hawley's mother, the couple married some months later, in December 1923—fighting, Murphy wrote, "all the way to the *mairie*."[94]

While Hawley and her mother settled into the Boulevard Raspail studio, Murphy plunged back into Montparnasse nightlife. "The drinking and bull-session companions of this time were Donald Ogden Stuart, Red Lewis . . . Robert McAlmon, Marcel Duchamp, Man Ray. One became automatically a member of this group. Iris Tree, Nancy Cunard and Mary Beerbohm were three English girls who lived in the quarter. At a party at

Nancy's, I spent several hours talking with [novelist] George Moore. On another occasion, I was invited to a party by Ford Maddox Ford, which was being given to introduce his friends to a young American writer, who turned out to be Ernest Hemingway. On many occasions, a group of us would be drinking with James Joyce, who would tell us stories of Dublin and whose wife would come to collect him late in the evening and lead him home. . . . One of my treasured possessions was a first edition of *Ulysses,* autographed to me by Joyce."[95]

Other gatherings were decidedly less literary. Murphy's memoir is studded with reminiscences of Comte Etienne de Beaumont's extravagant costume balls and the debauches of the Bal des Quat'z' Arts, the annual spring art students' event renowned for minimal garb and flagrant sexual escapades, to which he was invited by sculptor Constantin Brancusi. In addition to designing extravagant costumes for these parties, artists often took responsibility for the decor. Murphy's participation in one such event reveals a puckish sense of humor, while the piece he designed bears some resemblance to late twentieth-century performance and installation art. "Several of the artists in the quarter were decorating [theater] boxes for the independent ball," he recalled, "so I did one in which the box was the open laughing mouth of a huge face, the teeth being the people in the box. In the forehead of this face was a screen on which I projected a movie portraying the thoughts of the people in the box."[96]

For Murphy, it was a long way from the Rialto and the Rivoli. By the time he'd settled in Paris, he'd already lost or abandoned several opportunities in Hollywood and New York. He'd chosen, probably wisely, not to pursue a career as a studio art director. His musical short films were well received, but two attempts to build them into a viable franchise had not succeeded. In his haste to pursue his personal life, he'd all but dissociated himself from his first feature film.

In the States, Murphy was a young director struggling to break into a highly competitive industry. Montparnasse offered him an alternate image of himself: as an artist among other artists, absorbing influences far broader than anything the American film industry could provide. It was a radical change in perspective, which left him eager to pursue a different kind of filmmaking. The opportunity came with *Ballet mécanique.*

CHAPTER 3

VEXED AND DISPUTED

The Multiple Histories of *Ballet mécanique*

In terms of its origins and authorship, *Ballet mécanique* is easily one of the most contested artworks of the twentieth century. It's the sole film on which artist Fernand Léger is credited as a director; it's also the most identifiably avant-garde film in Murphy's oeuvre.[1] And while it's clearly a collaborative work, even now, more than eighty years later, the actual collaborators and the extent of each one's contribution remain open to debate.

An invigorating inquiry into the nature of cinema and visual perception in the guise of unfettered play, *Ballet mécanique* was one of the first films to be acclaimed as avant-garde art. It gained in luster over the following decades as experimental film emerged as a genre, and it remains a bellwether in cinema history.

The film opens with a short stop-action animation of Charlot Cubiste, the puppet that Léger, an avid Charlie Chaplin fan, created in homage to his favorite.[2] After another title, "Charlot présente le Ballet mécanique," that sequence is followed by shots of a dewy Katharine Hawley Murphy, eyes downcast and lashes fluttering, swinging in an old-fashioned garden. With a machine-gun burst of images—among them a man's straw hat, numbers, a typewriter, geometric shapes, wine bottles, machinery, and an isolated smile—the film then launches into an exuberant, determinedly low-tech fantasia on the Machine Age. Pumping machine parts, whirling pastry whisks, frantically swinging pots and pans, and other objects alternate, often at a split-second tempo, with amusement-park footage and prismatically fragmented close-ups of, among other things, the crested head of a parrot, the artist's model Kiki of Montparnasse, and Murphy himself, looking oddly uncomfortable under the camera's gaze. Memorable sequences include a series of eye-poppingly fast cuts between geometric shapes, a frenetic, stop-motion Charleston performed by a pair of mannequin legs and a mantle clock, and the endlessly repeating trudge of a washerwoman up a flight of stairs on a steep Paris street. Plot is nonexistent, visual sensation is all. "The whole thing is a mad, fantastic dance of unrelated objects," declared one critic.[3] "It gives those who see it a kick," wrote another. "It stimulates and excites them, creating its own story in their imagination. It is like a cocktail in an ice cream parlor."[4]

In the earliest known print of the film, the opening credit reads "F. Leger and Dudley Murphy present Ballet Mechanique"; and Léger's notes on the film, prepared as it was nearing completion in 1924, call it a "Film by Fernand Léger and Dudley Murphy."[5] But for several decades it was regarded as Léger's work alone, with Murphy's part in its creation barely acknowledged. Reedited versions by Léger obfuscated matters further. Throughout his life, Murphy regarded *Ballet mécanique* as one of his proudest achievements. But among his films, it most dramatically illustrates his recurring marginalization from his own projects.

As befitting a film that some consider cubist, the many histories of *Ballet mécanique* resist resolution into a single coherent narrative. Montparnasse in the 1920s was not a milieu that encouraged detailed record keeping, and documentation of the actual filmmaking process is scant. But in the decades that followed, almost everyone involved came forward with his version of events, none of which matched the others. Scholarship naturally ensued.

Léger was the first of the collaborators to write about *Ballet mécanique*, starting before it was completed. His primary concern, however, was the film's theoretical underpinnings, upon which he continued to elaborate in articles, lectures, and interviews through 1954, the year before his death.[6] George Antheil, who composed the music intended to accompany the film, later claimed to be the original impetus behind it; and at the time *Ballet mécanique* was made, Ezra Pound considered himself a prime mover on the project. A late entry into the authorship sweepstakes is Man Ray, who a few years before his death in 1976 told film scholar William Moritz that he and Murphy had done a significant amount of work together on the film but that he himself pulled out when Léger—brought in, he said, to bankroll the project—got involved.[7]

Among art historians and film scholars, accounts of the film's production are similarly varied. Some scholars, including Standish Lawder, firmly position Léger as its creator, with Murphy relegated to a vague subsidiary role. Others, such as Judi Freeman, depict Murphy as a crucial contributor and bring Man Ray into the collaborative mix. Still others, most egregiously Moritz, minimize Léger's contribution, crediting the film's creation almost entirely to Murphy and Man Ray.

In his memoir, Murphy's account of the film's genesis is characteristically offhand and succinct. "One day, when I was visiting Ezra Pound and talking about my work, he told me that a friend of his, Fernand Léger, wanted to make a movie. Also George Antheil, the young protégé of Stravinsky would like to make a movie.[8] So he brought the three of us together and we decided to make one."[9] The film's basic concept, he wrote, was "a belief that surprise of image and rhythm would make a pure film without drawing on any of the other arts, such as writing, acting, [or] painting."[10] In Paris, Murphy had met a wealthy American divorcée who'd lent him money for a movie camera, presumably the one he'd already used to shoot *The Syren*.[11] Despite the casual tone of his recollections, Murphy stated in plain terms the working arrangement for *Ballet mécanique:* he supplied the camera, Léger supplied the film. "So Léger and I financed our film equally," he wrote, "with the understanding that he would have the European rights of the finished film and I would have the American rights."[12] Regarding his working relationship with Léger, Murphy's description is brief and carefully worded to encompass not only their mutual ideas but his own improvisations: "We talked over ideas and I set out with my camera and the film, executing the ideas that we had talked over and photographing things that stimulated my imagination around Paris."[13]

Written some forty years after the film was produced, Murphy's account is disarmingly straightforward. There's practically no element in it, however, that isn't subject to an alternative reading by either a fellow collaborator or a scholar. To gain a broader understanding of the making of *Ballet mécanique* and Murphy's role in it, it's essential to consider the film as part of his cinematic oeuvre: to seek out continuities between *Ballet mécanique* and his previous productions, to examine the project's influences on his filmmaking sensibility, and to identify the cinematic strategies that Murphy took from it to other films. Considering *Ballet mécanique* from Murphy's point of view implies a somewhat different perspective on Léger's role in the film, as well as that of others who took part in its production. In the process, it may be possible to arrive at a more nuanced picture of a project that, despite the scholarly attention it has attracted over the years, remains something of a black box.

"Arithmetical Law" versus
"A Leg over Each Shoulder, Screaming"

The extreme contrasts that drive *Ballet mécanique* find a ready counterpart in the divergent personal styles of its creators. Léger was more than a decade older than Murphy (and several years older than Man Ray), and his bruising war experiences in the Argonne Forest and Verdun were a far cry from Murphy's daredevil stunts over the potato fields of northern Britain. By 1923, Léger was a mature artist with a methodical working style and a bulging roster of commissions and other projects. Murphy was young, gregarious, and energetic, a new arrival intent on absorbing as much of Montparnasse as he possibly could; while Man Ray, another recent American expatriate, was already making headway in the tumultuous scrum of the Parisian avant-garde.

Like many artists and writers in postwar Paris, Léger was an avid cinéaste. His friend, poet and novelist Blaise Cendrars, worked on Abel Gance's 1922 epic, *La roue* (The Wheel), and Léger was captivated by the film's experimental sequences.[14] Inserted into a sentimental, melodramatic plot, these sections featured rapid-fire cutting, jolting rhythms and violently contrasting imagery. They were a major influence on Léger, who after seeing *La roue* in production "wanted to make a film at any cost."[15]

Léger envisioned an experiment in formal design and visual content that "sustains an arithmetical law that is rather precise, as precise as possible (number, speed, time)."[16] In his 1924 notes on the film, prepared a few weeks before its premiere, his explanation of its structure is nothing if not precise. "An object is projected to the rhythm of 6 images a second for 30 seconds," he wrote. "3 images a second for 20 seconds. 10 images a second for 15 seconds. We persist up to the point when the eye and spirit of the spectator will no longer accept."[17]

With regard to cinema, Léger was a prolific theoretician who enthusiastically expounded on the medium as a visual art form. He was not, however, a filmmaker. He never acquired a grasp of basic filmmaking techniques in either shooting or editing, and frequently confused technical filmmaking terms.[18] The lack of fundamentals prompted him, if anything, to think *too* big. Some of the sequences he visualized for *Ballet mécanique* were almost lapidary in their intricacy—dividing the screen into nine equal sections, for instance, and running identical footage in each at a different speed.[19] Nor did Léger's disregard of technical limitations stop at cinema. At one point in planning *La création du monde,* a ballet production conceived with Cendrars, Léger proposed inflating animals, trees, and flowers with gas and launching them at the climactic moment of creation. According to Freeman, "the idea was discarded because complex machinery would have been required and the sound of gas would have made the music inaudible."[20]

Murphy, by contrast, was indisputably a filmmaker. At the time he started on *Ballet mécanique,* he'd recently finished his sixth musically inspired short film, *The Syren.* He'd also collaborated on at least one animation project and directed his first feature. He could readily supply the technical expertise, both behind the camera and in the editing room, that Léger lacked. He was quick, enthusiastic, and enjoyed collaborating.

As the only professional filmmaker on the project, however, Murphy wasn't simply contributing technical know-how; he was pursuing his career. His short films to that point had constituted an ongoing experiment in relating moving image to music.[21] And where Léger saw *Ballet mécanique* as an experiment in "arithmetical law," Murphy saw it as an extension of the concept he'd been successfully working with for the previous three years. The idea of visual music is crucial to *Ballet mécanique,* but instead of the classical works that inspired Murphy's previous films, the music in this case is jazz.

When work on *Ballet mécanique* began in 1923, jazz had already gathered France into its raucous embrace.[22] In the years before the war, the Parisian avant-garde had discovered traditional African art, its influence surfacing in everything from Constantin Brancusi's sculptures to Pablo Picasso's *Les demoiselles d'Avignon.* Now, with a small African-American enclave taking root in Montmartre, the avant-garde encountered a living black culture, and an intoxicating one at that. In smoky bars, clubs, and *boîtes de nuits* in Montmartre and Montparnasse, African-American jazz translated the speed, fragmentation, and simultaneity of postwar life into music: loud, discordant, polyrhythmic, and syncopated. For Paris, *le tumulte noir* was the sound of modernity itself.

Perhaps as much as the machine, jazz is the aesthetic ground from which *Ballet mécanique* springs. This is certainly true from Murphy's perspective. But Léger was also a great fan of jazz music and was later instrumental in persuading impresario Rolf de Maré to bring *La revue nègre*—and its star, Josephine Baker—to Paris in 1925.[23] George Antheil, composer of the music intended to accompany the film, often incorporated African-American musical themes and motifs in his work. With his companion Kiki, an artist's model and renowned Montparnasse figure, Man Ray was a regular at such jazz spots as le Grand Duc. As for Murphy, Paris may have given him his first sustained encounter with African-American music. For him, musicality and film were already tightly linked, but from *Ballet mécanique* onward, jazz and other African-American musical forms exerted a profound influence on his filmmaking, in visual aesthetics as well as in subject matter.

Along with an innate feeling for the musicality of film, Murphy brought a second key element to the making of *Ballet mécanique:* a sense of play. Léger may have been a jazz devotee, but his deliberate, theoretical approach was hardly jazzlike. Murphy's pleasure in cinematic improvisation and spontaneity stands in sharp contrast to Léger's calculated schematics. "I was intrigued to do something with the artificial legs that exhibit silk stockings," Murphy wrote, "and decided to do a stop motion dance with these legs around a clock. In bringing the legs to the studio, I drove through Paris in an open cab, with a leg over each shoulder, screaming. Even the Frenchmen were startled by this."[24]

Startled, perhaps, but not entirely unappreciative. In the early 1920s, the Parisian avant-garde was enthralled by America, especially the version they found at the cinema. France was still recovering from a devastating war fought largely on its own terrain, in which the better part of a generation had perished. For those who survived, the energy and verve of American movies—the cliff-hanging serials, cowboy shoot-'em-ups, and urban escapades filled with cars, skyscrapers, and machines—were as intoxicating as Paris was to Murphy. André Breton and Louis Aragon were avid fans of the old Pearl White serials; Aragon, Jean Cocteau, Francis Picabia, and Léger passionately admired Chaplin; and everyone, it seemed, turned out for Westerns. "I wish I were a trapper, or a bandit, a prospector, a hunter, a miner, or a sheep-shearer," declared Breton's friend, the dapper Jacques Vaché.[25] Poet Philippe Soupault especially admired what he called "American tempo," a reference not only to the early, undercranked films that had everyone moving at an antic pace but to the sheer vitality of American life on-screen. "We were living with passion through a most beautiful period," he wrote, "of which the U.S. cinema was the brightest ornament."[26]

Murphy's madcap ride with the mannequin legs reflects the energy and exuberance that he brought to *Ballet mécanique.* The sequence that he mentions—an ebullient, stop-motion Charleston—utilizes the sort of cinematic techniques that he likely picked up while making the puppet animation on Long Island with Gerome Brush, or perhaps the experimental film with Will Dyson in London in early 1923. Where some scholars find in *Ballet mécanique* a meticulous translation of Léger's visual style to the medium of film, others see a giddy spontaneity and sly, Dadaist sensibility that remain stubbornly at odds with Léger's theory-driven methodology. Murphy's freewheeling, improvisatory approach certainly offers one explanation of the film's stylistic leaps, but it may not be the entire story. If Man Ray is to be believed, work on *Ballet mécanique* was well underway before Léger entered the picture.

The Ghost in the Machine:
Man Ray and *Ballet mécanique*

On the evening of July 6, 1923, the leading lights of the avant-garde jammed the Théâtre Michel on the rue des Mathurins for a much-anticipated soirée: *Le coeur à barbe* (The Bearded Heart), a Dada extravaganza arranged by Tristan Tzara and his colleagues. It was a stellar lineup: premieres of musical works by Darius Milhaud, Igor Stravinsky, and Erik Satie, among others; poems by the likes of Cocteau, Apollinaire, and Soupault; and as the centerpiece of the evening, a play by Tzara, *Le coeur à gaz* (The Gas Heart). Also on the bill were three short films: Charles Sheeler's *Fumées de New-York* (known today as *Manhatta*), an abstract film by Hans Richter, and Man Ray's *Le retour à la raison* (The Return to Reason), with musical accompaniment by George Antheil.[27]

As Man Ray recalled in his 1963 memoir, *Self Portrait,* at that point he'd already begun experimenting with film. But it was Tzara who persuaded him to pull together the scant minute of footage that he'd accumulated and to fill out the reel with the cinematic equivalent of his cameraless Rayographs, made by placing objects directly on the film emulsion. Man Ray knew he didn't really have to show up with the film; as he noted, the Dada crew often promised surprise guests who never materialized, such as Charlie Chaplin. Nevertheless, the *Coeur à barbe* soirée promised to be the event of the season, and Man Ray was there, film in hand.

A loose montage of disparate images, *Le retour à la raison* featured shots of Kiki, her nude torso shadowed by a striped curtain, as well as several Rayograph-like images, including dancing pins and a glimmering snowstorm of crystals made by sprinkling salt directly onto film strips. Yet the film's creation may not have been quite as off-the-cuff as Man Ray would have us believe. According to film historian Deke Dusinberre, Man Ray painstakingly incorporated into the film a subliminal image of a nude woman—most likely Kiki—striking a lascivious pose in bed. Imprinted on the substrate of the negative, Dusinberre wrote, the image may be seen only when sections of the film are held up to the light by hand.[28] It was a finishing touch that the crowd at the Théâtre Michel would have undoubtedly appreciated had they only known.

By any standards, the Paris avant-garde was a tough audience, prepared to brawl at a moment's notice. On this particular evening, the reigning Dada crowd and the upstart surrealists were rival gangs ready to rumble. By the time Man Ray's film came on, surrealist leader André Breton had already broken the arm of one hapless poet, and Tzara himself had come under physical attack by both Breton and Paul Eluard.[29] "Monocles, furs, canes, diadems, language usually indulged in by chauffeurs flew about the theatre," reported Jane Heap, editor of the *Little Review*. "A dozen private fights were going on . . . canes clashed, mirrors and footlights smashed, the audience stamped and laughed and shouted: 'Put the police out . . . let's have this among ourselves.'"[30] Though only three minutes long, *Le retour à la raison* was not screened to the end; heavily spliced, it broke twice in the projector, bringing the show to an abrupt halt. The second break provoked yet another of the evening's melées, adding enormously to Man Ray's prestige among his fellows.

It was this sudden emergence as an avant-garde filmmaker that apparently brought Man Ray to Murphy's attention. It's logical to assume that Murphy, and for that matter Léger, was in attendance at *Le coeur à barbe*—virtually everyone was. "All the celebrities of Paris," wrote Jane Heap, "painters, sculptors, musicians, poets; foreigners of every title, and rich excitement-hunting Americans turned out for this ultra-modern show."[31] There is, however, no definitive evidence placing either Murphy or Léger at the event.

According to newspaper clippings in Murphy's collection, he may in fact have been in London that July—if not on the night of *Le coeur à barbe,* then later in the month—promoting the release of *The Syren,* the film he'd shot on Capri that spring. Between his time at the UFA studios in Berlin the previous autumn and the heady, cinema-as-art atmosphere he found in Paris, Murphy's European sojourn was already changing his ideas about film. As the London clippings demonstrate, he'd become markedly more sophisticated in presenting his own work. "These pictures are said to contain the unadulterated elements of the medium itself, namely rhythm, colour, tempo and balance," wrote one British paper. "In the endeavour to find the true expression of the cinema medium instead of constantly adapting literature and legitimate drama to the screen, often so unsuited to it, Mr. Murphy has arrived at a purer form of the picturisation of the images that are aroused by music."[32]

Whether Murphy attended the *Coeur à barbe* evening or merely heard about it later, he apparently sought out Man Ray as a collaborator. "One day a tall young man appeared with his beautiful blond wife, and introduced himself as a cameraman from Hollywood," wrote Man Ray in *Self Portrait*. "Dudley Murphy said some very flattering things about my work and suggested we do a film together. . . . I insisted on my Dada approach if we were to work together, to which he readily agreed." According to Man Ray, the two went on a few shooting expeditions together and set up interior shots for "tricky effects." But, he wrote, the collaboration was halted before much, if any, footage had been shot. "When Dudley appeared again, he announced that he was ready to go to work and would I purchase the film. I was surprised, thinking this was included with the technical equipment—that I was to supply the ideas only."[33] With that, Man Ray recalled, Murphy decamped for Léger's studio, saying that the painter had agreed to finance the film.

In a 1965 interview with Standish Lawder, however, Man Ray stated that he and Murphy had made "a few" of the exterior shots that were used in the final film.[34] And in Man Ray's 1972 interview with Moritz, a broader collaboration emerged, one that was hardly stymied for lack of film stock, instead producing a substantial amount of footage. According to Moritz, several of the film's signature images—including the kaleidoscopic shots of Murphy and the parrot, Kiki in matte white mime makeup, and the sentimental images of Katharine Hawley Murphy in the garden—were shot by Murphy in collaboration with Man Ray. It was only then that the pair ran out of money, Moritz wrote, and Léger was brought in, principally as a financial backer.[35]

For Man Ray, this was a deal breaker. Though part of the same broad artistic circle, he didn't think especially highly of Léger or his work. As informal portraitist to the Parisian avant-garde, he eventually photographed Léger; using his personal rating system, he gave the portrait a low six out of twenty, not out of dissatisfaction with the image, but because, to Man Ray, Léger's art was "so heavy it seems carved out of solid matter."[36] Bowing out of the project, Man Ray insisted that his involvement go completely unnoted, and it was, by both Murphy and Léger.[37] In his memoir Murphy made no mention of Man Ray in connection with *Ballet mécanique,* out of respect for Man Ray's wishes, perhaps, or because Man Ray's role in the film's creation was perhaps not as crucial as he himself remembered it. Or

conceivably Murphy, still denied his own credit on the film, was not prepared to extend it to another collaborator.

Other scholars have not been quite as generous as Moritz regarding
Man Ray's contributions to *Ballet mécanique* or as stinting about Léger's.
But most acknowledge Man Ray's hand in its style, particularly in the
filming of individuals and the outdoor shots. "*Ballet mécanique* undoubtedly had several shooting phases," wrote Jean-Michel Bouhours, "including a first one between Murphy and Man Ray and a second between
Murphy and Léger."[38] Freeman has pointed out that Man Ray published
several images that appear in the film, including kaleidoscopic renderings
of Kiki's face, as independent photographic prints and that others are
recorded as glass negatives in the Man Ray studio in Paris—persuasive
evidence for his collaboration on this footage.[39]

Man Ray understood the characteristics that the French so admired
in American films—unexpected juxtapositions, the frenetic "American
tempo," and close-ups used as purely visual elements—and emphasized
them in his own films, including *Le retour à la raison*. By 1923, when work
on *Ballet mécanique* began, these ideas were not uncommon among the
cinema-minded avant-garde. Léger himself had already discussed them
in his writings, including an essay on Abel Gance's *La roue,* published the
year before. But Man Ray and Léger were vastly different artists, and in
their respective hands, the same ideas would have taken significantly different form. Though it's unclear how much footage Man Ray and Murphy
actually shot together, Man Ray's Dada approach certainly had an influence on Murphy's filmmaking in *Ballet mécanique*. Whether directly or
indirectly, the film's staccato editing, jolting rhythms, and outlandish juxtapositions reveal traces of his sensibility as well as Murphy's and Léger's.

As Freeman suggests, Man Ray's involvement in *Ballet mécanique* likely
resulted in the creation of key images, including the ones involving Kiki.
In his 1972 interview with Moritz, Man Ray insisted that he and Murphy
had shot all the footage in which she appeared, pointing out, "You don't
loan out your mistress, do you?"[40] Murphy, for his part, noted only that
Kiki's "breasts and extraordinary face are used in *Ballet mécanique*."[41] Curi-
ously, in her own memoirs Kiki made no mention of the film (or of Léger
or Murphy), though she did discuss her work with another director.[42]
Repeatedly photographed by Man Ray and filmed by him for *Le retour
à la raison, Emak Bakia* (1927), and *Étoile de mer* (1928), Kiki was his collaborator as well as his mistress, and it's unclear whether she would have
participated in *Ballet mécanique* were it not for his involvement.

EROTIC OR NOT?

There's further reason to believe that Kiki's participation in the film might have been contingent on Man Ray's. According to Moritz (who presumably heard it from Man Ray in 1972), Murphy and Man Ray shot erotic footage of each other with their respective mates, to be intercut in brief flashes between shots of pistons and other pumping machine parts.[43] In his memoir, Murphy referred to one such sequence, though his description is more genteel. "Another scene showed a tremendous piston, brilliant and shiny, plunging up and down in a very phallic movement. This was followed by the bulging stomach of Katharine, who was now pregnant."[44]

Moritz has asserted that Murphy's print of *Ballet mécanique* included these erotic flashes and that Man Ray and experimental filmmaker James Whitney recalled seeing them at Murphy's screenings of the print in the 1940s.[45] "Those who remember the Murphy prints [*sic*] insist that it . . . contained many more scenes of Kiki and Katherine [*sic*] nude," Moritz wrote in a 1988 letter. "These scenes of nudity were integrated into the montage for their specifically erotic content, making the insistent pumping rhythms of the machinery ironically copulatory."[46] Freeman, too, has mentioned such a print. According to Murphy's son, filmmaker Michael Murphy, whom Freeman interviewed in 1982, Murphy's print contained not only the shot of Katharine's pregnant belly but also other nude, "particularly suggestive" images.[47]

From *Soul of the Cypress* and images and descriptions of his other films, it's evident that long before his encounters with the Parisian avant-garde, Murphy's cinematic aesthetic encompassed a refined eroticism of the "high class filler" variety. Against the churning creative life of 1920s Montparnasse—the Dada slugfests, sizzling jazz, and licentious artists' balls—his own tastefully seductive blend of myth and classical music must have struck Murphy as hopelessly out-of-date. In that inebriating atmosphere, he might readily have taken to the task of melding, in the name of art, an untrammeled sexuality with a broadly experimental cinematic style.

The intermingling of art and sexual intercourse was clearly an aspect of Man Ray's creative persona. In the early 1920s, visitors to his studio were sometimes shown his erotic images of lesbians and photographs of men and women in the act of sexual intercourse.[48] A few years later, Man Ray joined writers Louis Aragon and Benjamin Péret in creating the book *1929*, which featured childlike poems about the months of the year, written in

distinctly unchildlike language. It also included close-up photographs of
Man Ray and Kiki making love, taken with a camera set-up that Man Ray,
"the eternal *bricoleur*," had rigged himself.[49]

Given the artistic predilections of Murphy and Man Ray and the recollections of Man Ray and Murphy's son, Michael, it's likely that the original cut of *Ballet mécanique* did include at least some erotic footage. Yet
according to film curator Bruce Posner, who is assessing the existing versions of the film, none of them retains any of this footage beyond three
frames of a seminude Kiki.[50] What happened?

As far as Moritz is concerned, the conclusion is obvious: the ironically
intercut sequences of pumping pistons and sexual intimacies are "scenes
that Léger hired someone to cut out of the original and virtually destroyed."[51] In somewhat more guarded language, Freeman supports this
supposition. "It appears that all extant copies," she wrote, "which appear
to have been distributed only by Léger and as early as 1924, had these
passages deleted."[52]

No, It's MY Film: Other Contenders

"Wot'ells??" Ezra Pound wrote to his father. "Dudley Murphy, whom I
met in Venice in 1908, he being then eleven; turned up a few days ago. His
dad is a painter, he is trying to make cinema into art. ETC."[53]

Though cited elsewhere as having been written in July 1923, this letter
is not dated, save for an archivist's addendum incorrectly stating the date
as "October 1924?" In all probability it was written in late October 1923,
just before the premiere of *La création du monde,* the ballet production
that Léger conceived with his friend Blaise Cendrars.[54] Pound's offhand
comment about Murphy's visit marks the start of his involvement in *Ballet mécanique;* and though Murphy's memoir casts Pound as merely the
matchmaker for Léger, Antheil, and himself, his letters of the time hint at
a different story. "I have practically completed the film with Ezra Pound,
and it looks quite interesting," he wrote to his sister, Carlene, on November 16, 1923. "It is quite abstract—no people—only interesting forms."[55]
In a letter to his father a few days later, Murphy indicated that Pound, not
Léger, was financing the film at that point.[56]

A later letter from Pound to his father corroborates his involvement in
the project. Written in January 1924 from the Hotel Mignon in Rapallo,
Italy, it reads: "Certain amount of work in Paris Nov. & Dec. preparing

concert—general executive functions etc. . . . Also work on vorticism film—experiment interesting—but probably Murphy hasn't brains enough to finish the job in my absence or without pushing."[57] Though hardly a vote of confidence, his comments, along with Murphy's to his sister, point to Pound's involvement with the film in late 1923—as well as to his departure from it by early 1924, when he was already in Rapallo, where he remained through the spring.[58]

In his 1924 notes for the film, Léger mentions "an important contribution due to a technical novelty of Mr. Murphy and Mr. Ezra Pound—the multiple transformation of the projected image."[59] This comment suggests a likely focus for Murphy's work with Pound in November and December 1923: the footage shot with beveled, prismatic lenses. This makes sense; Pound had long been fascinated by fragmented images. As a leader of the British vorticist group, he had worked closely with photographer Alvin Langdon Coburn in the winter of 1916–17 to produce what the two called "vortographs": prismatically fragmented photographic images made using the "vortoscope," a kaleidoscope-like instrument rigged, as the story goes, from pieces of Pound's broken shaving mirror. *Ballet mécanique*'s multiple-image footage undoubtedly caught Pound's attention; in his January letter, he referred to it as a "vorticism film."

He was probably the only collaborator to think of it in those terms. Murphy had most likely learned about prismatic lenses while assisting Adelbert Ames, Jr., in his visual perception experiments at Dartmouth in 1921. In Man Ray's account of his work with Murphy, he wrote that Murphy had "some complicated lenses that could deform and multiply images, which we'd use for portraits and close-ups."[60] While Pound may have encouraged him in his use of the lenses, it's likely that Murphy had been experimenting with them, either independently or with Man Ray, before Pound came into the project.

In their memoirs, neither Man Ray nor Murphy mentions Pound's involvement in the film.[61] It's conceivable, though, that his support in the closing months of 1923 enabled Murphy and Man Ray to extend their collaboration. If, as Moritz wrote, Man Ray and Murphy had become intimate enough to film each other's sexual encounters, presumably the friendship had gone beyond a few strolls through the city. Man Ray's thoughts on Pound were somewhat warmer than his opinion of Léger. Pound had written admiringly of Man Ray's work in one of his "Paris Letters" for the *Dial*, and his financing of the project might not have precluded Man Ray's involvement with it.[62] "I knew him as a kindhearted man, always ready to help others," Man Ray wrote in *Self Portrait,* though "dominatingly arrogant where literature was concerned."[63]

During this period—autumn 1923—Pound was actively promoting the avant-garde pianist and composer George Antheil, whom he had met that summer. He wasted little time in bringing his young protégé onboard. Writing a score for *Ballet mécanique* was, musically speaking, right up Antheil's alley. He'd already composed several complex, dissonant works that served as inspiration for this latest opus, including the "Sonata sauvage," the "Airplane Sonata" (both 1921–22), and "Death of the Machines" (1923), the piece he called his "microscopic sonatina." (Though only a minute long, it had four complete movements.) By late 1923, his "Mechanisms" (1920–22) had been converted into mechanical player-piano rolls, being, in Pound's opinion, almost impossible to play by humans.[64]

In his 1945 biography, *Bad Boy of Music,* Antheil stood the usual story of the project's genesis on its head, portraying himself as the originator, with the other collaborators falling in line behind him. "I announced to the press [in October 1923] that I was working on a new piece, to be called 'Ballet mécanique,'" he wrote. "I said that I also sought a motion-picture accompaniment to this piece." Murphy supposedly answered the call, "flushed by Ezra Pound, who convinced him. Murphy said he would make the movie, providing the French painter Fernand Léger consented to collaborate. Léger did."[65]

As a motivating force behind the film, Antheil is fairly suspect. From the outset, the film and its score led remarkably separate lives. In his letters to Pound during this period, Antheil made little or no mention of the film; Man Ray and Murphy had likely begun filming after the Bearded Heart soirée in July and sometime before Antheil's October announcement. According to Freeman, Antheil didn't even see *Ballet mécanique* while he was composing, since it was being shot and edited at the same time.[66] At the film's premiere in September 1924, the score remained unfinished; Léger himself didn't hear it until the following summer. By then, its running time was more than twice as long as the film's. Antheil was nothing if not ambitious: he originally scored the piece for two grand pianos, three xylophones, four bass drums, a tom-tom, a siren, electric bells, three airplane propellers, and, by some reports, sixteen synchronized player pianos.[67] The player pianos apparently were a sticking point; at the time, no synchronizing machinery existed or could be built to handle them all. Antheil hastily reconfigured the score for one player piano and several human pianists, and his "Ballet mécanique" finally premiered in Paris, sans film, in June 1926. "The lad took himself seriously," the *New York Times* reported, "and at the end of four [player piano] rolls, had worked himself almost into holy roller frenzy. The spectators whistled, laughed, booed or applauded and private arguments diverted the interest of the audience while Antheil was still at the pedals."[68]

Léger's 1924 *Ballet mécanique* notes closed with "We have asked the composer, George Antheil, to make for [the film] a musical synchronised adaptation—thanks to the scientific process of Monsieur Delacomme, we hope to produce mechanically the sound and image absolutely simultaneously." Léger referred to French inventor Charles Delacomme, who, working with the player-piano company Pleyel, had developed a system intended to synchronize film running in a projector with a player-piano roll. Freeman cited a January 1924 payment of three hundred francs from Murphy to Delacomme "for his services on the film," but it's unclear what those services were.[69] Murphy's November 1923 letter to his sister, Carlene, indicates that he thought he was almost done with the film at that time. So it's conceivable that Delacomme was preparing it, in some way, for synchronization. But with Antheil's score more than a year away, it's unlikely that Delacomme was synchronizing *Ballet mécanique* to its music.

He might have been working on a different film. Freeman noted that Delacomme was involved in synchronizing an earlier Murphy project, *Valse de Mephisto*.[70] Murphy himself makes no mention of this film, nor does it turn up in any of his press clippings. Perhaps it is a version of *Danse Macabre* with French titles, synchronized by Delacomme. Conceivably it could be this film, rather than *Ballet mécanique,* for which the three-hundred-franc payment was made. Although Delacomme and his company, Synchronisme-Cinématographique (later Synchro-Ciné), prepared Léger's prints of *Ballet mécanique* from the late 1920s into the 1930s, there is no record of him actually synchronizing a print of the film to its music.

OVERLAPPING SCENARIOS

By autumn 1923, enough footage had been shot on *Ballet mécanique* to send Murphy into the editing room with Pound and, by mid-November, for Murphy to consider the film almost completed. But it didn't wrap up until mid-1924, several months after Pound had left the project.

In the interim, Léger entered the picture, brought in, by all accounts, by Pound. The poet lived around the corner from Léger's studio, and the two were friends; they admired each other's thinking about art, modernity, and machines. As coeditor, briefly, of the *Little Review,* Pound was instrumental in publishing Léger's writings. In 1923, Léger dedicated his two-part essay, "The Esthetics of the Machine," to Pound.[71]

Leaving for Italy, Pound fretted about Murphy's ability to complete the film without him; in his letter of January 1924, he plainly said so. For his part, Murphy may have been fretting, too, though not about the film. Late 1923 was a time of personal turmoil. Earlier that year, his mother, Caroline Bowles, had returned to the United States from Europe, her health failing. In November, while Murphy was in the editing room with Pound, she died.[72] At the same time, Katharine Hawley's mother, who was still living with the couple in their Montparnasse studio, exerted increasing pressure on them to marry. In early December, amid much argument, they finally did. With Pound's departure soon after, Murphy needed another financial partner to continue the project. He may have had the camera, as he wrote in his memoir, but he still needed someone to buy the film.

Léger's involvement with *Ballet mécanique* probably overlapped Pound's to some extent. Given Léger's crowded schedule, however, it may not have been by much. Through late summer and early autumn of 1923, while Murphy and Man Ray were presumably on their shooting excursions through Paris, Léger designed and built an elaborate set for Marcel L'Herbier's 1924 film, *L'inhumaine:* a futuristic scientific laboratory in which the film's climactic scene was enacted. In late October, les Ballets suédois premiered *La création du monde,* the ballet that Léger had conceived with Blaise Cendrars and for which he designed the sets and costumes. And in January, he began teaching at l'Académie moderne, an art school that he started with artist Amédée Ozenfant. By 1924, Léger had a bustling studio and was juggling a number of commissions; things were so busy that some of his students were contributing to his paintings, in the fashion of a Renaissance atelier.[73]

Considering the footage that Murphy had already shot and edited for *Ballet mécanique,* on his own and with Man Ray and Pound, Léger came into a project that had already started taking shape—even if it wasn't, as Murphy had thought, practically finished. Léger had been contemplating making a film for some time. In a December 1922 letter to Pound, for example, he discussed the optimal conditions for such an undertaking (which included collaborators for scenario, decor, and technical expertise); in a letter to fellow cinéaste Jean Epstein a few months later, he sketched out ideas for an elaborate animated film that was never realized.[74] After writing and thinking about cinema for years, he at last had an opportunity to put his theories into action.

Ballet mécanique is thought to have been completed by July 1924, probably six months or more after Léger joined the project. It's likely that the film was finished sometime in the summer, but it might have been as late as September. Art historian Christopher Green, for one, based the July completion on the July 24 date inscribed on Léger's notes on the film, as printed in *L'Esprit Nouveau* (no. 28). Green pointed out that one of the sequences in the film, which arranges and rearranges the words "On a volé un collier de perles de 5 millions," was apparently inspired by a newspaper headline, "Un collier de 5 millions. On l'a volé naturellement," which appeared in *L'intransigeant* on September 10, 1924. He suggested that this sequence is an addition to the finished film.[75] It might be; however, given Léger's propensity for extended experimentation and the lack of a firm date for Murphy's departure from Paris, it's conceivable that editing on the film continued past the completion of Léger's notes about it, with Murphy and Léger together making last-minute changes and additions.

Hollywood cranked out full-length feature films in a fraction of the time it took to complete *Ballet mécanique*. But Léger was fastidious in his cinematic experimentation—mathematically so, as his notes indicated. However, until the film was finished, those experiments were mediated by Murphy, who did the actual shooting and editing. Though Charlot Cubiste, the Chaplinesque figure that opens and closes the film, is Léger's creation, Murphy, with his knowledge of stop-motion techniques, may have done the actual animation.[76]

Freeman has written that Léger functioned as *Ballet mécanique*'s "co-ordinator," who "helped to choose images and create rhythms present in the completed film."[77] This is probably a fair assessment of his role, with one significant omission: he put up a considerable chunk, if not all, of the money. Had *Ballet mécanique* been a Hollywood film, Léger might have been called its producer. His influence is undeniable, but his available time was limited; during this period he had so many projects in the works that Freeman, for one, wondered "how he still managed to produce pictures, travel, and teach in the years after 1920."[78] Despite Léger's considerable input, Murphy remained the primary day-to-day sensibility on the project. Of the principal collaborators, he was the only one involved in *Ballet mécanique* from start to finish. He had initiated the film, working first with Man Ray and then Ezra Pound before Pound brought Léger into the project. And while he was keenly aware of his collaborators' abilities and quick to pick up on whatever they brought to the project, he was the only one who had been, and would remain, a professional filmmaker.

In his subsequent films, Murphy was not always as fully committed to narrative as Hollywood might have liked. But in no other film would he abandon it as completely as in *Ballet mécanique*. All three of his collaborators undoubtedly encouraged him in this pursuit, and he responded in kind. Once Murphy returned to the film industry, however, narrative immediately reappeared and, even in his most inventive works, never left.

Even so, *Ballet mécanique* had a lasting effect on Murphy's filmmaking. Despite the constraints of Hollywood film form, characteristics of *Ballet mécanique*—the heightened emphasis on cinematic rhythm, the playful exploitation of visual perception, and, insofar as possible, the primacy of visuality over narrative flow—remained part of his cinematic style. Take, for example, the kaleidoscopic imagery that is one of *Ballet mécanique*'s visual signatures. Murphy utilized the technique to striking effect in *Black and Tan* (1929) and to a lesser extent in *The Love of Sunya* (1927) and *The Sport Parade* (1932). A decade later, the concept of multiple imagery resurfaced in altered form in the soundie *Alabamy Bound* (1941).[79]

Beyond questions of technique and style, *Ballet mécanique* marked a broader turning point. Before the film, Murphy's cinematic production had been largely limited by his self-imposed "visual symphony" format. From all indications, *The Syren,* the film he completed just before initiating *Ballet mécanique,* was of a piece with his previous musically inspired work. The explosively creative milieu of Montparnasse, the increased exposure to African-American jazz, and the avant-garde thinking that gave parity to film as a visual art inspired in him the desire to make a different kind of film. The concept of filmmaking that Murphy took away from *Ballet mécanique* was both blessing and curse—blessing, in that it clarified his visual sensibility and pushed him to further explore the musicality of film; and curse, in that this film-as-art approach would prove immensely difficult to work with in Hollywood. Even more difficult, as it turned out, was an essential task that he might well have taken for granted: keeping his name on the film.

Pushed Out of the Picture

Soon after *Ballet mécanique* was completed, Murphy and Léger parted ways. On September 24, 1924, the Internationale Ausstellung neuer Theatertechnik (International Exposition for New Theater Techniques), organized by

Frederick Kiesler, opened in Vienna. According to an article the following day in the Viennese newspaper *Neues 8 Uhr-Blatt,* Léger gave a lecture and showed *Ballet mécanique* as part of the opening night event.[80] It was the film's public premiere.

Murphy, meanwhile, returned to the United States. Katharine Hawley Murphy, whose "bulging stomach" had been filmed by Murphy and intercut into the piston sequence, was well along in her pregnancy and had gone home ahead of him. Still nurturing feature film aspirations, Murphy was eager to get back to Hollywood. Ironically, his efforts to reenter the industry mainstream resulted in his returning to France for several months, working with director Rex Ingram on *Mare Nostrum* (1926).[81] With that protracted absence, it wasn't until March 1926, more than a year after its completion, that *Ballet mécanique* premiered in New York. Which version of the film was shown—and whose print—remains in question.

In early 1926, Frederick Kiesler came to New York to stage an American version of his international theater exposition, organized with Jane Heap of the *Little Review.* The event was eagerly anticipated, with advance coverage appearing in the *New York Times* some six weeks ahead of the scheduled February 15 opening. Though delayed by almost two weeks, once it did open on February 27, the International Theatre Exposition was a great success, garnering wide press coverage and enough attendance to warrant holding it over for an additional week, to March 21. Presented in the Steinway Building on West Fifty-seventh Street, the exposition featured works from sixteen countries, including not only France, the USSR, and the United States but also Latvia, Belgium, and Poland. Pablo Picasso, Henri Matisse, Francis Picabia, and Georges Braque were among the artists whose theatrical designs were exhibited. Léger was represented by designs for his two Ballets suédois productions, *The Skating Rink* (1922) and *La création du monde.*

In addition to organizing the exposition with Kiesler and editing the *Little Review,* Jane Heap belonged to a coterie of passionate film devotees. By 1926, film societies and ciné-clubs devoted to experimental, foreign, and artistic cinema were springing up throughout Europe and the United States. In New York, one of the preeminent film groups was the International Film Arts Guild (originally the Film Guild), directed by Symon Gould. A second organization, the Film Associates, Inc., presented public premieres in New York and distributed selected films to theaters and film societies around the country. Both Heap and Kiesler were members of its advisory council.

In the program booklet for the International Theatre Exposition, an advertisement for the Film Associates announced a screening of Marcel L'Herbier's *L'inhumaine,* under the film's American title, *The New Enchantment.*[82] Presented on Sunday, March 14, at the Klaw Theatre on West Forty-fifth Street, the program also included "an abstract film as an indication of the new experimental films to be presented in April." The abstract film was *Ballet mécanique.*[83]

Though *The New Enchantment* earned lengthy reviews, the premiere of *Ballet mécanique* generated scant notice, much of it dismissive or bewildered. After *The New Enchantment* finished, reported Mordaunt Hall, "an even stranger production was put forth in which there was everything from pats [*sic*] and pans to a swinging girl, a glimpse of an amusement park and red circles—a film which would make the most confused effort of a futurist or cubistic artist seem as plain as a pikestaff."[84]

A few days later, on Thursday, March 18, the film received an encore screening before a packed house of homegrown cinéastes, "earnest individuals who believe in using the words 'art' and 'cinema' in the same breath," as the *New York Evening Post* put it.[85] The event was the opening night of the International Film Arts Guild's subscription series at the Cameo Theatre. In addition to *Ballet mécanique,* the program included Charlie Chaplin's *The Pilgrim* (1923) and *Color Dynamics,* a prismatic abstract short produced by the Eastman Kodak Laboratories. *The Three Wax Works* (1924), an expressionist feature by German director Paul Leni, rounded out the bill.

For some New York critics, the repeat screenings allowed them to get their bearings with the film. Some ten days after he saw *Ballet mécanique* at the Cameo, Richard Watts, Jr., wrote in the *New York Herald Tribune:* "It is disturbing and downright silly, but it is undeniably arresting. And it does push back the borders of camera possibilities, does provide one with a vague and distant half-glimpse of what can be done by the cinema in the way of rhythmic effects, camera angles, symbolisms, and all the other pet phrases of optimistic film radicals."[86]

In its Viennese incarnation two years earlier, Kiesler's theater exposition had hosted the world premiere of *Ballet mécanique.* According to his widow, Kiesler had kept the print shown there.[87] If so, given that Kiesler was on the Film Associates' advisory council, it's quite possible that the first New York showing of *Ballet mécanique,* the Film Associates' screening at the Klaw, used his print. But Murphy, back in New York after his stint on *Mare Nostrum,* was part of the same filmgoing circle. He'd already become acquainted with Symon Gould and was helping to program the International Film Arts Guild's schedule at the Cameo that spring, which included frequent screenings of *Ballet mécanique*.[88]

While it's unclear whose print was shown at the New York premiere, it's likely that the one screened at the Cameo was Murphy's. In his memoir he made no mention of the International Theatre Exposition or the presentation at the Klaw but described the scene at the Cameo. "There being no score to accompany the film," he wrote, "I got a Negro drummer from Harlem, who played on drums, tin washpans and washboards, and who would watch the film as he played interpretations in his own far-out manner, to the images which excited him on the screen. The audience at these showings got so excited that they would create near-riots in the theatre."[89] Writing in the *New York Telegram* that spring, Gould seconded Murphy's description of the screenings, mentioning both the film's "unique and original accompaniment of drums only" and the "mild psychic hysteria" of the audience.[90]

Moreover, Gould's description offers some indication that Murphy's print—in other words, his original edit of the film—differed significantly from later versions. "Sex, a nude female form, now seductive, now distorted," Gould wrote of the film. "And the satirical touch at the end, movie-wise, a daisy-dotted field, two figures home-wending and the orchestra ironically chiming in with 'Home, Sweet Home.'"[91] According to Posner, these descriptions don't match any sequences in extant versions of *Ballet mécanique*, all of which originated with Léger.[92]

Interestingly, *Ballet mécanique* premiered in London on the same date as its New York debut at the Klaw: March 14, 1926. There has been some speculation that the print screened in London was one of Murphy's. The thinking is that he must have stopped in London on one of his trips from Europe, after either *Ballet mécanique* or *Mare Nostrum*, leaving a print with the film society there.[93] This is unlikely. According to both Léger and Murphy's son, Michael, Murphy had only one print of the film.[94] Moreover, the information in the program notes appears to have come from Léger, suggesting that he was the source for the print. "Mr. George Antheil was engaged in the composition of music for this picture," the notes read, "but, according to Mr. Léger, his music is not likely to be suitably ready for some time and a jazz accompaniment suggested by Mr. Léger will accordingly be played instead. Mr. Léger is a Paris artist who has frequently painted aspects and arrangements of mechanical objects. Mr. Murphy is an American. The titling of the picture has been retained in French."[95] Had the information come from Murphy, presumably it would have been his name, not Léger's, mentioned three times in eight lines.

Too, in the spring of 1926, London was probably the furthest thing from Murphy's mind. Having spent a relatively unproductive few months in France as part of Rex Ingram's retinue, he was eager to reestablish himself in the States and in the film industry. Soon after returning, he apparently worked as an assistant on Alfred Santell's *Dancer of Paris* (1926).[96] Now, with *Ballet mécanique* making its New York debut, Murphy energetically pursued press coverage for himself and the film, looking to attract attention not only from the moviegoing public but from studio executives as well.

In "When Is It a Moving Picture? Dudley Murphy Helps to Answer the Question," an article in *Moving Picture World,* he spoke with aplomb on such cinematic matters as dynamic repetition, contrast, editorial rhythm, and percussive effects. "I believe the secret of Chaplin's success lies in his consummate knowledge and feeling for tempo," he was quoted as saying. "It is surely one of the reasons for the success of [King Vidor's] 'The Big Parade.' When the troops are coming to France—left, right—left, right, boom, boom, on and on they come. Repetition. The strength of this sequence is due to this repetition. . . . Repetition is one of the basic factors in all art and films can use it to more advantage than almost any other art form because of the time element." It may have been conventional wisdom among the cinéastes of Montparnasse, but it was engagingly fresh to American ears. "Murphy knows a pile of things about a motion picture camera," the writer noted. "He can make it do almost anything the human imagination conjures up." Though the article undoubtedly piqued interest among film audiences, Murphy had a larger goal in mind. "*Ballet Mecanique* should certainly be put into country-wide distribution," the closing paragraph read. "But more important still, one of the big producers of full length pictures should grab young Mr. Murphy and lead this son of Erin and America gently but firmly by a contract to a more or less secluded studio spot where he can have an opportunity to advance the art and the attraction power of the *moving picture.*"[97]

Reporting on New York movie openings, the *Los Angeles Times* picked up on Murphy's pitch. Noting that several "futuristic films made abroad" were to be shown with an upcoming Ernst Lubitsch retrospective at the Cameo, reporter Helen Klumph singled out Murphy as a filmmaker for Hollywood to watch. In a paragraph titled "Develops Ideas," she called

him "a young man who is likely to cause quite a stir in the picture industry one of these days. . . . Now and then he makes weird experimental
short pictures. But instead of basking then in the praise of his highbrow
friends, he goes out and gets a job as assistant—assistant director or cameraman. . . . On such young men rests the future of the picture business—
men who are developing an individual technique while studying at close
range the methods of the crafty and box-office-wiz [directors]."[98]

Hollywood had a chance to judge for itself a few months later, when
the Photoplay League—a West Coast counterpart to New York's film
societies—screened *Ballet mécanique* at a theater in Sherman (now West
Hollywood) on July 12, 1926. It was the group's premiere program; the bill
included, among other films, *The Three Wax Works, Prismatic Polygraphs,*
the German drama *Shattered* (1921), and a 1914 Charlie Chaplin–Mabel
Normand short. Prints were supplied by the International Film Arts Guild,
making it likely that Murphy's version of *Ballet mécanique* was the one
shown. Industry luminaries turning out for the gala premiere included
producer B. P. Schulberg, directors Ernst Lubitsch, Clarence Brown, and
Josef von Sternberg, and actors Adolphe Menjou and Dolores Del Rio.[99]

None of the films took the audience by storm—not even *The Three
Wax Works,* whose director, Paul Leni, was one of the evening's honored
guests. Critical response to *Ballet mécanique* was mixed. "While the 'Ballet Mechanique' is a rather interesting short subject to view, and is provocative of much discussion, one would be quite justified in taking the
whole thing as something in the nature of a practical joke," wrote Tamar
Lane in the *Film Mercury.* "The producers of this hodge-podge assert that
it is a serious attempt at something or other, and many spectators profess
to see much in it. I, for one, however, refuse to be hoodwinked."[100] But to
Edwin Schallert of the *Los Angeles Times, Ballet mécanique* was one of the
strong points of the program, "decidedly interesting among the novelties
presented." He readily grasped the film as "an expression of rhythm with
animated things. This picture tells no story, but is distinctly one of effects
strikingly achieved with pots, pans, chairs, tables, and other familiar objects
not gifted with personality, but that seem to assume one for the time of
their animation."[101]

The Photoplay League's initial program left Hollywood with little appetite for more, and the organization soon folded. Studio filmmakers may
have been intrigued by futuristic films made abroad, but their interest lay
primarily in invigorating the hometown product. Hollywood had no ready
niche for a radically visual, nonnarrative production like *Ballet mécanique*

or, at least initially, for its promising young codirector. As the industry continued to consolidate and the feature film moved toward a consistent, recognizable form, Murphy's dream of cinematic experimentation at a major studio appeared less and less likely.

In New York, Murphy handled the distribution of *Ballet mécanique* himself, using his one print. He took the same kind of personal, small-scale approach he'd used in the early distribution of his first films. "I had the print, which I kept in the closet of my apartment," he recalled. "When I got a booking, I would take the print in a taxi to the theatre, collect the rental in advance. When the showing was over, return the print to my closet, so that I was not only the film's director, but also its distributor. The film had cost $150 and got $100 a showing. This was the perfect way to market a film."[102]

Eventually, though, Murphy sought a wider audience. In May 1928, some two years after *Ballet mécanique*'s American premiere, a small item in the *Los Angeles Times* announced that the film would go into national distribution through FBO, the studio for which Murphy was then working.[103] Around the same time, FBO acquired distribution rights to Robert Florey's experimental short, *The Life and Death of 9413—a Hollywood Extra* (1928). Unlike *Ballet mécanique,* Florey's film had been an unequivocal hit with the Hollywood cognoscenti and had done well in its New York premiere; FBO reportedly released it to more than seven hundred theaters nationwide.[104]

It's unlikely that *Ballet mécanique* enjoyed similar distribution. In his memoir, Murphy made no mention of a national release, nor did his personal clippings files include notices for screenings outside New York. Murphy had no negative for the film, so exhibition prints would have had to be made from his copy. If such prints were actually made, apparently none survives.

It's possible that FBO intended to develop a niche market distributing experimental films. But less than six months after the announcement about *Ballet mécanique,* FBO was folded into RKO, a newly created division of RCA that also absorbed Pathé and the Keith-Albee-Orpheum theater circuit. Distributing futuristic short films fell off the agenda. Florey moved on to other production arrangements, making his next film under the auspices of United Artists. Distribution of *Ballet mécanique* apparently reverted to Murphy's closet.

Lack of national distribution left him vulnerable to competition. In 1931, gallery owner Julien Levy apparently obtained a 16mm print of *Ballet mécanique* from Léger.[105] Thinking to sell short films to collectors in limited editions, Levy screened it in his New York gallery in 1932.[106] A few months earlier, in late 1931, Léger himself screened *Ballet mécanique* at the Arts Club of Chicago.[107] And in the mid-1930s, the fledgling Museum of Modern Art acquired at least one print of the film.

The first copy of *Ballet mécanique* to enter MoMA's collection appears to have been a 35mm print acquired from Léger by Iris Barry, founding curator of the MoMA film library, when she traveled to Europe in 1936.[108] In 1939, Léger gave the museum a 16mm version that he may have previously shown there in 1935, featuring a sequence of rapidly alternating geometric shapes meticulously hand-colored by Gustav F. O. Brock, one of the last masters of this specialty.[109] According to Moritz, in the 1930s MoMA also acquired release prints and 35mm materials from the Cinémathèque française.[110] Regardless of how the film entered the collection, one point is clear: the French-language titles on MoMA's circulating prints make no mention of Murphy as codirector, referring to the work as "un film de Fernand Léger."[111]

In addition to deleting Murphy's name from the credits, the prints in MoMA's collection effectively squelched his distribution of the film. "A number of people I interviewed," wrote Moritz, "including Man Ray, James Whitney, and Harry Hay . . . remember that Murphy was rather bitter about this," since the film societies and small theaters that would have otherwise rented his print, with his credit intact, "were now showing MoMA prints with these French titles that omitted any mention of Murphy."[112]

More to the point, MoMA's version of *Ballet mécanique* was not the film that Murphy made. If erotic footage existed in his original cut—and Gould's description seems to indicate that it did—it had been eliminated. What's more, Léger continued to reedit the film long after the collaboration with Murphy ended. At least four distinct versions of *Ballet mécanique*, as well as variants of these versions, are known to exist in archives and cinémathèques around the world.[113]

This count includes the "Kiesler print," a 35mm nitrate print originally held by Frederick Kiesler, who had organized the international theater expositions in Vienna and New York in the 1920s. Now in the collection of Anthology Film Archives in New York, this print is longer than and substantially different from the others and is generally considered the earliest of the extant versions. That doesn't necessarily mean, however, that it's the original version. Léger began reediting the film almost immediately after its completion. Regardless of the point at which he and Murphy finished their collaboration in the summer of 1924, it's likely that the version that Murphy carried out of the editing room was not the one Léger showed in Vienna in late September. Freeman, who inspected the original Kiesler print at Anthology, noted "minute and extensive frame by frame cutting," not the sort of treatment that's normally given to a print destined to run repeatedly through a projector.[114] Moritz wrote that the Kiesler print "contains large sections that are copied in black-and-white from an edited original (probably Murphy's finished edit), and among those passages are frames that show signs of having been copied from a tinted original."[115]

It is likely that none of the extant versions of the film originated with Murphy. As noted, he owned a single 35mm print, which he used for his initial New York bookings, later screenings, and whatever dealings he had with FBO. According to William Moritz, this print was destroyed in a fire in California some time after the 1940s.[116]

WHOSE FILM IS IT, ANYWAY?

As Moritz has observed, *Ballet mécanique* is a film made by committee—and, one might add, a rotating committee at that. Murphy was its only consistent member and the least renowned of its collaborators. At the time the film was made, Léger was an established artist and a public figure. Man Ray and Ezra Pound were well regarded in avant-garde circles and found broader acclaim soon after.[117]

Murphy wasn't the only collaborator to disappear from *Ballet mécanique*. Neither Man Ray nor Pound even made it into the film credits. Yet in the beginning, Murphy had been openly acknowledged by Léger as a full partner in the film's creation, only to see himself erased from its history like a disgraced Soviet functionary from a Kremlin photograph. For someone who, as Bouhours says, "[passed] himself off willingly as a modest but zealous subordinate," Léger did a remarkably thorough job of securing sole claim to the film's authorship.[118]

At the same time, it must be pointed out that *Ballet mécanique* remained in the public eye largely through Léger's efforts. Through the decades, he continued to write about and discuss the film and frequently screened it as part of his lectures in the United States and elsewhere.[119] Léger secured a level of international interest in the film that Murphy alone was unlikely to have generated, ensuring its lasting fame. The price, however, was several decades in which Murphy lost virtually all directorial credit for the project. In a 1951 letter to Virgil Thomson, George Antheil—who'd gone on to become a composer and musical director for Hollywood films—remarked that even then, years later, Murphy felt that he'd been "bilked by Pound and Léger in proper recognition of the fact that he, and not they, had the major part to do with making *Ballet mécanique*."[120] Antheil himself concurred. Writing to Thomson a few weeks later, he commented that "Léger and Pound pretended to have produced" *Ballet mécanique,* but in reality, they "supplied some ideas, and the money."[121] As Man Ray drily noted in *Self Portrait:* "And that is how Dudley realized the *Ballet mécanique,* which had a certain success, with Léger's name."[122]

Though *Ballet mécanique* is a milestone in avant-garde cinema and one of the achievements of which Murphy was most proud, its impact on his career was equivocal. Despite his immersion in what was arguably the pivotal cultural milieu of the early twentieth century, he had never lost sight of his goal of becoming a successful studio director. And while *Ballet mécanique* was crucial in the formation of his filmmaking style, it all but ensured that his style would not be the type that Hollywood was looking for. Murphy wanted to pursue a mainstream film career *and* make experimental "art" films. With the sensation that *Ballet mécanique* created in its New York and Los Angeles screenings, he hoped to gain the opportunity to experiment further under the aegis of a major studio. The looser, more casual Hollywood he'd left behind in 1920 might have accommodated such an arrangement. In the Hollywood he was returning to, it was impossible. While he was in Europe, the American film industry had become increasingly standardized and businesslike. In theory, at least, Hollywood had no objection to experimental films—its enthusiasm for Florey's *Life and Death of 9413* indicates as much. But it preferred the homegrown variety, especially as a means of identifying promising talent, like Florey, that could work within the system. Murphy's vision of studio-sanctioned cinematic art was no longer practical, if it ever had been. It was, however, persistent, and it colored his dealings with the film industry for the rest of his career.

In the long run, Léger had a shrewder grasp of how to exploit the film than Murphy did. Destined largely for film societies and museums, *Ballet mécanique* was accorded the status of cinematic art; in his writings, interviews, and lectures, Léger vigorously reinforced the connection between the film and his artistic output in other media. Murphy, on the other hand, saw no inherent disjuncture between popular culture and the avant-garde; even though *Ballet mécanique* was as far from the mainstream as a movie could be, he continued to consider himself a professional filmmaker, not an artist who made films. As a result, he was caught between the two identities. He became known as an "arty" director at a time when Hollywood had little use for art. In the industry, his association with *Ballet mécanique* didn't do for him what he hoped; conversely, his identification with Hollywood may have weakened his perceived claim to the film.

For Murphy, the die was cast when MoMA received its prints of *Ballet mécanique* in the 1930s. Even as a relatively new institution, the museum's distribution capabilities far exceeded the limits of his informal one-man operation, reaching the art-house and ciné-club markets much more effectively than Murphy or even FBO might have done. The version of *Ballet mécanique* circulated by MoMA became not only dominant but also, given the museum's prestigious modern-art imprimatur, authoritative in this country. As a result, Murphy's credit and authorship were lost to scholars as well as to the general public. Lawder's foundational work, *The Cubist Cinema,* for instance, was published in 1975, a year before discovery of the Kiesler print. With research largely drawn from the MoMA version, the book not surprisingly assigned authorship for *Ballet mécanique* squarely to Léger, dismissing even the possibility of Murphy as cocreator.

Whose film it is and whose creative stamp it most clearly bears are questions as irresistible as they are irresolvable. I would contend that no one "true" version of *Ballet mécanique* exists or for that matter has ever existed—that virtually from the start, Murphy and Léger emerged from the editing room with two distinct versions of the film, of which each man believed himself the primary auteur. For Léger, the editing on his version never really ceased. Even in his final years, he was planning a color remake with Cinémathèque française cofounder Henri Langlois.[123] In Murphy's case, his purest vision for the film was lost with the only copy of his version. Had he had the foresight, the business sense, and the spare cash to make an additional print or two, the history of *Ballet mécanique* might have played out somewhat differently.

CHAPTER 4

INTO THE MAINSTREAM

Murphy returned from France in late summer or early fall of 1924. By then, Katharine Hawley Murphy had taken up residence at an informal art colony on her great-aunt's estate in Croton-on-Hudson, New York. Looking for film work, Murphy remained in New York City while Hawley Murphy waited out her pregnancy upstate. The work came quickly enough, but instead of uniting the couple it separated them further. One of the first people Murphy had called on in New York was J. Robert Rubin, secretary of the newly merged Metro-Goldwyn Pictures. Rubin pointed him toward Rex Ingram and *Mare Nostrum*.

It was in many ways an inspired match. Ingram was a Yale-trained sculptor who at one time had shared a studio with Thomas Hart Benton, and he brought an artist's eye to his moviemaking. Strikingly lit, elegantly composed, his films were profoundly visual and romantic, driven by the sheer drama of their imagery. A studio director since 1916, Ingram had catapulted a little-known Rudolph Valentino to fame in *The Four Horsemen of the Apocalypse* (1921) and did the same for Ramon Novarro in *The Prisoner of Zenda* (1922). Though only a few years older than Murphy, Ingram was at the height of his career in 1924. His films made millions worldwide, and his name on the marquee was as much of a box-office draw as most movie stars'. Along with D. W. Griffith and Cecil B. DeMille, he was frequently acclaimed as one of the cinema's great directors.

Ingram was a perfectionist who thought nothing of tearing apart and redoing a set, down to the paint on the walls, to satisfy his compositional sense. He routinely overscripted, shooting far more scenes than could

69

possibly fit into a single feature. Editing was a protracted and painful process. (On *Mare Nostrum* he shot, by his editor's estimation, more than a million feet of film.)[1] Arrogant and mercurial, he resisted authority in any form. He was generous to those he favored but quick to renounce them for the slightest transgression; once lost, his good opinion was impossible to recover. Charismatic, attractive, and sexually adventurous, Ingram was critically acclaimed and spectacularly successful—everything that Murphy aspired to be and more. "He was one of the handsomest and most glamorous men I have ever seen," Murphy recalled. "When I showed him some of my films, he engaged me to work with him on his forthcoming picture. But instead of Hollywood, he said we sail for Paris Wednesday morning."[2]

Murphy had caught the director at a defining moment in his career. Despite Ingram's immense success, by 1924 he was no longer content in Hollywood. The system that had given important directors complete control over their own pictures—enabling him to create his colossal hits— was on the way out, supplanted by a web of business-savvy producers who reported not to individual directors but to the studio heads. The merger of Ingram's studio, Metro, into Metro-Goldwyn Pictures (soon to be Metro-Goldwyn-Mayer) put Louis B. Mayer, whom he thoroughly detested, in control of production. As one of the industry's top money-makers, Ingram had clout and didn't hesitate to use it. He'd already spent time in Nice while shooting his previous film, *The Arab* (1924), and he now demanded his own production center there. None too graciously, the studio complied. *Mare Nostrum* was the first project scheduled for the new facility.

Fresh from Paris, with the avant-garde aura of *Ballet mécanique* still upon him, Murphy made a strong impression on Ingram, who'd had little European experience himself. Most likely Hermann's artistic reputation didn't hurt, either, nor Murphy's easy affinity with the Dublin-born director's Irish roots. Signing on to *Mare Nostrum,* Murphy joined a company of Ingram regulars that included writer Willis Goldbeck, cameraman John F. Seitz, editor Grant Whytock (who would later edit Murphy's *The Emperor Jones*), and Ingram's wife and leading lady, Alice Terry. The initial phase of the project took place not in Nice but in Paris. "We were put up in a first-class hotel," Murphy wrote, "and there followed 6 months of preparation, during which time Ingram was working on the script with Goldbeck." For the rest of the team, there was little to do but wait. "We were on salary and expenses, but we only had to make an appearance at the office once or twice a week," he recalled. "My job was doing research on some undersea sequences, getting costumes designed for mermaids."[3] Ingram had no knowledge of Paris, so Murphy's informal duties involved introducing him to the city, its cultural life, and elegant restaurants not overrun by American tourists.

Though it's unclear precisely when in 1924 Murphy returned to the States after *Ballet mécanique,* a letter to Katharine Hawley Murphy, dated Armistice Day, placed him back in Paris with Ingram by the end of October, anxiously awaiting her arrival. "We are to be here till the last of December and we could be together most of the time as work doesn't really start till then," he wrote. "Then we go to Spain for a few weeks . . . and I would be with you till February 15th, about, when we would go to Naples. . . . We would come back here after three or four weeks in Naples and have the spring together."[4] As Murphy's letter implied, the script for *Mare Nostrum* called for extensive location shooting, including Barcelona, Naples, Pompeii, and stretches of the French seacoast. From start to finish, the film took some fifteen months to complete. Working back-to-back on four films for other directors, Alice Terry didn't arrive in France until well into 1925, leaving Ingram to continue developing the script while a second-unit crew headed by Seitz—and presumably including Murphy—shot the Barcelona material with Terry's costar, Spanish actor Antonio Moreno.

Meanwhile, Katharine Hawley Murphy, nearing the end of her pregnancy, arrived in Paris in late 1924. The couple's son, Michael, was born in the American hospital in Neuilly on January 11, 1925.[5]

Though Murphy's schedule on the project was relatively light, the demands of new fatherhood didn't mix with production work for a director as volatile as Ingram. A few months into the film, Murphy was elbowed aside by Harry Lachman, an American expatriate painter in whose studio Murphy had shot parts of *Ballet mécanique.* It was easy to see why Ingram came to prefer Lachman. He was an artist, spoke fluent French, had lived in Paris longer than Murphy, and had entrée to a broader swath of Parisian society. He also knew how to work the French bureaucracy, a talent that Murphy never had need to develop. When the purchase of the Nice facility became snarled in legalities, Lachman was able to cut the red tape or at least hire the lawyer who did. As a result, he became the manager for Rex Ingram Productions, and Murphy became one of several individuals whose work on *Mare Nostrum* was not acknowledged in its credits.[6]

Like *The Four Horsemen of the Apocalypse, Mare Nostrum* was adapted from a novel by Spanish writer Vicente Blasco-Ibañez. A sordid tale of World War I–era love and espionage that leaves virtually no survivors, the film did not do well at the box office. Nor were the Hollywood trade journals inclined to be gracious. Earlier in 1924, Ingram had commented to the French papers that he found Europe so congenial that he could never make a film in Hollywood again. The industry press, notably Louella Parsons, wouldn't let him forget it.[7] Calling *Mare Nostrum* "unquestionably draggy," *Variety* chided Ingram for allowing "his sense of the dramatic to run rampant at times." In a backhanded rebuke, the paper noted that "Ingram has been away from these shores a long time. It wouldn't do him any harm to take a jaunt back home if for nothing else than to sit around, talk with the boys, and glance over what they're doing in picture work. Some of the footage here reveals that absence in Ingram's work."[8]

It may have been good advice, but Ingram didn't take it. He remained abroad for the rest of his film career, which lasted through four more productions. *Mare Nostrum* marked the beginning of his decline, which was exacerbated by the arrival of sound film a few years later. Ingram turned out two more features for MGM, *The Magician* (1926) and *The Garden of Allah* (1927), neither of them particularly successful. He then bought the Nice studio, independently producing his last two movies: *The Passions* (1929) and *Baroud* (1931), his only sound film. At that point he retired from filmmaking, devoting himself to travel, sculpture, and writing.

If his work on *Ballet mécanique* encouraged Murphy to pursue a non-Hollywood filmmaking style, the association with Ingram gave him a non-Hollywood business model to match. It's evident from his memoir that Murphy admired Ingram a great deal, not only for his success, but for the way he exploited it to place himself beyond the studios' tightening grasp. Ingram worked independently of the MGM hierarchy; the end credit for *Mare Nostrum,* for instance, calls it an "Ingram-Metro-Goldwyn" production. Apparently he even insulted his nemesis, Louis B. Mayer, with impunity. Murphy recalled one episode in which Ingram, forced to acknowledge Mayer in a hotel dining room in Paris, introduced him as "Louis B. Merde."[9] Though Murphy's success in the industry never approached Ingram's, he was haunted by Ingram's vision of a Hollywood away from Hollywood—a distant, semi-independent production center that maintained only the most tenuous, advantageous connection to its patron studio. He would attempt to re-create this arrangement or something like it in three different countries over the course of his career.

"Finding His Job"

Mare Nostrum premiered in New York in February 1926, a little over a month before *Ballet mécanique* had its American debut at the International Theatre Exposition. Leaving *Mare Nostrum* some months before its completion, Murphy presumably returned to New York by mid- to late 1925.

The New York to which Murphy returned was far more louche than the city he'd left in 1922. As Bruce Kellner has noted, the height of the Roaring Twenties found Manhattan in a decadent mood, with a determined appetite for trifles—mah-jongg, crossword puzzles, cocaine and bootleg liquor, bee-stung lips, Ouija boards, the Charleston—and an insatiable taste for nightlife. Some six years into Prohibition, speakeasies had leveled the cultural landscape. No one, it seemed, went to the opera or to symphony concerts, lectures, or museums; they were jamming the cabarets or phoning orders to their bootleggers.[10] Tossed into the cocktail shaker of Prohibition, once-steadfast class distinctions blended in a frothy new social concoction. In night clubs and speakeasies, refined young ladies shimmied alongside shop clerks and chorus girls, while their Ivy League dates talked gangster slang and African-American musicians set a syncopated tempo for the Jazz Age. Scrambling to escape police raids or sitting knee to knee in overpacked paddy wagons further eroded social barriers.

With *Ballet mécanique* lending its own note to New York's cultural frisson, Murphy made his way through a circle that included Algonquin Round Table regulars and writer Carl Van Vechten, a legendary cocktail-party host whose nightclubbing sorties to Harlem added a distinctive kick to the city's Prohibition culture. But cocktails were one thing and work was another, and in this regard *Ballet mécanique* did little for Murphy during that first year in New York. Hollywood was slow to take notice, and before long Murphy had to accept whatever work came his way. In spring 1926, while the film was still causing a stir at the Cameo, he was hired for a short production called *Finding His Job,* an assignment he undoubtedly would have refused if he could. "This light love story is used as a pleasant means of presenting the propaganda of the [Bedford] Garden Club," noted the *New York Times,* "the object of which is to show the public what harm can be done by a carelessly thrown lighted cigarette or the tearing of blossoms from young trees. . . . Mrs. James S. Metcalf received much applause for her scenario of this film, which was directed by Dudley Murphy."[11]

As a follow-up to *Ballet mécanique,* it was hardly worth the celluloid it was printed on. But with a toddler at home and another child on the way, Murphy could not afford to be choosy. His divorce from Chase and lengthy stay in Europe, which had continued even as his mother weakened and died, caused Murphy's father to cool toward him. Hermann's fatherly advice and helping hand were offered less frequently, and Murphy was now the one eager for contact. A few days after the *Times* mention of *Finding His Job,* he dropped Hermann a quick note, telling of a French film about children that he was editing and enclosing a few press clippings, the *Times* piece probably among them.[12] "Do write me soon and let me know how you are at least," he admonished.[13] But by September, correspondence had not picked up, despite the birth of the Murphys' second child, Poco, in August. "Please write," Murphy added in closing his letter of September 15. "I'm going to try and make my letters weekly instead of bi-annual. Also I would like to hear from you once in a while."[14]

If Murphy needed confirmation that Hollywood had no idea what to make of *Ballet mécanique,* he got it in one of the next assignments to tumble in. As the first project for her new production company, film star Gloria Swanson had chosen to make *The Love of Sunya* (1927), an adaptation of a 1917 play that had been previously brought to the screen in 1919. In the film, a Hindu mystic discloses to a young woman what the future would hold for her with each of her suitors, revealed through consultations with a magic crystal. Impressed with the visual impact of *Ballet mécanique,* Swanson hired Murphy to create the special effects for the crystal sequences. Here was the industry's use for abstract cinematic art with a European touch: special effects for the kind of exotic mumbo-jumbo that it cranked out by the bushel.

What's more, it didn't work. As a special-effects man, Murphy was apparently a disaster. "He foundered at each technical problem, and soon we were running behind schedule," Swanson wrote in her autobiography.[15] (Art dealer Julien Levy, at the time an aspiring filmmaker, was Murphy's assistant on the project, and he too recalled endless delays on the set.)[16] At the same time, little in Murphy's experience had prepared him for dealing with a waning but still powerful movie star nervously embarked on her first self-produced film. "I panicked at the thought that I might fail in the dramatic as well as the technical aspects of the picture and be a laughingstock," Swanson wrote. "I began working sixteen- and eighteen-hour days, and the only results seemed to be more delays and second-rate effects."[17] Eventually, she recalled, someone was found to help resolve the technical issues: George de Bothezat, an émigré Russian aeronautics engineer who in 1922 had developed a prototype helicopter for the U.S. Army. Between them, Murphy and de Bothezat managed to create effects that satisfied Swanson and her director.

Despite the behind-the-scenes difficulties, Hollywood liked what it saw. "Dudley Murphy's echo of the photographic technique which riveted attention to his 'Ballet Mecanique' is employed with sound logic in . . . the imaginary episodes which constitute the greater part of the picture," wrote a reviewer in the *Los Angeles Times*.[18] Evidently Swanson thought highly enough of his creative sense, if not his technical expertise, to engage him again for the animated titles in her 1930 film, *What a Widow!* "Joe Kennedy had insisted on unique titles at the start of the picture," she wrote, "principally so that no one would miss the one that said, 'Joseph P. Kennedy presents'; therefore I got Dudley Murphy to create something extra special."[19]

NARRATIVE TAKES OVER

Even so, Murphy's future clearly did not lie in cinematic special effects. Screenwriting proved a more likely field and a surer path to feature film directing. Sailing from Europe into New York Harbor, Murphy had been struck by the dynamism of the city skyline and its palpable energy. "New York, in fact, the whole sweep of the American scene, fascinates me," he told writer Matthew Josephson. "Nobody realizes how strange the life that is going on right under our noses is. I am trying to get the fantastic speed and rhythm of this jazz age into a film." Josephson noted that Murphy "is working now on a feature film of New York life. It has never been done yet, as Flaherty has done the Eskimos or the South Sea Islanders."[20]

When Fritz Lang first glimpsed the New York skyline in 1924, he responded with the dark fantasia of *Metropolis*. By contrast, what Murphy had in mind was literally a film about the skyline—specifically, New York skyscrapers and the men who put them up. "I met a steelworker who lived in the Village," he recalled, "who gave me all the technical terms and some of the spirit of the men who walked the beams and built these fantastic buildings."[21] Quickly writing "Skyscraper," he started shopping the treatment to the studios.

In Hollywood, the tightly centralized, cost-efficient system that had sent Rex Ingram sailing off to Nice was starting to pay off for MGM. The

studio was enjoying a run of comparatively on-time, on-budget hits such
as King Vidor's 1925 *The Big Parade.* By the late 1920s, MGM's innovative
approach was widely regarded as a model of industry efficiency, and several other studios implemented similar management plans.

Not all directors, however, were willing to surrender fiscal (and in many
cases creative) control over their films, especially not those, like Ingram,
who'd enjoyed near-complete autonomy. One holdout was Cecil B.
DeMille. A Hollywood pioneer, in 1914 he'd directed the first American
feature-length film, *The Squaw Man,* in a rented horse barn on the corner
of Selma Avenue and Vine Street. Through a series of mergers, that original studio, the Jesse L. Lasky Feature Play Company, had been folded into
Paramount; and despite the runaway success of his 1923 spectacle, *The
Ten Commandments,* the supremely autocratic DeMille and studio head
Adolph Zukor (a stealthy, taciturn man nicknamed "Creepy") had never
gotten along. In January 1925, the feud came to a head, and DeMille left
Paramount. He bought the old Ince Studios and the Producers' Distribu-
tion Corporation, combining them to establish a new venture, the Cinema
Corporation of America.

In New York, Murphy pitched "Skyscraper" to the story editor for
DeMille's company, who liked it well enough to send it on to DeMille
himself. The company purchased the rights and engaged Murphy to work
on the scenario at its West Coast studio. After the lengthy detour of *Mare
Nostrum* and the ill-assorted, incidental work that New York offered,
Murphy finally made it to Hollywood. He rented a small beach house
in Venice, up the street from Janet Gaynor, who would soon win the first
Academy Award for Best Actress. Katharine Hawley Murphy remained
back East, where her family could help care for the children as she pursued her own career as a dancer.

His fervor to get started put Murphy at an immediate disadvantage.
The first two films that DeMille made for his new enterprise had done
poorly at the box office, leaving the company in precarious financial
straits. While Murphy waited impatiently for an audience with the great
man, DeMille was engrossed in finishing *King of Kings* (1927), the grand
spectacle intended to pull the company out of its fiscal bind. Presumably
the last thing DeMille had the time or inclination for, at that point, was a
story conference with an overeager new writer. And though Murphy may
have been in sympathy with DeMille's concept of independent production, he was all but incapable of acquiescing to the director's autocratic
persona, even when it was clearly politic to do so. "I subsequently had an

audience with DeMille to tell my ideas for the treatment of the story," he wrote. "I was ushered into his magnificent office, on the floor of which was a big bear rug. He sat behind an enormous desk with a powerful light shining on me and he sitting in the shadow. I paced up and down trying to tell the story and somewhat blinded by the light, I kept tripping over the bear rug. I finally removed the rug, which was *lèse majesté,* and turned the light around so that it shone directly on DeMille's face. I didn't get very far with the story when the audience came to an abrupt end."[22] With it went Murphy's career at the studio.

"Skyscraper" was assigned to a succession of scenarists, including a junior writer named Alissa Rosenbaum, recently emigrated from Russia. She would eventually enter the public arena as the novelist and philosopher Ayn Rand. In the beginning, though, she was merely one among thousands of film-industry foot soldiers. She worked at DeMille's studio until it closed in 1928, then moved on to the wardrobe department at Paramount. "Skyscraper" was her first assignment as a screenwriter. "It was the story that gave me the most trouble," she later commented.[23] She fared little better than Murphy had, emerging with a scenario that diverged sharply from his original treatment but bore an uncanny resemblance to *The Fountainhead* in rough-draft form. The studio rejected it.

The screenplay for *Skyscraper* (1928) was eventually written by Tay Garnett, an experienced scriptwriter who went on to direct such films as *China Seas* (1935) and *The Postman Always Rings Twice* (1946). Directed by Howard Higgin, the film starred William Boyd (of later *Hopalong Cassidy* fame) as the smart, scrappy ironworker Blondie and Alan Hale as his burly sidekick, Swede.[24]

The plot follows a conventional arc. The two men compete for an attractive chorus girl, who chooses Blondie; he loses the use of his legs saving Swede from a terrible accident, then rejects the girl in a wave of self-pity; thanks to Swede's self-sacrificing machinations, it all turns out right in the end. On paper, it's a far cry from "the fantastic speed and rhythm of this jazz age" that Murphy was looking to capture in his New York film, and nothing at all like *Ballet mécanique.* But despite its conventional plot, *Skyscraper* has a great deal of verve and an eye for working-class life, down to the slang-filled intertitles, that few American films of the time can claim. The characters are stock figures, but they're well played (Boyd's in particular), and the skyscraper scenes capture the energy, humor, and rough camaraderie of a construction site. When Blondie and Swede start brawling over a practical joke one has played on the other, for instance, the foreman comes to break it up; the two of them turn on him, knocking him out and propping him up with an illegal bottle of gin, guaranteeing that he'll be picked up by the cop on the beat.

Variety called *Skyscraper* "a program picture of the very top grade" and compared its winning combination of comedy and sentiment, "tinged with a certain whimsical quality," to an O. Henry story. "Beautifully acted and ably directed," the paper decreed, adding that the titles were "brightly written, fit in pat, and are never self-conscious."[25] The *New York Times* reviewer Mordaunt Hall, however, took a dim view of such lowbrow goings-on. "A wild attempt to glorify the steel riveter is now on view at the Paramount Theatre," he wrote, calling it "a rather crude and none too edifying subject. . . . Dudley Murphy, who aimed at high art in his futuristic screen contribution, 'Ballet Mechanique,' is credited with the original yarn of 'Skyscraper,' which was twisted into its present form by Elliott Clawson and Tay Garnett."[26]

In the *Times* review, the two ends of Murphy's filmmaking spectrum collided. Hall couldn't comprehend the maker of a "high art" film like *Ballet mécanique* as the originator of such a determinedly mass-market piece of entertainment and assumed that Murphy's original story had been "twisted" by others. In fact, the final script of *Skyscraper* closely followed his concept for the film, at least as recalled by Ayn Rand. In notes accompanying the publication of her own architect-centered "Skyscraper" scenario, she commented that Murphy's original story "involved two tough construction workers who were in love with the same girl. The events consisted of them throwing rivets at each other, or almost falling off the girders; they fight but they are really the best of friends—it was that kind of story." Nor did Rand think highly of the finished film, which she called "a lousy picture."[27]

Though both *Ballet mécanique* and *Skyscraper* were inspired by modernity—the speed, rhythm, and jazz that Murphy found so exhilarating—they couldn't have been more dissimilar. Yet the disjuncture isn't inconsistent with Murphy's filmmaking sensibility. He saw himself as a filmmaker not for the cultured few but for everyone, not for cinéastes but for moviegoers. From the beginning, he'd brought an art-inflected, emphatically visual sensibility to his filmmaking. But *Ballet mécanique* excepted, his work was destined for movie theaters, not museums, and good box office was as important to him as good reviews.

After collaborating on *Ballet mécanique* and working with Ingram, Murphy would have happily signed on with any studio that allowed him to continue experimenting with cinema. But his struggles in New York after *Mare Nostrum* had demonstrated the futility of that career path. Hollywood simply wasn't interested. By the same token, independent filmmaking paid erratically and poorly, and he'd had enough of that. Feature film directing had always been his goal; it now appeared to be his only real choice. Having displayed his capacity for experimentation in *Ballet mécanique,* he understood the need to demonstrate his mastery of narrative film form—audience-pleasing, salable, Hollywood-style narrative—as essential to reaching that goal.

Two Shots at the Big Time

Once he got to Hollywood, Murphy's screenwriting finally brought him his chance at feature film directing. In 1927, he pitched one of his stories, "Stocks and Blondes," to William Le Baron, vice president in charge of production at FBO Studios. "I was determined that I was going to try to get to direct my story, and for an hour I walked up and down in front of the gates of the studio," he recalled, "practicing the Coué system of positive thinking.[28] I had many arguments [as to] why I should direct. . . . I told Mr. Le Baron the story and he liked it and asked me how much I wanted for it. I told him I also wanted to direct it, being prepared with my arguments. He said, 'OK, but I would like you to direct another one first.' So, in a split second, I had become a feature director."[29] It was under Le Baron's auspices that FBO announced national distribution of *Ballet mécanique* a few months later.

By October 1927, Murphy had plunged into preparation for both *Stocks and Blondes* (1928) and Le Baron's film *Alex the Great* (1928), for which he wrote the screenplay. "I have been working a blue streak the last two months, getting out the continuity of *Stocks and Blondes* and now I have had to rewrite *Alex the Great*," he wrote to Katharine in late November 1927. "I just had a conference with the supervisor on it and there has to be some changes and more work on the story before I can start shooting, so while casting and getting my staff together and doing all the preparations for shooting I also have to write the continuity some more." Murphy had frequently lived apart from his family, staying in New York City while they were in Croton-on-Hudson, but with the cross-country separation and Murphy's philandering tendencies, the marriage was starting to fray. "NO, one Italian dancer does not mean more than three of you, and get your mind at rest on that score, PLEASE," he wrote. "There can be nobody I believe that can fill your place in my heart or life. Write me darling please and tell me everything."[30]

Despite his protestations, Murphy's social life was hardly suffering. That year, his name began to surface in local society columns, as a guest at noteworthy dinner parties or a participant in impromptu Hollywood events.[31] By the 1930s, his directing assignments were reported in industry newsbriefs, and as the decade wore on, he turned up in the gossip columns with increasing frequency.

Alex the Great was released in spring of 1928, opening in New York in late April. Starring former vaudevillian Richard "Skeets" Gallagher, the film recounted the exploits of a country boy who manages to find love and riches in New York City. It was not a success, as a short but scorching *Variety* review attests. "This is the story of a Vermont rube who sold 50 automobile trucks to a department store proprietor by recognizing a picture of the prop's pet cow, Betsy Ross, hanging on the wall," the reviewer wrote. "It's just as bad as it sounds. . . . Dudley Murphy, the director, has made a generally botched job out of a typical H. C. Witwer fresh guy yarn. The detail particularly is clumsy, unnatural, and annoying."[32] The *New York Times* was marginally more positive, conceding that "there are scenes which are good and scenes which are bad and some which are neither. . . . It is all a hectic affair which jumps and flashes around something like a trout on the end of a line."[33] Foreshadowing Murphy's work on *Black and Tan,* the reviewer noted that the film's best scene took place in a nightclub.

Murphy's own project, *Stocks and Blondes* (1928), was released later that year. Also starring Gallagher, it fared little better. The *New York Times* called it "a somewhat dismal exposé of the famous Wall Street. Mr. [Albert] Conti is a good actor and Mr. Gallagher can be; both of them in 'Stocks and Blondes' stumble over their interference. . . . Mr. Gallagher, who was the reporter in 'The Racket,' seems to feel the need of direction."[34] The *Chicago Tribune* considered it "a neatly turned comedy drama, mighty well directed" but conceded that Gallagher's character "is likely to give you a pain in the neck and a woozy feeling in the stomach and an itch in your kicking foot."[35]

As feature film careers go, it was not a brilliant start but it was a start nevertheless. Early 1926 had found Murphy in New York City, fresh from the avant-garde heights of Montparnasse and the sweeping romanticism of *Mare Nostrum;* 1928 saw the release of two Hollywood features under his name. In little more than a year, he had parlayed a highly experimental short film into the beginnings of a mainstream film career.

As Murphy looked to move up the film industry ranks, however, the industry was itself undergoing a transformation, centralizing production in the hands of strong executives and winnowing out directors who couldn't accept the new regime. By 1928, Hollywood was also wrestling with the greatest challenge it had yet faced. Sound would change every aspect of commercial filmmaking, from aesthetics to business practices, production to exhibition.

Accustomed to exerting control over his own small projects, Murphy, like Ingram, did not fit smoothly into the emerging studio system. Other experimentally minded filmmakers such as Robert Florey went on to lengthy directorial runs without the setbacks that marked Murphy's career. But Murphy aspired to something loftier than the usual industry fare; despite everything, he still wanted to make hit movies that could stand as art. As he struggled to establish his credentials and prove his ability to handle the kind of narrative films that Hollywood wanted, he continued to look for opportunities to stretch the studios' increasingly standardized approach to filmmaking. Interestingly, those opportunities came with the transition to sound.

CHAPTER 5

THE BEGINNING OF THE
AUDIBLE PERIOD

On a Friday in early August 1926, while *Mare Nostrum* was wind-ing down its run at the Criterion and *Ballet mécanique* was still causing the occasional ripple at the Cameo, a film called *Don Juan* opened at the Warner Theater on Broadway at Fifty-second Street. Produced by Warner Bros. and starring John Barrymore, it was the first movie to showcase the new Vitaphone sound system.

For Warner Bros., Vitaphone was an immense gamble. A second-string studio that had never broken into the top ranks, Warner was in precari-ous financial shape in 1926. Sound film had been a tantalizing goal since the early days of cinema, when Thomas Edison first tried to synchronize phonographic recordings to film. Workable sound systems had existed since the early 1920s, but the technology was problematic—systems didn't hold sync, or they produced poor-quality sound—and movie audiences seemed perfectly content with silent film, which by the mid-1920s had reached its height as an art form.

Like most of Hollywood, Warner initially thought the advantage of sound lay in music and effects, not in dialogue. Originally shot as a silent, *Don Juan* remained, in essence, a silent film. The sound track carried little more than an orchestral score and the effects of clashing swords in a dra-matic dueling scene. But the short films that accompanied the premiere of *Don Juan* gave a stronger indication of what the new system could deliver. The program opened with a short speech by Will Hays, president of the Motion Picture Producers and Distributors of America, welcoming Vita-phone to the film industry. Hays's address was projected with strikingly

Dudley Murphy (right) with his mother, Caroline Bowles Murphy, and sister, Carlene, c. 1904.

Dudley Murphy at the piano with Carlene, c. 1907.

Murphy and Carlene, c. 1913.

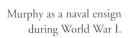

Murphy as a naval ensign
during World War I.

Hermann Dudley Murphy, *Self Portrait,* c. 1900. Museum of Fine Arts, Boston; gift of Carlene Bowles Murphy Samoiloff, daughter of the artist. Photograph copyright Museum of Fine Arts, Boston.

Hermann Dudley Murphy, *Dudley Murphy,* c. 1916.

Chase Herendeen, Murphy's first wife, in *Soul of the Cypress* (1920). Photographs courtesy of the Library of Congress/Motion Picture, Broadcasting, and Recorded Sound Division.

Chase Herendeen (left) c. 1920, when *Soul of the Cypress* was filmed; (below) a decade later as Broadway showgirl Chase Herendon. Photographs courtesy of Jerry Herendeen Moderwell.

Dudley Murphy and Katharine Hawley, early 1920s.

Katharine Hawley in *Aphrodite* (1920).

Aphrodite: Hawley as the goddess of love emerging from the surf at Laguna.

Aphrodite: (above) an inscription on the reverse of this photograph reads, "Santa Monica—Aphrodite prays for the return of Adonis' spirit"; (below) a scene shot at the Theosophical Center at Krotona, with one of its decorative white structures in the background.

Katharine Hawley in
Ballet mécanique (1924).
Slide courtesy of Anthology
Film Archives. Photograph by
Arunas Kulikauskas.

Dudley Murphy in
Ballet mécanique. Slide
courtesy of Anthology Film
Archives. Photograph by
Arunas Kulikauskas.

Kiki of Montparnasse in
Ballet mécanique. Slide courtesy
of Anthology Film Archives.
Photograph by Arunas Kulikauskas.

Ballet mécanique: the
stop-motion Charleston.
Slide courtesy of Anthology
Film Archives. Photograph
by Arunas Kulikauskas.

St. Louis Blues (1929): (above) Bessie Smith sings; (below) barroom scene with Smith at right. Behind her is a waiter spinning a tray on his fingertips, an incidental motif that Murphy included in several films. Photographs courtesy of the Library of Congress/Motion Picture, Broadcasting, and Recorded Sound Division.

Black and Tan (1929): (above) a frame from the kaleidoscope sequence, with Duke Ellington at the center; (below) the deathbed scene. Shadowed silhouettes also appear in Murphy's soundie *Yes, Indeed!* (1941). Photographs courtesy of the Library of Congress/ Motion Picture, Broadcasting, and Recorded Sound Division.

Dudley Murphy in a studio portrait from the 1920s. Photograph courtesy of the Murphy Family Collection.

Dudley Murphy with his sister, Carlene Murphy Samiloff, in the early 1930s.

synchronous, intelligible sound. This revelation was followed by a lineup of musical shorts, which included the New York Philharmonic Orchestra playing the overture to Wagner's *Tannhäuser;* violinist Efrem Zimbalist performing Beethoven; tenor Giovanni Martinelli singing "Vesti la Giubba" from *I Pagliacci;* and Roy Smeck, "the Wizard of the String," soloing on Hawaiian guitar and ukelele.

Virtually all the New York papers turned out for the premiere. With few exceptions, the reviews were glowing, at least for the Vitaphone sound. Writing in the *New York Times,* Mordaunt Hall called it "a marvelous device," proclaiming that "the future of this new contrivance is boundless."[1] *Variety* noted, "The public opening was at $10 a seat Friday night. Saturday and Sunday the house was stormed by the public at each of the two performances daily."[2] Equally heartening was the jump in Warner Bros. stock, from fourteen dollars and change to thirty-two, in the first few days after the premiere.[3] Within three weeks, the studio announced that all twenty-six regular features on its 1926–27 schedule would be available in Vitaphone versions—that is, with orchestral score and sound effects—in addition to the usual silent format.[4]

A little over a year later, in October 1927, the studio premiered *The Jazz Singer.* Only partly a talkie, its sound track spotlighted songs by Al Jolson and a few lines of dialogue scattered through an otherwise silent film with orchestral accompaniment. Jolson was one of the most popular entertainers of the era, and the public responded not only to his musical performances but to his relaxed, informal chatter. Shrewdly marketed and later rereleased, by the early 1930s *The Jazz Singer* had grossed $2.6 million on production costs of $422,000.[5] In July 1928, not quite a year after *The Jazz Singer* premiered, Warner took its next leap with *Lights of New York,* the first "100% All Talking Picture," which posted even larger profits, grossing one million dollars on a paltry outlay of twenty-three thousand.[6]

None of these, it must be said, was a great film. *Don Juan* was a big-budget production, and *The Jazz Singer* had Jolson, but on purely cinematic terms they left a great deal to be desired. Gratuitously inflated from two reels to seven, the gangster film *Lights of New York* was even worse. ("This 100 per cent talkie is 100 per cent crude," sniffed *Variety.*)[7] One thing, though, was clear: the moviegoing public wanted sound and plenty of it, and they weren't particular about the films it came in. No matter that only a handful of theaters were actually equipped for it; the few that were did nonstop, turn-away business. Regardless of how magnificent or artful, silent movies suddenly seemed not only obsolete but antediluvian.

The fascination with sound prompted a boom in short films. While the studios scrambled to develop 100 percent talkies, short subjects—which were faster and cheaper to produce than features—helped to sate audience demand. Inspired in part by the variety and pacing of vaudeville, early sound shorts relied heavily on performers: singers, musicians, comics, and the like. These films soon came to replace the live acts that had previously opened movie programs, accomplishing what Murphy, with his Visual Symphony films, had attempted a few years earlier. Vitaphone shorts released in 1927 and 1928 featured everyone from Martinelli singing opera to George Burns and Gracie Allen in a wisecracking comic routine.[8]

In its sometimes riotous mix of high and low culture, the production of early sound shorts took its cue not from feature films but from radio. A world away from the arcane shortwave technology of Murphy's childhood, broadcast radio had swept the country in the early 1920s, instilling an appetite for sound years before the talkies appeared. Radio unfurled an exhilarating range of voices, languages, and dialects, fostering a wholesale reinvention of the way Americans spoke. Suddenly everyone, especially in the big cities, was talking slang. Modernity acquired a linguistic dimension, one that hinged on knowing what a "palooka" or "baloney" was, how a "dame" differed from a "tomato," or what it meant to say "my dogs are barking." Language became a way of pulling cultural turf away from the upper-class elite, a reassertion of the democratic impulse expressed in the most colorful, nose-thumbing terms. If Prohibition meant everyone getting illicitly drunk together, it seemed only fitting that they speak a common language while they did.

Though Warner Bros. bolted ahead with sound film, other studios were slow to come to terms with it. Several were reluctant to make the intensive investment of time and capital required to switch over to sound production, and some executives still saw it as a novelty that would quickly blow over. Few, if any, understood the radical changes that sound would wreak on film aesthetics and the industry. Within months, though, even the most reluctant studios were scrambling to master the new technology. Director and screenwriter William C. deMille, older brother of Cecil B. DeMille, described 1928 as the year "when our nice comfortable little world was suddenly turned upside down and we all lay flat on our backs listening to the voice of God speaking through a microphone."[9]

Even so, the change didn't happen overnight. Not only did the studios have to retool their facilities for sound production, movie theaters had to be converted as well. Wiring a theater for sound was expensive and could take weeks. In 1927, there were an estimated twenty-five thousand movie houses in the United States, the majority of them in small towns. According to a *Film Daily* survey, by July 1929, only 5,251 theaters had been wired for sound.[10]

Behind the transition was a high-stakes corporate struggle for dominance in the emerging field of sound-film technology. Despite zealous attempts, Warner Bros. could not effect a Vitaphone monopoly. AT&T, the studio's partner in the venture, quickly recognized that Warner's chokehold was stifling the interests of the communications corporation. AT&T created a new division of its Western Electric subsidiary, Electrical Research Products, Inc. (ERPI), to develop sound-film technology with other studios.

Vitaphone was a sound-on-disc system with sound tracks recorded on sixteen-inch-diameter discs that resembled phonograph records. The discs for a given film were played on turntables that were ganged to the film projector on a driveshaft, which kept the machines running in sync. In early 1927, Fox Film, another second-tier studio, introduced Movietone, a sound-on-film technology similar to the one that eventually became the industry standard. Though a rival to Vitaphone, the Movietone system was no challenge to AT&T; it also used Western Electric technology. But AT&T did have a corporate competitor: RCA, which in mid-1927 introduced Photophone, another sound-on-film system. Late to market and hampered by quality issues, Photophone didn't pose a serious threat at first. In early 1928, when most of the major studios finally committed themselves to sound film, AT&T's Western Electric technology was the acknowledged winner.

In 1935, RCA would have the satisfaction of seeing most of the major studios switching to Photophone. In 1928, though, it could claim only two small prizes: Pathé and Murphy's studio, FBO. At the time, both were controlled by financier Joseph P. Kennedy, who'd gone into a joint venture with RCA to develop sound theaters. In 1928, Kennedy and RCA head David Sarnoff merged the two studios into a new production-exhibition conglomerate, RKO, which was itself part of RCA.[11] At this point, Kennedy bowed out of the movie business, some five million dollars richer.[12]

A vital ingredient in the new venture was the chain of two hundred vaudeville theaters of the fraying Keith-Albee-Orpheum circuit, which had been converted into movie houses. From a production perspective, RCA had three immediate needs: to supply its new theaters with product, to demonstrate the Photophone system to its best advantage, and to refute the claims of poor sound quality and loss of sync. To that end, the company set up a production facility in New York City, at Sixth Avenue and Twenty-fourth Street.

Words, Then Music

Launching his Hollywood career in 1927–28, Murphy was caught in the sound-film backdraft. He wrapped up work on *Alex the Great* and *Stocks and Blondes* as *The Jazz Singer* and *Lights of New York* were sending shock waves through the industry. When Joseph Kennedy merged Pathé and FBO in late 1928, he put William Le Baron in charge of production at both studios. Facing the formidable task of consolidating the two facilities and converting them to sound, Le Baron no longer had time to nurture new directors, especially one whose initial forays had been less than stellar. With Hollywood offering no immediate prospects, Murphy returned to New York. There, he was hired by RCA to write and direct sound shorts to showcase its Photophone system.

Trolling for inspiration, Murphy found it at the Algonquin Round Table. Two years earlier, in 1926, he'd been a frequent guest at the daily luncheon party and was on familiar terms with several of the regulars. "I was an audience of one with five humorists," he recalled. "[Alexander] Wolcott would say something brilliant and amusing and the other[s]," including George S. Kaufman, Marc Connelly, Ring Lardner, and Robert Benchley, "would deadpan their reaction, impatient to get on themselves, while I would roar with laughter."[13] It was Harold Ross, founding editor of the *New Yorker*, who "had the idea that my proposed short films might be some of the sketches that Connelly had written for the Dutch Treat Club. . . . so I adapted a screen play of Marc's sketch, 'The Traveler,' which was the story of a man buying a ticket at a window in Grand Central Station . . . but unable to decide which place he wanted to go." As Murphy recalled, "It was a very amusing sketch and made a delightful two-reel film."[14]

The Traveler (1928) was well received by the RCA/RKO hierarchy, and Murphy made another: *The Burglar* (1928), also based on a Connelly sketch. In it, Connelly himself played a wealthy Park Avenue collector insulted by a burglar who insists that his prize artwork is a fake. No prints of either film are known to survive.[15]

In addition to spending time with the Algonquin crowd, Murphy again fell into the social orbit of Carl Van Vechten, whom he'd met during his New York *Ballet mécanique* heyday. Van Vechten was a discerning music, dance, and literary critic and the author of several novels. He was also one of the first white New Yorkers to spend time in Harlem, initially through his friendship with Walter White, future director of the NAACP. He actively promoted artists whose work he admired, such as Langston Hughes and Countee Cullen. It was through Van Vechten's influence, for instance, that Hughes's first book was published and his poems appeared in *Vanity Fair*. Van Vechten's nightclubbing helped put Harlem on the map for cosmopolitan midtowners and established him as the "white master of the colored revels," as one foreign visitor declared.[16] Small's, a Harlem club with a racially mixed clientele, was renowned as his after-hours headquarters.

Though married, Van Vechten was flamboyantly gay, with a taste for ornate bracelets, ruffled shirts, and on occasion, the red and gold silk robes of, as one friend put it, "the dowager Chinese empress gone berserk."[17] He was an avid socializer and an inspired host, and the parties at his West Fifty-fifth Street apartment attracted a dizzying crowd that included "most of the Negroes whose work had even then commanded some attention," along with the likes of Salvador Dalí, Helena Rubenstein, Somerset Maugham, and publisher Horace Liveright. "If the guests found Carl's Prohibition bar impressive," wrote his biographer Bruce Kellner, "they could easily find themselves equally intoxicated on the entertainment, usually supplied by one another."[18] George Gershwin might sit down at the piano one night, a Native American perform war dances the next; or Bessie Smith would sing the blues, followed by an operatic contralto from Peru. At one such gathering, Murphy met Miguel Covarrubias, the deft, witty, Mexican-born caricaturist for *Vanity Fair* who was one of Van Vechten's protégés. Covarrubias became Murphy's companion and guide on his nightclubbing trips uptown.

"Not long ago nobody knew much about Harlem," wrote *Variety* in January 1928. "In a remarkably short time due to New York Negro commercial progression, the international fame that its theatrical celebs achieved, the popularity of books having the section as its locale . . . these and a host of other reasons have made Harlem one of the best known spots in the entire world."[19] An ad for Small's, appearing that month in the *Inter-state Tatler*, an African-American newspaper, put it more succinctly: "In fact, the most fastidious Ofay hawks prefer Harlem to Broadway."[20]

Returning to New York after more than a year in California, Murphy found the city's drunken, insouciant urbanity as convivial as Montparnasse or early Hollywood. Uptown nightlife loomed large in his personal land-scape. "Like many whites in artists' circles he had a zest for Harlem glitter," wrote film historian Thomas Cripps, "and boasted of his Negro connec-tions and of liaisons with black women."[21] Murphy, for his part, saw it in cinematic terms. "[I] fell in love with the characters and exciting jazz," he wrote. "I felt I must capture this excitement in a film."[22]

Radio had already kindled enthusiasm among white audiences for African-American music: spirituals, minstrel routines, and above all, jazz. The arrival of sound film only accelerated the demand for black music and subjects. "Negro sketches, which were almost an unknown quantity before this talking picture business, are now finding more and more spots on Eastern programs," wrote industry commentator Arthur W. Eddy in 1929.[23] As critic Harry Alan Potamkin put it, "Sound has made the Negro the 'big thing' of the film movement."[24]

As sound took over, the eloquent metaphors, evocative allusions, and striking visual compositions of silent film were flung onto the cultural dust heap. Film historian Scott Eyman has noted that the literal silence of silent films had an abstracting effect on stars and story lines, making actors seem younger than they were. Sound, on the other hand, made them seem older. Instead of silent film's stylized emoting, something different was re-quired by sound: fast-talking, street-smart types who'd seen and done it all.[25] "Reality is what is wanted in pictures," director Frank Capra wrote in the 1931 *Cinematographic Annual*, "not symbolic touches and beautiful settings for mere beauty's sake."[26]

Though the first short sound films were, by and large, recorded perform-ances—like radio or phonograph records with visual adjuncts—by 1928, those performances were increasingly framed by some kind of narrative pretense, however slight.[27] Backstage dramas were among the earliest plot lines. They had the added advantage of putting surrogate audiences on-screen, giving performers, whose bows to the phantom movie audience felt awkwardly out of place, someone to respond to.

For his third film for RCA, Murphy returned to his earliest inspiration, music. This time he opted for popular over classical, settling on the hit song "St. Louis Blues." "I approached W. C. Handy, who sold us the rights and who did a special arrangement of his classic piece," Murphy recalled. "I got Bessie Smith, the greatest blues singer of all times, to play the part of the St. Louis Woman, and wrote a story for the film, suggested by the lyric."[28] Though Murphy credited Covarrubias with introducing him to Harlem, it's likely that he learned of Bessie Smith through Van Vechten, who'd first heard her sing in late 1925. ("I believe I kissed her hand," Van Vechten later recalled of that first meeting. "I hope I did.")[29]

For the film, Murphy was especially interested in re-creating the authentic feel of an uptown club. "I rehearsed the piece in a loft in Harlem and then brought a group . . . from Harlem to our studio," he wrote.[30] "To capture the spirit, I had created a set which was more or less a duplicate of a Harlem night club and peopled it with the real people who frequented this Harlem night club.[31] I gave them beer to drink while we set up the cameras and rehearsed in the studio."[32]

Given his familiarity with early systems for synchronizing film with live music, Murphy readily adapted to the technological demands of sound-film production. Knowing that the musical performance was the core of the film, he devised an effective technique for filming Smith, who was not entirely at ease in front of the camera. He set up four cameras, "synchronized to the master sound track, so that I would not have to stop the action for close-ups or moving shots and could run the music and song without a break. When the crowd was completely relaxed with the beer and the spirit of the night club, I called for action and a continuous scene, which ran 10 minutes, was photographed. Bessie Smith's close-ups were taken with a 6″ lens from 20 feet . . . so that there was no self-consciousness on her part, which might have occurred had the camera been close to her."[33]

Shooting with multiple cameras ganged to a master sound track wasn't uncommon in early sound films. As late as 1932, some scenes at Paramount, for instance, were shot with ten cameras.[34] But with a jittery star, a multicamera setup was essential to Murphy's concept for St. Louis Blues. His direction yielded relaxed, fluid performances by all three principals: Jimmy Mordecai, Isabel Washington, and Smith.

The film opens on a stairwell crap game, a scene that's neatly stolen by a comic janitor who takes a cut of the action. Jimmy (Mordecai) enters the game with a bankroll gotten from his woman, Bessie. As he rolls, Bessie's rival (Washington) suggestively rubs the dice on her hip for luck, and Jimmy wins big. The two go to his room, where Bessie soon bursts in on them. Slapping and chasing the other woman out, she cajoles Jimmy, reminding him of all the money she has lavished on him. Abasing herself, she crawls to him and clings to his leg, but he rebuffs her with a kick and storms out. On the floor, reaching for the liquor bottle, she croons the opening lines of the song. The scene moves to a club where Bessie continues singing as the chorus joins in. Jimmy makes a triumphant, dancing entrance, charming Bessie so he can lift the money from her garter. He sneeringly rejects her again and leaves, as the film ends with a close-up on Smith singing the last notes of the song.

Murphy's efforts to construct natural cinematic performances pushed him to integrate music and narrative as fully as possible. At the time, sound editing was in its infancy and the technology was primitive, so sound edits could be noticeably abrupt. Filmmakers, Murphy included, quickly discovered that cutting the picture to a running sound track, rather than the other way around, resulted in a smoother, more continuous edit. The editing on *St. Louis Blues* reinforces its fluid, low-key style; once Smith starts singing, the sound track on the tune runs continuously. The opening few bars are sung in her room. The image fades to black as the sound track plays across the cut, fading up as she continues to sing without a break, standing at the bar in the saloon. Such techniques have long since become standard, but in 1929 few musical performances were edited with such assurance or sense of narrative flow.[35]

Smith was known for her unpredictable temper, especially after drinking; despite being on cordial terms with Van Vechten and his wife, actress Fania Marinoff, she'd slugged Marinoff—a petite, effusive woman—to the floor when she'd taken the liberty of kissing Smith farewell at one of their gatherings. ("Get the fuck away from me!" she reportedly yelled. "I ain't never heard of such shit!")[36] But the singer was pleased with *St. Louis Blues*. When it was finished, Murphy recalled, she turned up at his door with a case of gin, ready to celebrate. The result, he wrote, was "one of the best parties I have ever given."[37]

St. Louis Blues earned Murphy a rave in *Variety*, substantially longer than the reviews for either of his Hollywood features. "A pip short, directed and authored by Dudley Murphy . . . a colored dramalet running a little short of two reels, pungent with tenseness and action and replete with Aframerican local and other color," it read. "Plenty of atmospheric props and hotsy-totsy trimmings which may get by the censors on the ground of authenticity, for it certainly rings true." Murphy's handling of the narrative didn't escape notice, either. "A clever iris-out from [Smith's] prostrate position on the tenement floor into her besotted condition in a honky-tonk, standing against the rail, has the recording blend in from one scene to the other without lyric interruption, yet effectively indicating a time span," the reviewer wrote. "The predominant keynote of 'St. Louis Blues' is its low-down colored hotch-cha-cha aura."[38]

But low-down hotch-cha-cha didn't sit well with everyone. "The singing in this new subject is effectively recorded and the scenes in a cabaret thronged with blacks are adroitly filmed," wrote Mordaunt Hall in the *New York Times.* "It is, however, a sordid study in which there is a decided vein of vulgarity. It may be realism, but it is spoiled by being distasteful."[39] According to one source, the NAACP, appalled by the image of African-American life presented in the film, tried to have it banned.[40]

It's difficult to assess what the African-American community thought of *St. Louis Blues* or to what extent black audiences had access to the film. Smith was a popular entertainer, and notices of her stage performances appeared with some regularity in the African-American press; but the only mention of *St. Louis Blues* in a major African-American paper was a five-line item in the *Chicago Defender.* It noted only that production had begun on a film based on the song, with "many well known persons in the cast."[41] No reviews or other notices appeared, either during the film's production or after its release.

There are several possible reasons for this. The film was released in the summer of 1929, a time when many movie houses were not yet wired for sound, including theaters in black communities. Although a notice in the *New York Amsterdam News* indicated that talkies had made their debut in Harlem in January 1929, when *Lights of New York* appeared at the Lafayette Theater, it's unclear how quickly sound technology made its way into African-American theaters around the country—and without sound, *St. Louis Blues* would have lost much of its appeal. It's possible that the NAACP did attempt to stifle coverage of the film and that it succeeded. Less likely is that the black press balked at the film and chose not to cover it, even when it did play in local theaters.

Whatever the African-American community may have thought of *St. Louis Blues,* it was a solid hit on the Broadway movie circuit. Richard Watts, Jr., who had struggled with and ultimately admired *Ballet mécanique,* was especially complimentary. "Not the least important quality is that [*St. Louis Blues*] suggests what an important director Dudley Murphy gives evidence of being," he wrote. "He has ideas and feeling and it is therefore pleasant to find him smashing in on the consciousness of the screen world again."[42]

St. Louis Blues premiered in New York in late August 1929, on a bill with *Bulldog Drummond* (1929), the talkie debut of British actor Ronald Colman. That film had been an immediate hit when it opened in May; unlike many less fortunate actors, Colman had a lightly accented, unstilted speaking voice that perfectly matched his debonair on-screen persona. Moved to another Broadway theater after its premiere run ("first time at popular prices"), the film continued to generate enthusiastic response among moviegoers. Even so, *St. Louis Blues* soon crashed the theater's advertising campaign. A series of ads in the *New York Herald Tribune* tells the tale. When *Bulldog Drummond* opened at the Rialto after a lengthy run at the Apollo, the ad of Sunday, September 1, 1929, made no mention of *St. Louis Blues*. A week later, on Sunday, September 8, an ad approximately twice as large still touted Ronald Colman but added five lines of copy: "Extra! Added Attraction! The Jazz-Epic of American Tragic-comedy. 'ST. LOUIS BLUES' featuring Bessie Smith. Harlem life in song, music, and dance!" Subsequent ads in the September 15 and September 22 issues continued to promote *St. Louis Blues,* calling it "20 minutes of rare talkie!" and "the Jazz Epic of American Tragi-comedy that's startling New York!"[43]

A full-page ad in the September 4, 1929, issue of *Variety*—the same issue that carried the paper's enthusiastic review—confirmed the film's hit status in New York. Under the headline "Blazing Sensation Overnight on Bway," the copy read: "White Hot Dramatic Show Stopper Leaves Em Cheering in the Aisles! Two reel riot opening week with 'Bulldog Drummond' at Publix Rialto, New York held over indefinite. . . . ST. LOUIS BLUES . . . all dialog smash . . . with most stirring musical and vocal setting at the moment of moaning to press. . . . From original song by W. C. Handy. Directed by Dudley Murphy. With Bessie Smith, famous Victor recording artist and host of negro [*sic*] singing and dancing artists."[44]

In his memoir, Murphy recalled the film's snowballing success. "Much to the amazement of the theatre manager," he wrote, "so many people called to ask when *St. Louis Blues* went on, that the short, which originally had not been billed in lights, was now billed as big as the feature, and was held over for many weeks."[45] Nationwide, bookings were more spotty than the critical acclaim might suggest. Many exhibitors in smaller markets declined to take the chance on such "hotsy-totsy" material, and African-American at that. Even so, RCA was delighted with the film's success and quickly commissioned another.

FINE PHOTOGRAPHIC TRICK STUFF

Murphy followed *St. Louis Blues* with a second film set in Harlem. Inspired by Duke Ellington's free interpretation of Chopin's "Funeral March" in his "Black and Tan Fantasy," Murphy wrote "a simple scenario, in which . . . Ellington's sweetheart, when dying, asks him to play the 'Black and Tan Fantasy.'"[46]

Completed in November 1929, a few months after *St. Louis Blues, Black and Tan* is richer than Murphy's description implies. The film opens with Ellington at the piano in his tenement apartment, working up the song with his horn player.[47] A pair of movers arrive to repossess the piano, bumbling their way through a comic routine that is saved from offensive stereotyping, barely, by the sly, improvisatory use of language.[48] The stalemate is resolved by the arrival of Ellington's girlfriend (Fredi Washington), who bribes the movers with bootleg gin. Washington is a nightclub dancer who works to support Ellington's composing. She has a heart condition and cannot tolerate the strain of performing; nevertheless, she insists on going onstage that night.

As in *St. Louis Blues,* Murphy takes particular care with the transitions between scenes. The apartment sequence fades to a moment of black before coming up on a close-up of Ellington's hands at the piano. The camera pulls back to reveal him playing at the nightclub, a stylish art deco set with a mirrored floor. At this point, narrative yields to spectacle, as a troupe of five tap dancers, assembled in ascending height, takes the stage. They dance with near-mechanical precision, the pattern of their movements reflected in the mirrored floor before them. The performance runs almost three minutes, with Ellington and his band well in the background.

Near the end of the dancers' second number, the film cuts repeatedly to Washington backstage, feeling faint and starting to swoon. As the film shifts to her point of view, an extended sequence of kaleidoscopic imagery evokes her increasing disorientation. Ellington's face, the band members, and the already multiple, machinelike dancers—presented in a time-bending repeat of their just-completed performance—are further fragmented and multiplied by the lens.

Lasting another two-plus minutes, this kaleidoscopic sequence is, in part, a visual essay on concepts previously explored in *Ballet mécanique.* Like music, the extended segment is structured as theme and variation: first, the straightforward precision dancing behind the mirrored floor, then, via Washington's perception, a fragmented, even more machinelike rendition of the same performance. The kaleidoscope images are more complex than any in *Ballet mécanique,* juxtaposing the moving dancers with Ellington and his orchestra. As a whole, the sequence is a sophisticated refinement of the human-machine tropes of the previous film. At the same time, it prefigures Busby Berkeley's concept of multiple human bodies united in a precise, aesthetically pleasing machine conceived for the camera. Having spent the first part of the film constructing a standard version of cinematic time and space, Murphy, in this extended sequence, sketches out a more visually driven alternative that almost pulls away from the narrative construction that preceded it.

Almost, but not quite. Unlike *Ballet mécanique,* the visual strategies in *Black and Tan* ultimately serve an ongoing narrative, and once the kaleidoscopic spectacle ends, the story quickly resumes. Mastering her dizziness, Washington goes onstage, clad in little more than beads, to perform a wildly shimmying dance. Filmed from below through a transparent floor, a shot of her spinning legs is strongly reminiscent of similar shots in René Clair's avant-garde short film *Entr'acte*—another pentimento, perhaps, of Murphy's Paris years. After less than a minute, the frenetic performance ends in Washington's collapse. The unfeeling nightclub boss quickly orders her carried offstage and brings on a plumed chorus line, demanding that Ellington continue playing. Ellington goes into the next number, just long enough to musically cover a few provocative leg shots, then abruptly stops and walks off with the band.

The film fades to black, coming up on a stark shadow frieze of upraised arms and musical instruments. The scene once again is the apartment, but the comic realism of the opening sequence is supplanted by somber spectacle. Singers and musicians crowd around the bed where Washington lies dying. She asks Ellington to play the "Black and Tan Fantasy," and the music segues from mournful spirituals to a full-out performance of the title number by band and choir. Portraying Ellington from Washington's point of view, the film depicts his face gradually blurring "like a guttering candle," as Jonathan Rosenbaum has written. The camera shows Washington's death, then returns to the blurred close-up of Ellington's face—a shot that, narratively speaking, can no longer be justified by Washington's point of view. The film fades out on Ellington, "thereby collapsing the film's co-ordinates of space as well as time," wrote Rosenbaum, "into the realm of pure idea, or pure music; and both slowly fade away in the same flickering breath."[49]

In themselves, the visual strategies in *Black and Tan* aren't groundbreaking, drawing as they do on techniques developed in *Ballet mécanique* and other avant-garde films. Instead, the film's experimental nature lies in the use of these strategies to push the narrative envelope: to interrogate the rapidly standardizing Hollywood style in terms of how much purely visual, nonnarrative digression it might successfully absorb and to explore the impact of that material on the narrative film form. This approach would reach its apogee with Busby Berkeley's string of three 1933 hits—

Footlight Parade, Gold Diggers of 1933, and *42nd Street*—for which the choreographer created extravagant, machinelike spectacles without benefit of kaleidoscopic lenses. At the time *Black and Tan* premiered in late 1929, however, Berkeley's first film, *Whoopee!* (1930), was almost a year away, and Murphy's work was hailed for its visual innovations.

As the laboratory for this experiment, *Black and Tan* was intended for popular audiences, not the rarified ciné-club circuit. For Murphy, avant-garde cinematic strategies were fair game for mainstream filmmaking, and no approach was too sophisticated for the moviegoing public. In *Black and Tan,* hot jazz, sexy showgirls, and a sentimental story line coexist with near-abstract visual sequences that engage the sheer pleasure of gazing at the screen. It's fascinating that Murphy chose to do this—to deliberately reemphasize the visual—in a movie specifically conceived to foreground sound. In 1929, sound film had not entirely lost its aura of novelty with either the public or the film industry, and the standard sound-film form had not quite solidified. With *Black and Tan,* Murphy seized this brief moment of technological experimentation, understanding it as an opportunity to expand the constricted visual vocabulary that had come into play with sound films. In 1926, he thought that *Skyscraper* would fulfill his vision for a New York film that imaginatively interpreted "the life that is going on right under our noses . . . the fantastic speed and rhythm of this jazz age."[50] But with its visually emphatic, musically inspired approach, *Black and Tan* came much closer to achieving that vision.

Sharing similar settings, musical inspirations, and some performers, *St. Louis Blues* and *Black and Tan* are generally considered companion films. In both, Murphy demonstrates a sure command of sound-filmmaking technology and the aesthetics of the short sound film. Cinematically, though, they're quite different. *St. Louis Blues* is a straightforward if minimal narrative, centered on Smith's musical performance and distinguished by thoughtful, well-devised visual and aural transitions. By contrast, *Black and Tan* deliberately departs from the narrative norm. One of the signal characteristics of Murphy's filmmaking is the alignment between innovative visual strategies and the musicality of African-American jazz. It's a crucial premise of *Ballet mécanique,* and it reemerges with increased sophistication in *Black and Tan.*

Coming on the heels of *St. Louis Blues, Black and Tan* was another critical success for Murphy and RCA. The music, acting, and direction all won praise, and Murphy's visual experiments were singled out as enhancing the film's overall dramatic effect. "Very fine production of jazzy colored atmosphere, expertly directed," wrote *Film Daily*. "Duke Ellington and his all-colored orchestra put over the hot jazz, and how. . . . Fine photographic trick stuff that is beautifully done." The final verdict: "A novelty done with class that should go big anywhere."[51]

In the months following its premiere, the film appears to have reached a national audience. A list of sample sound-film programs in Chicago movie houses in April 1930, for instance, noted that it played at the Central Park theater for three days,[52] and an article in the *New York Amsterdam News* indicated that in August 1930 (some nine months after its release) *Black and Tan* opened at the Sunset Theatre in Harlem. Describing the film as "stark realism photographed in a startling manner," the *News* called it "one of the most remarkable pictures to be brought to the screen."[53] In upstate New York, the *Rochester Times* described it as "a film in which artistic photography, imaginative direction and excellent acting are combined with rare balance which give it a lasting beauty and significance. Ten years from now this film will be listed among the notable achievements of the beginning of the audible period."[54] In terms of its reception at the time, *Black and Tan* was a cinematic experiment that succeeded in both critical and popular terms—that is, insofar as a film about an African-American subject could succeed in the United States in 1929.

Racial Realities

In their production, distribution, and reception, *St. Louis Blues* and *Black and Tan* are inseparable from the racial realities of the day, both in the film industry and the country at large. America in the 1920s may have been discovering African-American music, culture, and slang, but in film at least, the process almost inevitably occurred at the hands of white interpreters, who brought with them their own prejudices and preconceptions. There was, of course, a small but tenacious African-American film industry, its leading producer being Oscar Micheaux, but its audiences were limited to black communities, particularly in the segregated independent movie theaters of the South.[55] For the most part, white audiences' glimpses of black life were mediated by white writers and performers, who spoke what one scholar has termed "entertainment dialect."[56]

Murphy was one of several artists of the time, from George Gershwin to Eugene O'Neill, who took an interest in depicting African-American life. Cripps has referred to these individuals as "Negrophiles"; David Levering

Lewis called them "Negrotarians"; and Michael Rogosin labeled the phenomenon "racial cross-dressing."[57] Their motivations were complex and
at times contradictory, including admiration or affection for black culture,
a desire to improve the status of African Americans in the cultural mainstream, and fascination with the exotic. The potential for creative and
financial reward could not be overlooked, either. As Lewis drily noted,
"Afro-American material could yield handsome returns."[58] Or as Carl Van
Vechten testily complained, "Are Negro writers going to write about this
exotic material while it is still fresh or will they continue to make a free
gift of it to white authors who will exploit it until not a drop of vitality
remains."[59]

Like many white artists, Murphy saw African Americans as emblematic
of urban modernity, and his films often conflated blacks with performance
and spectacle. According to family and friends, his interest in African-
American culture wasn't necessarily motivated by politics or a sense of
social injustice; instead, he seized upon a highly stylized view of black culture as a crucial element of his filmmaking vocabulary. In this he was not
alone. Around the country, blacks faced virulent discrimination in housing, employment, and education; in the South, lynching was still a powerful tool of white terrorism. But in Hollywood, in 1929, African Americans
were suddenly hot.

That year, the studios released several productions with all-black casts,
including the feature films *Hearts in Dixie, 200 Native Entertainers,* and
notably King Vidor's *Hallelujah!* Though Vidor's film was widely acclaimed
for its artistry, it struggled at the box office along with the others, particularly in the South, where mainstream exhibitors strenuously objected
to the increasing number of films on African-American themes. Though
movies like *Hearts in Dixie* and *Hallelujah!* were generally well attended
by urban black audiences, they were considered outdated, if not quaint. A
New York Amsterdam News article on *Hearts in Dixie,* for instance, noted
that the story "is one of the old-time Negro in the heart of the Southland.
Whether it is one that does the Negro justice now is a debatable one."[60]

Hallelujah! met with a similar response. Though the *New York Amsterdam News* supported the film, other African-American papers were dismayed at its treatment of religion, and black urban audiences sometimes
laughed outright at the depiction of rural characters. The Baltimore-
based *Afro-American* reported that at the film's Harlem premiere, "King
Vidor's intended dramatics brought forth peals of laughter at the wrong
moment."[61] *Hallelujah!*'s dismal reception threatened to swamp Murphy's

films as well. It's conceivable that *St. Louis Blues,* released around the same time, wasn't promoted to African-American theaters for fear of a similarly negative response. A brief notice about *Black and Tan* in the *Afro-American* stated that "Dudley Murphy . . . although discouraged at the flop of 'Hallelujah,' has just completed a short cinema sketch featuring Duke Ellington and the Cotton Club orchestra."[62]

Unlike other all-black films released in 1929, *St. Louis Blues* and *Black and Tan* presented urban blacks in modern settings. Most of the characters were poised, attractive, and self-possessed—a striking contrast to the prevalent Hollywood depictions of blacks on-screen. Greater Los Angeles in the 1920s was a rigidly segregated metropolis, which offered few points of contact among racial and ethnic groups. Murphy may have been one of the few directors in the industry to have become acquainted with the lifestyle of urban African Americans, even on the level of Harlem nightclubbing and socializing, and to have made a point of portraying it on-screen. *Black and Tan* was popular with black and white audiences alike; five years after its premiere, a 1934 news item announcing its rerelease noted that the film was "still holding the box-office record for a short subject."[63]

St. Louis Blues and *Black and Tan* inspired an interesting ambivalence in later scholars, who on the one hand faulted the films for having been made by an outsider with a limited understanding of black culture and, on the other, praised them for having succeeded as well as they did. For Cripps, the transition from silent to sound film was one of black cinema's richest periods of development—though not for black filmmakers, for whom the cost of sound technology remained prohibitive. "With the irony implicit in American racial arrangements," he wrote, "Negro cinema hopes were placed in the hands of . . . the most improbable lot of whites," of whom he considered Murphy "the most unlikely *and* the most successful."[64]

In their discussions of Murphy's work, both Cripps and Donald Bogle focused on *St. Louis Blues* rather than *Black and Tan.* Though he described its plot in detail, Cripps devoted little attention to *Black and Tan* in cinematic terms, making no mention of Murphy's visual experimentation. In *Toms, Coons, Mulattoes, Mammies, and Bucks,* Bogle did not mention the film at all. While he admired *St. Louis Blues* for its candor about black life, Bogle found it marred by overstatement.[65] Cripps, however, considered *St. Louis Blues* "the finest film of Negro life up to that time," noting that "in every instance old stereotypes took on new dimensions."[66]

Murphy's African-American films are best understood in light of Hollywood's brief fascination with all-black movies in the late 1920s. In this context, *St. Louis Blues* and *Black and Tan* acquit themselves reasonably well—better, in retrospect, than many such films of the early sound era. Murphy himself didn't transcend the prejudices of his day, but he demonstrated respect for the performers whose work inspired him and a certain willingness to get out of the way. Directing with an openness to improvisation and a sensitivity to the fluidity of musical performance, he worked inventively with the technology and aesthetics of sound film, and trusted his own taste. In the process, he created two enduring works of African-American cinema at a time when such films were the rare exception. Critically well received and popular with audiences, *St. Louis Blues* and *Black and Tan* earned him a chance at the kind of major directorial projects that had been his goal from the beginning. Instead, he fell afoul of a determined socialite and a strand of pearls.

CHAPTER 6

NOT MURDER BUT MAYHEM

Hollywood Again

The success of *St. Louis Blues* did not go unnoticed by the film industry. In late September 1929, while Murphy was still at work on *Black and Tan,* a brief item appeared in the *New York Journal American.* "Dudley Murphy, one-time cameraman, has been signed by Paramount as a short subject director on the staff of the Long Island studio," it read. "Murphy has produced several original musical shorts, utilizing his knowledge of screen photography to develop an unusual technique. One of his recent subjects, 'The St. Louis Blues,' is now at the Rialto, where it has attracted wide comment from press and public."[1]

After its Hollywood sound stages had been destroyed by fire in early 1928, Paramount shifted sound production to its East Coast facility in Astoria, Queens, under production head Walter Wanger.[2] One of the actresses under contract to the studio was Gilda Gray, a now-forgotten icon of the 1920s best known for popularizing "the shimmy." Gray had starred in two silent features: *Aloma of the South Seas* (1926), which had done well for Paramount, and the less successful *Cabaret* (1927), a sordid tale involving a nightclub dancer, a tough detective, and a gangster. It fell to Murphy to bring Gray into the sound era with a two-reel musical short—something similar to *St. Louis Blues* but presumably even more successful. Murphy hoped that the assignment would finally win him a directing slot on a feature-length sound film.

Once again he turned to popular music for inspiration. Devising a plot from the lyrics of the song "Frankie and Johnny," he scripted and directed the film, which was eventually called *He Was Her Man.* Though publicly touting it with enthusiasm, privately he was not entirely pleased, feeling that it lacked the "vitality" of his African-American productions. But it accomplished its purpose, winning him an appointment with Wanger to discuss his directing future at Paramount. Murphy eagerly anticipated the meeting. "At the time I was doing [the film] for Wanger, Preston Sturges was writing for Paramount—his play, *Strictly Dishonorable,* having been a hit on Broadway. Also, [director and producer] Monta Bell was there at that time, as was Lubitsch," he recalled. He was thrilled at the prospect of joining such notable colleagues and "keenly looking forward to the next step up the ladder."[3]

Since his return to New York, Murphy had been living in a penthouse apartment in an office building at 18 East Forty-first Street, while Katharine Hawley Murphy remained in Croton-on-Hudson, raising the couple's two children. Faltering since Paris, the marriage had continued to unravel, and the penthouse was a de facto bachelor pad, which he sometimes shared with a former brother-in-law, John Barbour. "My apartment, being close to the theatrical district, was always open and on many occasions I would come home and find people assembled for a late snack," he wrote. "Fats Waller, who was playing in a show on 46th Street, used to come up and compose on my piano. My apartment being in an office building, no one was ever disturbed by noise."[4]

The night before his appointment with Wanger, Murphy came home from the theater to meet Barbour. According to Murphy, Barbour arrived at the apartment first. He reluctantly admitted a woman whom Murphy had recently begun seeing, the estranged wife of a prominent bond broker. Apparently drunk, she'd demanded to be admitted. Finding Murphy out, she'd insisted on waiting. Murphy and Barbour both offered to escort her home, but she adamantly refused. Tired and exasperated, the men retired to their respective rooms, leaving her on the couch. The next morning, the maid arrived to discover her dead body. The following day, January 16, 1930, Murphy was front-page news.

"Woman Found Dead in Film Man's Rooms" was the lurid headline in the *New York Times.* "Director and Friend Say Mrs. Harriet Adler, Broker's Wife, Called Late at Night," ran the subhead, followed by "Marks on Her Throat" and "Officials Lay These to Pearls She Wore—Order a Thorough Investigation Today." Although the article noted that death was attributed to natural causes and that neither Murphy nor Barbour had been detained, "in some manner" the string of pearls that Adler had been wearing "had been pressed against [her] throat until they left tiny indentations in her flesh. These ligature marks and a slight discoloration of the face hinted strongly enough at possible strangulation" to require a precaution-ary autopsy.[5]

No stranger to publicity, Murphy was at ease in the flourishing celeb-rity culture of the late 1920s. He enjoyed seeing his name in print and during this period engaged a clipping service to keep track of his press mentions nationwide. They included a flurry of syndicated notices related to *He Was Her Man* and celebrity-oriented items that "spotted" him in Broadway restaurants or touted him as a Rudy Vallee look-alike.[6] Only days before, the syndicated column "Broadway Films" had mentioned his new fur coat, "so large and ferocious looking that several colleagues sug-gested it be chained up when not in use," and a joke of his had appeared in Walter Winchell's column under the writer's trademark "Heheheh."[7] But a knack for working the gossip pages hardly prepared Murphy for the maelstrom of media attention that Adler's death provoked. "There now followed," he wrote, "a horrifying day as reporters started crowding into my apartment and snapping pictures and interrogating Barbour and myself. . . . I was not arrested nor held, but was told not to leave town pending the outcome of the inquest. When I emerged from my building, I was greeted by newsboys, brandishing papers with screaming headlines: 'Society Woman Choked in Movie Director's Penthouse.' To relieve my tension and brave the world, so to speak, I went to 21 for lunch and was greeted kiddingly by Jack and Charlie, 'Have a drink, murderer.'"[8]

When Murphy called Walter Wanger to explain his missed appoint-ment, the possibility of his directing at Paramount evaporated. The studio moved swiftly to minimize any spatter from the negative publicity. Writ-ten not twenty-four hours after the fact, the *New York Times* article ended by noting that "at the Paramount offices it was said that [Murphy] had directed one 'short' for them but was connected no longer with the orga-nization."[9] The studio apparently went to even greater lengths to distance itself from the scandal. Though syndicated newspaper columns in Decem-ber 1929 and January 1930 carried numerous mentions of the upcoming release of *He Was Her Man,* in the months that followed the film was not reviewed, even briefly, in *Variety* or the *New York Times*—indicating, per-haps, that it was not released at all. No prints are known to exist.[10]

The day after the story broke, the *Times* buried a brief follow-up in its inside pages. An investigation found that Adler had died of "acute alcohol-ism and the pressure of a choker necklace" caused by the position of her body as she lay passed out on the couch.[11] Though Murphy was officially exonerated, he noted with uncharacteristic understatement, and more than a touch of irony, "My brilliant career had a temporary set-back due to this unfortunate occurrence."[12]

Hollywood Looks Good

Adler's death was national news, but nowhere was the spotlight as relentless as New York.[13] Faced with a floodtide of miserable publicity, Murphy had little choice but to leave town. He drove down to Florida, then cross-country to Los Angeles with Reed Howes, who'd starred in Murphy's first feature, *High Speed Lee.* Together they rented a small house on Doheny Drive between Sunset and Santa Monica boulevards.

While directing his short films for RCA and Paramount, Murphy had continued to write scenarios and scripts for other projects. He cowrote the story for *Jazz Heaven* (1929), an amiable if rambling romantic comedy about a country boy making good in Tin Pan Alley, which made clever use of a radio broadcast in its plot.[14] In early 1929, he'd tried to interest RCA in a feature-length script called "Rhapsody" and had started discussions with Sonora-Bristolphone, a small film-sound equipment company, to direct a film based on "a story of colored life by Carl Van Vechten."[15] Apparently neither of these projects was realized, but Murphy continued to draw on his story-, scenario-, and scriptwriting abilities for paying work when directing jobs were scarce. The hasty return to Hollywood was such an occasion. It was several months before he picked up a directing assignment. In the interim, he worked on two drafts of the script for Tod Browning's *Dracula* (1931), earning a credit for additional dialogue.[16]

At the end of 1930, almost a year after Adler's death, an item in the *Los Angeles Times* noted that Murphy—"the clever writer who has been distinguishing himself in the picture world for the past four or five years"—had been signed by MGM to write a series of sports films.[17] The first, tentatively titled *Fore,* was slated to star golfer Leo Diegel and John Mack Brown, one of the leads in *Jazz Heaven,* with Murphy directing. Murphy did write and direct an MGM short called *A Lesson in Golf,* which was released in January 1932. He made no mention of the film in his memoir, however, and little is known about it.[18]

By 1931, Murphy had signed on with Paramount again, not Wanger's New York facility but the main Hollywood studio run by his rival, B. P. (Ben) Schulberg. A February 1931 article in the *Los Angeles Times* noted,

"We've been used to thinking of Dudley Murphy as a writer, but it seems that he has long cherished the ambition to be a director, and has indeed one independent picture to his credit. Now Paramount is gratifying his ambition by signing him as director on a long-term contract. It is on the cards that Murphy shall direct 'Confessions of a Co-Ed' when the picture goes into production."[19] A second item referred to him as a "young director whose unique camera effects have established him as a revolutionary in screen technique"—a legacy, presumably, of *Ballet mécanique* and *Black and Tan*.[20]

But when *Confessions of a Co-ed* (1931) reached the screen, Murphy was billed not as director but as codirector. In this he was one of the many casualties of Schulberg's decision to hire Broadway directors inexperienced in film. David O. Selznick, who worked under Schulberg from 1928 to 1931, recalled that "the whole Paramount studio was hipped at the time on the idea that pictures should be directed by stage directors because of their greater experience in directing dialogue."[21] Murphy's credit was shared by David Burton, a theater director whose previous two films had also been made with Hollywood codirectors. "I supplied the visual element and photographic technique, while he took care of the dialogue," Murphy wrote. "By this time, sound had completely come in and no silent pictures were being made."[22]

Even though Murphy's own recent hits were sound films, they were inspired by music, not the spoken word. Plot, character, and dialogue, the linchpins of the classical Hollywood film, were seldom the dominant elements in his filmmaking. To his dismay, he found that he could not embrace the emerging conventions of the medium. "To me and those of us who had learned to tell a story in images," he wrote, "the advent of sound had set the technique of picture making back several years."[23]

Murphy was not alone in his thinking. Hollywood in the late 1920s and early 1930s was littered with directors who, having survived the transition to centralized production, couldn't adapt to the aesthetics of sound. They included major commercial directors such as Fred Niblo (*Ben Hur,* 1925), Clarence Badger, who'd directed Clara Bow in *It* (1927), and Herbert Brenon (*Beau Geste,* 1926). Veteran silent-film director William C. deMille, who'd done two to four films a year in the early 1920s, saw his career plummet. Disdainful of sound film as an art form, he believed its highest purpose lay in bringing grand opera to the masses.[24] Even Clarence Brown, who enjoyed a decades-long career after sound, regretted the changeover. "I think that silent pictures were more of an art than the talkies ever have been," he later commented. "Too many people let the dialogue do their thinking for them, do the plot exposition for them, do everything for them. Silents were . . . subtler, I guess."[25]

As a codirector at Paramount, Murphy fared better than many of his contemporaries, though he might have wished for a better film to work on. Set on a college campus, *Confessions of a Co-ed* is the convoluted tale of four students and their love lives. Peggy (Claudia Dell) and Patricia (Sylvia Sidney) fall for the same smooth talker, Dan (Phillips Holmes). In his pursuit of the two, he manages to get Peggy expelled for misbehavior and seduces Patricia shortly before being expelled himself and heading to South America. In desperation, Patricia marries Dan's friend Hal (Norman Foster). She's under the impression that Hal knows that she's carrying Dan's child, not his, since she'd asked Peggy to tell him; but Peggy never did. Three years later, Dan returns from South America and the truth comes out. "But no muddle is beyond the motion picture producer when he desires to give the audiences a happy ending," wrote Mordaunt Hall, "and the case of Patricia and Dan is no exception." The two realize their love for one another and, over Hal's objections, decide to marry. *Confessions of a Co-ed* was allegedly adapted from the diary of an anonymous college student. As Hall observed, "It is no wonder that the author . . . should prefer to remain anonymous, for it is a most trivial and implausible story." For him, the film's direction was "nothing to arouse any great degree of enthusiasm."[26]

Even so, Murphy brought a few characteristic touches to the project, including his approach to the extras casting. As in *St. Louis Blues,* where he peopled the nightclub scene with Harlem habitués, here he chose his bit players from sororities on the UCLA campus, rather than through the usual Hollywood casting call. He was particularly proud of having successfully grappled with Schulberg and Selznick over his choice for a minor singing role: a promising young vocalist named Bing Crosby, for whom *Confessions of a Co-ed* was an early screen appearance.[27]

SAME STATION, DIFFERENT TRAIN:
HOLLYWOOD AFTER SOUND

By the early 1930s, the basic elements of the Hollywood studio system were solidly in place, along with most of the production executives who would dominate the industry over the next decade. Gone were the days of the omnipotent film director and script ideas told and sold over cocktails for a hundred dollars. With its squadrons of technicians and heavy production costs, sound had standardized the movies. No longer were they vehicles of individual expression, however magnificent or quirky. Rigorously organized, factorylike production was the norm, along with easily replicated plots and characters. Writers, directors, and production heads struggled to come up with winning cinematic formulas in a suddenly transformed medium. Similar changes were afoot on the commercial side. Before sound, the film industry had been a sizable and profitable business. With millions invested in new technologies and powerful bankers sitting on the boards of most studios, it was now *big* business.

No sooner had sound begun to reach small-town movie screens than the Depression took hold. While at first the film industry considered itself proof against economic disaster, by 1933, three of the top five "integrated majors" (Paramount, Fox, and RKO) had gone into bankruptcy or receivership.[28] Shrewd fiscal management was now a necessity, and the industry was dominated by cost-efficient, bottom-line executives such as Irving Thalberg, Darryl F. Zanuck, and Schulberg.

The system required of film directors a certain diplomatic dexterity and an astute grasp of their place in the hierarchy. Laboring under an outdated concept of the director's role—part avant-garde film artist, part Rex Ingram—Murphy in these years demonstrated neither the skills nor the understanding to exploit the industry power structure or even to avoid running afoul of it. Hollywood was a small, single-industry town with a demonically efficient grapevine. Sylvia Sidney, star of *Confessions of a Co-ed,* was, as he recalled, B. P. Schulberg's girl, and as he ruefully admitted, "Had I been a better politician, I would have played up to her."[29] Instead, he apparently responded as he usually did with attractive women. Decades later, he wrote, "[Schulberg] asked me if I ever knew why I was let out of [the contract with] Paramount. . . . [He] told me that Sylvia had told him that I was on the make for her when I was doing this picture."[30] Even as an ambitious director eager to make his way through the system, Murphy was impervious to its implicit ground rules. "I had very little respect for the politics of the movie business," he wrote, and it's hard to dispute that conclusion.[31]

Murphy made one more film for Paramount before being released from his contract: *Twenty-four Hours* (1931). On this project, his credit slipped to associate director under Marion Gehring, another import from the Broadway stage. Adapted from a novel by Louis Bromfield, one of Murphy's colleagues on the *Dracula* screenplay, the film's action unfolds within the span of a single day. Disheartened by his wife's infidelity, a hard-drinking millionaire (Clive Brook) sets off into a snowy New York night. He ends up going home with a beautiful nightclub singer (Miriam Hopkins), passing out drunk in her living room while she goes off to bed alone. That night, her gangster husband returns and kills her, and the millionaire is arrested for the murder. Meanwhile, a rival gang leader kills the murdering husband in revenge for a previous killing. The millionaire is exonerated when detectives find the killer's fingerprints on a liquor bottle in the singer's bedroom. Realizing that his drinking is the cause of his ruined marriage, the millionaire decides to sail off, freeing his wife (Kay Francis) to seek her happiness elsewhere. The film closes with the wife unexpectedly joining him on the ocean liner, willing to give the marriage another try.

Twenty-four Hours was well-received by the critics. Mordaunt Hall called it "well directed and beautifully photographed," while *Variety* described it as "the essence of the old time society drama, only superbly dressed up in modern accessories. . . . Altogether an absorbing bit of fiction." The review cited specific cinematic touches that, though impossible to attribute conclusively to Murphy, bear the mark of his style, especially in their attention to visual transitions. "The passage of time is indicated intermittently by tricky camera shots at all sorts of clocks scattered through the city," *Variety* wrote, "views across house tops to some towering skyscraper clock blurred in a flurry of snow. Chimes ring the hour, too."[32]

The film was a modest hit, but for Murphy its greatest impact was personal: it brought Miriam Hopkins into his life. "There is a myth that one can fall in love with a girl on the screen," Murphy wrote. "I had seen a picture which [Ernst] Lubitsch had made in New York with a lovely blonde actress . . . and I had actually fallen for her on the screen."[33] Hopkins was incandescently beautiful, with an elegant sense of comic timing. The movie Murphy saw was Lubitsch's *The Smiling Lieutenant* (1931); Hopkins was about to star in another for him, the sparkling *Trouble in Paradise* (1932). Though Murphy's involvement with Hopkins lasted only a few months, he considered it the most intense love affair of his life.[34]

In July 1931, while he was immersed in his new romance, Katharine Hawley Murphy filed for divorce.[35] Since their return from Paris in the mid-1920s, the couple had lived largely apart, and he'd spent little time with her or the children. Five years later, Hawley Murphy was ready to make the final break. Caught up with Hopkins, Murphy didn't object. It wasn't long, though, before the actress moved on to other conquests, leaving him devastated. "Now I was truly carrying a torch," he recalled. "I had bought an open cockpit Butler Blackhawk plane, which I kept at the Santa Monica airport and being in a suicidal frame of mind, I used to do tail-spins, seeing how near the ground I could come before pulling out."[36]

By the end of the year he'd found solace in an unlikely quarter. "One day, Fletch, my old secretary from New York, gave a cocktail party for me to meet a beautiful young girl who was also carrying a torch. . . . Our mutual misery drew us together and when we left the party, we took a long drive to Laguna," Murphy wrote. "Suddenly realizing the hour, Josephine ('Jo-Jo') said her father"—Fox executive and former New York City commissioner Joseph Johnson—"would never forgive her for staying out so late. So I suggested we carry on to Tiajuana [*sic*] and get married. We proceeded to do so."[37]

Within days, the spur-of-the-moment elopement hit the gossip columns. "Never was the town more shocked than by Josephine Johnson's marriage to Dudley Murphy, in whose New York apartment a wealthy lady was found strangled by her own pearls a couple of years ago," reported one New York paper.[38] The *New York Times* noted that the bride was eighteen years old; the bridegroom, thirty-four.

After the exhilaration of the elopement, married life with a teenage stranger was a sobering reality. Looking back, Murphy admitted, "It was unfair to Jo-Jo to marry her, feeling the way I did for Miriam."[39] Oddly matched as they were, the two gave the marriage a try. In early 1932, Murphy bought a spacious, Spanish-style house on Amalfi Drive in the Pacific Palisades. Recently repossessed by a bank, it was a bargain at twenty-five thousand dollars, "with a small down-payment and mortgage payments of about what I had formerly paid for rent." Set in the midst of a lemon grove, the house was at least a quarter-mile from the nearest neighbor, and Murphy recalled, "Jo-Jo and I were very happy there."[40]

Selznick Steps In

The deepening Depression left the film industry facing plummeting attendance, increasingly finicky audiences, and mounting losses. The system that had efficiently cranked out hundreds of movies a year now discovered that quantity alone was no longer a guarantee of profitability. As they floundered for workable strategies, the studios were torn between the predictability of production-line mediocrities and the costly gambles of "prestige" productions.

The economic turmoil sent executives scrambling from studio to studio with increasing frequency. By 1933, Walter Wanger had gone from Paramount to Columbia to MGM. Darryl F. Zanuck, locked in an irresolvable power struggle with Harry Warner, left Warner Brothers to form Twentieth Century Pictures, forerunner of Twentieth Century-Fox, with former United Artists executive Joe Schenck. In 1931, Selznick left Paramount, attempting to set up as an independent producer before becoming head of production at RKO. Like Wanger, he ended up as a unit producer at MGM in 1933.[41]

Murphy and Selznick had first crossed paths at Paramount, where Selznick oversaw production on *Confessions of a Co-ed* and *Twenty-four Hours*. One of the most successful producers in Hollywood history, Selznick had a near-infallible grasp of what film historian Thomas Schatz called "the holy trinity of the studio system": budget, star, and genre.[42] A passionately hands-on producer, he was at heart an independent and in 1935 formed his own company, which produced such classics as *Gone with the Wind* (1939) and *The Third Man* (1949). In his memoir Murphy made frequent reference to Selznick, and it appears that the two got along well. Selznick may have appreciated Murphy's eye for talent—evident in his casting of Bing Crosby in *Confessions of a Co-ed* over Selznick's own strenuous objections—or possibly Murphy's avid defense of his filmmaking decisions, which in Crosby's case involved paying a portion of the singer's fee out of his own directing salary.[43] In any event, when Selznick became head of production at RKO in 1931, Murphy moved with him. Mandated to reduce costs and beef up revenues, Selznick fired most of the directors under contract at RKO and brought in replacements on a picture-by-picture basis. On that footing, he gave Murphy his first assignment as sole director of a feature-length talkie.

The film was *The Sport Parade* (1932).[44] Starring a strapping young newcomer, Joel McCrea, it recounts the story of a star collegiate football duo, Sandy Baker (McCrea) and Johnny Brown (William Gargan), once their days of varsity triumph are over. Straight-arrow Johnny takes up a career as a sports editor, but Sandy falls prey to the blandishments of an unscrupulous promoter and chooses to coast on past glories. His personal appearances flop—no one's interested in yesterday's heroes—and professional football is too crude for his gentlemanly sensibilities. Johnny comes to the rescue, bringing him onto the newspaper's sports staff and generously sharing his column and byline. Finding himself falling for Johnny's girl, Irene (Marian Marsh), Sandy quits the paper and cuts himself off from his friend. Down on his luck, he goes back to the crooked promoter, who sets him up as a wrestler and arranges for him to throw an important match. Irene shows up in his dressing room and declares her love for him, but it's only when Johnny, in the audience with Irene, starts volubly rooting for him that Sandy reverses himself and wins the match. By the closing frames, he's also won the girl, with Johnny's blessing.

It's a common enough plot for a 1930s romantic comedy, but the film's conventional surface concealed a distinctly homoerotic undertow. "*The Sport Parade* is a barely disguised tribute to bisexual male bonding, garnished with abundant, lovingly shot displays of McCrea's physique as viewed in almost every configuration," wrote Richard Barrios, who noted that a preliminary draft of the script featured Sandy jauntily singing about "a bisexual built for two."[45] Given the force field of attraction between Sandy and Johnny and the camera's bodily obsession with McCrea, Irene doesn't stand a chance.

Barrios credits Murphy with articulating the script's homosexual subtext, and the film supports this assertion. The locker-room sequences, with their masculine camaraderie, have energy and verve, while the love scenes between Sandy and Irene fall flat. In the final wrestling match, the camera's gaze does seem inordinately focused on McCrea's thinly clad derriere. However, Murphy also insisted on a rewrite of the initial script, which had included writer Corey Ford's barely veiled allusions. "I felt that it should have another writer," was his only explanation.[46] He had cast humorist Robert Benchley, an acquaintance from the Algonquin Round Table, in the role of the sports announcer and arranged for Benchley to do an additional draft. "This angered the original writer," he wrote, "who made a funny crack about me, 'God have Murphy on us.' It is too bad he didn't have the same sense of humor in the script."[47] In Benchley's hands, his own character—whom Mordaunt Hall described as a "bibulous and haphazard radio announcer, who chuckles over his mistakes and yawns while trying to describe a sprint in a six-day bicycle race"—became one of the strong points of the film, which Hall pronounced "quite a satisfactory entertainment."[48]

The Sport Parade is studded with the kind of visual play found in Murphy's earlier sound films. In the opening scene, a slow camera zoom into Benchley's large, square microphone dissolves into a wide shot of the football gridiron. Later, another zoom closes in on a photograph on a café wall, which comes alive as it fills the frame. An exit sign starts spinning, dissolving into a spinning automobile wheel, which then dissolves into an office wall clock. And Dizzy, the perpetually inebriated news photographer (played by Skeets Gallagher, star of Murphy's silent features *Alex the Great* and *Stocks and Blondes*), sees nightclub dancers fractured and multiplied, *Black and Tan*–style, through a kaleidoscopic lens.

Murphy was by no means the only industry director to retain an emphasis on visual play for its own sake. But the preference threw him increasingly out of step with the Hollywood mainstream. In the wake of sound, cinematic experimentation had all but disappeared; with so much money invested in the new technology, the stakes on every production were too high. As a result, Murphy's filmmaking style began to seem old-fashioned, a holdover from the silent era and from his own earlier experiments. Strategies that had appeared fresh in 1929, pushing the narrative envelope in *Black and Tan,* no longer had the same impact a scant three years later. Instead, some of *The Sport Parade*'s visual flourishes tend to thwart its narrative. The kaleidoscopic sequence depicting Dizzy's drunken point of view, for instance, is a moment of unsublimated spectacle that stops the narrative cold. Jutting awkwardly from the film's overall flow, such disjunctures speak eloquently of the difficulties Murphy encountered in fitting his filmmaking style into the emerging sound-film aesthetic.

Most directors adapted or perished, but another who grappled with the narrow conventions of the standard sound film was Rouben Mamoulian. A Russian-trained Broadway theater director, Mamoulian started working in film soon after sound came in. His films include *Applause* (1929) and *Love Me Tonight* (1932), both highly innovative in their sound treatment and editing. Like Murphy, Mamoulian foregrounded visual play as well as a sophisticated use of sound and music. Though more successful, Mamoulian also had his difficulties with the industry; in a career lasting almost thirty years, he made only sixteen films.[49]

With its vestiges of a more visually emphatic style, *The Sport Parade* demonstrates how divergent the aesthetics of silent and early sound film really were. It points to how compelling (and visually austere) early narrative sound film could be, even in a formulaic production. And it offers a clear indication that the imperatives of the early sound-film form could not accommodate, and largely excluded, the image-based aesthetics of silent film. Just the year before, Frank Capra had admonished industry professionals that "'directorial touches' and photographic 'scenic splurges' should be kept out of a picture. They detract from the story. Excellence in direction is reached when the audience never thinks of the director's work. . . . The minute the audience becomes conscious of the 'machinery' of a picture, they forget the story."[50] Deliberately designed to make audiences aware of the machinery, Murphy's visual touches attempt to enrich the viewing experience while loosening the storytelling and its grip on the viewer. But the strategy doesn't work. Awkwardly perched on the film's narrative framework, Murphy's visual embellishments are little more than scattered reminders of what was lost when silent film vanished.

One other distinguishing characteristic of Murphy's earlier sound films resurfaces in *The Sport Parade:* its fictional world is inhabited by a broader mix of people than are usually found in Hollywood features. With respect to African Americans, that world almost unavoidably reflects the prevalent attitudes of the times. The film's nightclub sequence opens with a shot of African-American performers doing a jazzy "jungle" dance number, followed by their cultural opposite: black tap dancers elegantly attired in top hats and tails. These two performances are the subject of the drunken photographer's kaleidoscopic vision, recalling Fredi Washington's illness-induced visions in *Black and Tan.* Here, in a film lacking an African-American context, the effect is disconcerting, suggesting that blackness, linked to performative display, is a precondition for this type of visual play.

The film's only African-American character is Alex, Sandy's masseur. A sympathetic and supportive figure, he lets Sandy know that he's bet on him to win the wrestling match, even though he knows it's been rigged. However, Alex also has to submit—not once, but twice—to having his head rubbed vigorously (presumably for luck) during the match by one of Sandy's Dartmouth buddies.[51]

What is arguably the most enlightened depiction of African Americans is also the briefest. As the final wrestling match builds to its climax, Murphy cuts away to quick shots of audience members absorbed in the action. He cuts to a stylish, well-dressed African-American couple, intently rooting for Sandy to win, then cuts back later to the woman as she cheers Sandy's triumph. Donald Bogle has pointed out that "even in crowd scenes, Hollywood has traditionally presented a lily-white world with not a single Black face in sight," as if the African American "did not exist as just an ordinary everyday citizen."[52] Portrayed as neither objects of ridicule nor comic relief, the black couple are accorded the same treatment from Murphy's camera as other members of the audience.

Murphy slips one more near-subversive encounter into his cutaways. In the film's first wrestling match (which does not feature McCrea), he cuts to a couple watching the action, a stereotypically gay pair who find the ring action too violent for their sensibilities. One turns to the other, saying, "Oh, God, this is just brutal. Let's go!" and they head for the exit.

Such incidental appearances by homosexual characters were not uncommon in the pre-Code films of the early 1930s, which saw the increasing occurrence of gay and lesbian characters, cameo roles, and narrative
subtexts.[53] In a February 1933 article entitled "Tsk, Tsk, Such Goings On,"
Variety noted that "producers are going heavy on the panz stuff in current
pix."[54] But even in that permissive climate, Murphy's flash of gayness went
beyond the norm. As Barrios pointed out, "The look and manner of this
unidentified pair really feels like the unfeigned real thing. And just before
the camera cuts away from them, one takes the other's hand in his—a rare
public display of affection that establishes that the pair, whatever the writer
and director want the audience to think of them, really is a romantic duo."[55]

In *The Sport Parade,* Murphy inventively worked the seams of the
classical Hollywood film form—transitions between scenes, cutaway shots
usually dismissed as filler—to shift the film toward his own cinematic sensibility. The unadorned narrativity of the early sound film was replaced by
a more stylized, visually inventive treatment. And the on-screen populace
that 1930s Hollywood depicted as white and straitlaced became, in brief
throwaway moments, more inclusive.

The Sport Parade gave Murphy a good indication of what he could hope
to achieve within the confines of the mainstream film industry and standard Hollywood film form. He'd always wanted to be a Hollywood director and had worked more than a decade to attain the level of success that
he'd finally achieved. He tried to be satisfied with it; eventually he was not.
After a break of some months, that dissatisfaction led to the definitive turning point of *The Emperor Jones.* Meanwhile, art once again assumed an important, if momentary, role in his life.

CHAPTER 7

BETWEEN PICTURES

By the time he'd settled into the Amalfi Drive house with Jo-Jo in early 1932, Murphy had been back in Los Angeles for about two years. Though the Depression struck the city hard, its population continued to grow. It had already swelled to more than two million, powered by its top industries: agriculture, oil, and the movies.

Los Angeles politics were volatile and extreme. Unlike San Francisco, L.A. was a hardline antiunion town. The film studios stood firm until unions were federally mandated by the National Industrial Recovery Act of 1933. Across the region labor conflicts frequently flared into violence, especially in the agricultural empires of the Imperial Valley. Upton Sinclair, erstwhile friend and neighbor of Murphy's mother, Caroline, may have been raising socialist hell in Pasadena, but the Los Angeles Police Department had its own Red Squad, which targeted the Socialist and Communist parties with a vengeance. The city's nonwhite population had jumped to 14.2 percent in 1930, a larger proportion than any major city other than Baltimore. But its African-American population had grown to only thirty-nine thousand, fewer than 2 percent of the total.[1]

Culturally, the city continued to develop. The two major art schools, the Otis Art Institute and the Chouinard Art Institute (later Cal Arts), were well established, and smaller institutions had sprung up as well. Modern art was gaining acceptance in the city's museums, and galleries and dealers proliferated, fueled in part by the collecting interests of the Hollywood elite. An expanding community of bibliophiles—businessmen, lawyers, and wealthy film professionals, among others—browsed among an increasing number of bookstores, rare book dealers, and private clubs. By 1930, architect Richard Neutra had moved to the city and established his practice, and art critic Arthur Millier had begun writing regularly on art for the *Los Angeles Times*.

In spring of 1930, acclaimed Soviet film director Sergei Eisenstein came to Hollywood at the enthusiastic urging of David O. Selznick at Paramount. Predictably, no film resulted from his sojourn. Selznick's personal admiration for the director didn't prevent him from strongly advising Paramount to discontinue Eisenstein's project, an adaptation of Theodore Dreiser's *An American Tragedy*. In an October 8, 1930, memo to B. P. Schulberg, Selznick called Eisenstein's adaptation "the most moving script I have ever read. . . . When I had finished it, I was so depressed that I wanted to reach for the bourbon bottle. . . . I think it an inexcusable gamble on the part of this department to put into a subject as depressing as this one, anything like the cost that an Eisenstein production must necessarily entail."[2] Eisenstein's agreement with the studio was canceled less than six months after it was signed. The project was handed to Josef von Sternberg, who couldn't have cared less about its political overtones. Released in 1931, his version came off as flat and half-hearted. It not only fizzled at the box office but prompted Dreiser to sue the studio.

Murphy evidently knew and spent time with Eisenstein during his blighted tenure at Paramount.[3] In a later interview, he would recall the Soviet director's enthusiastic embrace of *Ballet mécanique*.[4] At this point in Murphy's career, however, the contrast between Eisenstein's cinematic theories and *Confessions of a Co-ed* must have been piquant indeed.

But if his filmmaking preferences inclined uneasily toward Eisenstein's, Murphy's social life was pure Hollywood. In the nearly fifteen years that he owned it, the house on Amalfi Drive was the scene of many memorable parties. At one such celebration, Murphy recalled, "I had [acclaimed concert pianist] José Iturbi and Fats Waller. Each wanted to play the other's style of music. At this party, Charlie Chaplin told many of his fascinating stories and did his monologue of the Frenchman and his wife and her lover. . . . Another party I gave for Jock Whitney, and it was at that party that David Selznick [got] Whitney and his sister, Joan Payson, to back him in *Gone with the Wind*. I remember a fight between Clark Gable and Selznick (?) in the kitchen during the course of the party."[5]

Murphy also became a fixture in local gossip columns, racking up considerable print in 1932 alone. In May, for instance, he was "espccially pleased" with the new Club Airport Gardens (a favored watering hole of fellow pilot Howard Hughes), because "he said he could land his plane across the way and then come in for a dance and dinner."[6] In October, he got into a nightclub brawl with Greta Nissen's husband, prompted by Murphy's dance-floor attentions to the actress. ("'It was all over in a minute,' Murphy said yesterday. '. . . everything was peaceful and has been forgotten by this time.'")[7] Gambling in Caliente, Mexico, in November with an unnamed comedian, the two lost all. "Dudley made a grab at the comedian's false teeth. Wanted to bet them. In the scrimmage the teeth were broken. . . . When he gets them fixed he threatens to bite Dudley with them."[8] A few weeks later, the subject was fashion: "And is Dudley Murphy trying to pull a Gable? He's seen constantly, even on the hottest days, in a bright yellow, high turtle neck."[9] As the year drew to a close, Murphy prepared to direct *Now You See It,* an RKO biography of magician Harry Houdini starring Adolphe Menjou; another item gleefully reported the two of them at a dinner meeting of the Society of American Magicians, encountering rubber cutlery, a levitating plate, and other tricks.[10]

Despite his ease in the Hollywood social landscape, as a filmmaker Murphy still aspired to something more meaningful. For him, Eisenstein and his theories would have offered a bracing counterbalance to night-clubs, yellow turtlenecks, and the usual studio assignments. But the Soviet director was arguably not the most radical of Murphy's acquaintances during this period. In May 1932, soon after Murphy bought his house on Amalfi Drive, the Mexican muralist and painter David Alfaro Siqueiros arrived in Los Angeles to teach a course in fresco painting at the Chouinard Art Institute.[11] Through his friendship with Siqueiros, Murphy, in his usual ad hoc, freewheeling way, had an unexpected hand in twentieth-century art history.

A militant socialist and labor organizer as well as an artist, Siqueiros had been an officer in the Mexican Revolution, a representative of the new Mexican government in Spain, and a key organizer of the Syndicate of Technical Workers, Painters, and Sculptors, the group that had sparked the mural movement in Mexico. Jailed by an increasingly reactionary government in 1930, then confined to the outlying town of Taxco, he chose exile in Los Angeles over continued house arrest at home.[12]

Siqueiros was welcomed by L.A.'s art world as well as its Mexican-American community. Director and art collector Josef von Sternberg, whom Murphy knew socially, was particularly helpful in bringing the artist into the United States. Sternberg quickly commissioned a portrait from Siqueiros and assisted him in getting his paintings to Los Angeles after they'd been detained by the Mexican government. On May 9, 1932, an exhibition of Siqueiros's lithographs opened in Jake Zeitlin's downtown bookstore. A few days later, a show of his paintings, mural designs, and other works opened in the Stendahl Ambassador Gallery. By mid-June, Siqueiros and a team of local artists and students were at work on a mural in the courtyard of the Chouinard Art Institute. In October, he and a larger team completed a second, much bigger mural on the exterior wall of the Plaza Art Center on Olvera Street.

Neither of these murals fared well. This was due in part to the experimental materials and techniques that Siqueiros used on them and his determination that they be fully exposed to the elements, "in the free air, facing the sun, facing the rain, for the masses."[13] Airbrushing paint onto a surface of waterproof cement, Siqueiros and his teams, known as the Bloc of Mural Painters, were able to produce finished work quickly. For Siqueiros, this meant a more fluid approach to composition than he'd experienced in his previous mural projects, done in Mexico more than a decade earlier. Unfortunately, the experimental surface started to erode almost immediately, especially in the case of the Chouinard mural, which, according to eyewitness accounts, either flaked off or washed away in the first rainstorm.[14]

Adverse weather conditions, however, were the least of it. The Chouinard mural, *Workers' Meeting,* depicted a crowd of construction workers, arms linked, listening intently to a red-shirted speaker on a soapbox flanked by a black man and a white woman, each with a child. At the mural's dedication on July 7, 1932, Siqueiros delivered a stinging critique of North American imperialism to a crowd of eight hundred. A fiery anticapitalist oration might have gone over well in left-leaning San Francisco, but Los Angeles was hostile territory. *California Arts and Architecture* magazine tartly observed that "the art of fresco in this country will languish until it is able to free itself from the sorrows of Mexico and the full red glow of Communism."[15] Within the year, all traces of *Workers' Meeting* were obliterated by whitewash.

A similar fate awaited the Olvera Street mural, *Tropical America.* At the time, prominent civic leaders, including Otis Chandler and Christine Sterling (owner of the building on which the mural was painted), were turning the neighborhood into a folkloric re-creation of a Mexican village. They looked to Siqueiros to provide the appropriate decor. The mural's subject, however, was hardly that. It was an uncompromising assault on U.S. imperialism in Latin America, with its central image—painted by

Siqueiros alone, under cover of darkness on the night before the work's unveiling—depicting a Mexican campesino bound to a double cross, crowned by a triumphant North American eagle. Describing the unveiling in the *Los Angeles Times,* Millier wrote, "When the scaffolding finally came down . . . onlookers gasped. No one but the author had been able to visualize the close-knit powerful design so long shaded and concealed by those scaffolds."[16]

The audience gasped, to be sure, but aesthetics weren't the issue. *Tropical America* was as potent an indictment of imperialism and capitalist exploitation as Los Angeles was likely to see, and despite its artistic significance it was doomed. Within months, the Plaza Art Center was forced to paint over any sections plainly visible from the street. Years later, Christine Sterling would renew the lease on the building's upper floors only with the proviso that the fresco be completely painted over. By the 1970s, the decades spent "in the free air, facing the sun, facing the rain" had taken their toll, and scant trace remained of either the whitewash or the paint it covered. So little of the original pigment was left that full-fledged restoration was out of the question. Despite a lengthy, multimillion-dollar conservation effort in the 1990s, spearheaded by the J. Paul Getty Trust, today *Tropical America* is a ghostly shadow of the 1932 original.[17]

It was during the painting of *Tropical America* that Murphy met Siqueiros. Reuben Kadish, one of the local artists who worked with Siqueiros as a member of the Bloc, recalled that John Huston arranged Murphy's introduction. According to Murphy, however, film director Mal St. Clair, whom he'd known since his teenage days in Pasadena, brought him down to Olvera Street and introduced him to the artist.[18] "Siqueiros and I became great friends," he wrote, "and to help him out I put all my furniture from my house in the garden and held a three day exhibition of Siqueiros's paintings in my Amalfi Drive house. I got a very distinguished clientele to come and Siqueiros sold about ten of his paintings. Charles Laughton bought two, Walter Wanger bought one and Josef von Sternberg bought one.[19] In gratitude for my help, Siqueiros offered to do a mural for me on the wall of the enclosed patio."[20]

From the outset, Murphy's generosity may have been prompted by his desire for such a work. According to Los Angeles artist Fletcher Martin, another of Siqueiros's assistants, Murphy approached him with a request to be introduced, saying "Wouldn't it be great if Siqueiros would do a fresco on the wall in my garden?"[21] Siqueiros may have been as eager for the project as Murphy, if not more so. By the time *Tropical America* was unveiled in October, the artist's six-month visitor's permit had expired. A deportation order had been issued, and federal agents were actively searching for him. A major commission at an upscale private home deep in a lemon grove was just what Siqueiros needed, and he most likely leaped at the opportunity. For this reason, the arrangement may have been more of a business deal than a gesture of gratitude; Siqueiros perhaps painted the mural in lieu of rent, as Arthur Millier later asserted.[22]

It's worth noting that during this time Murphy's father was still actively pursuing his own steadfastly conservative career in art. A few years earlier, he'd become chairman of the Boston Art Club, succeeding a chair who'd been ousted for encouraging modern art, which Hermann Dudley Murphy publicly referred to as "that crazy stuff." Called upon for a statement, he declared, "We think these modernistic paintings are the work of only a small minority . . . the majority of the painters in the club are conservative rather than extremists."[23]

Though Hermann had extended financial assistance to Murphy in buying the Amalfi Drive house, relations between father and son remained cool. By the early 1930s, they were pursuing entirely separate lives at opposite ends of the country. In most things, Murphy's taste diverged sharply from his father's, and art was no exception. As a figurative painter, Siqueiros was hardly as "modernistic" as some of his international contemporaries. Even so, it's unlikely that the mural for Murphy's garden would have won Hermann's approbation. Originally titled *Delivery of the Mexican Bourgeoisie Born of the Revolution into the Hands of Imperialism,* it soon became known as *Portrait of Mexico Today.* Painted on the semienclosed, roofed walls of a structure in Murphy's backyard, using traditional fresco techniques, it's the only one of the artist's Los Angeles murals—indeed, the only one north of the Mexican border—to have survived.

At thirty-two feet long and eight feet high, *Portrait of Mexico Today* is a compact, tightly defined composition. The long back wall is divided by painted columns that echo the structure's wooden support columns. The center section of the back wall depicts two indigenous women and a child posed on a stepped platform reminiscent of a pre-Columbian pyramid. The right section, devoid of figures, continues the platform-pyramid with greenery behind. The left section depicts the figure of a Mexican revolutionary whose red mask has slipped, revealing the features of political strongman and former president Plutarco Elias Calles, a revolutionary hero who had grown increasingly powerful, conservative, and corrupt. Bags of gold at his feet represent his betrayal of the people. On a narrow wall directly facing the Calles panel is a portrait of financier J. Pierpont Morgan, a suggestive reminder that one of his employees, Dwight Morrow, was the United States' ambassador to Mexico during the Calles era. The side-wall panel between them depicts the bodies of two martyred workers, implicating both Morgan and Calles in the violence that killed them. On the right side wall, opposite the fallen workers, a fighter dressed in what looks like a Soviet Russian uniform takes aim at Morgan.[24]

Originally Siqueiros had planned a mural of flower girls grouped around a fountain, precisely the kind of folkloric theme that Otis Chandler and Christine Sterling would have been gratified to see on Olvera Street. But Murphy insisted on stronger subject matter, pushing Siqueiros to create the most personal of his Los Angeles works: a trenchant statement on contemporary Mexican politics reflecting his own bitter experience of the Calles regime.[25] The resulting mural was, as one recent scholar put it, "a pivotal work in his career and in the history of mural art."[26]

According to Murphy, Siqueiros, his wife, Uruguayan poet Blanca Luz Brum, and their eight-year-old son (nicknamed "Dinamito") took up residence at Murphy's home. Reuben Kadish, who assisted on the project, has disputed accounts of Siqueiros and his family actually living on the property, but artist, family, and crew clearly spent long stretches of time there.[27] This proved something of a trial, particularly for Jo-Jo. Siqueiros usually painted between midnight and three or four in the morning and wasn't inclined to be quiet about it. As Bloc member Fletcher Martin put it, "There was always a sense of elation and accomplishment after the night's work."[28] Worse still was Dinamito—"properly named," wrote Murphy, "as he was a most destructive and obnoxious child." After about two months, "with the fresco half-finished, Jo-Jo gave me an ultimatum: 'Either the Siqueiroses have to go, or I go.' I tried to explain to her how important it was to have this work of art finished, but she was adamant and left for New York."[29]

Siqueiros stayed to complete the work. Soon after, in November 1932, his deportation order was finally carried out. Given the continuing reactionary climate in Mexico, he opted to spend 1933 in South America, where he painted another mural in a suburb of Buenos Aires.[30]

Murphy took great pride in *Portrait of Mexico Today* and entertained lavishly at the Amalfi Drive house. He lived there until 1946, when he sold the property to Minna and Willard Coe. Ironically, Coe was a nephew of J. P. Morgan and did not take kindly to Siqueiros's depiction of his relation. Despite Murphy's repeated attempts to dissuade them, the couple planned to have the work painted over, making Siqueiros three for three in terms of murals lost to Los Angeles. "It wasn't until [Carlos] Chávez, the famous Mexican conductor . . . raved about the mural," wrote Murphy, "telling them how lucky they were to have it, that they decided not only to preserve it, but to install special lighting and use it as a background for their entertaining."[31]

In 1986, the Amalfi Drive property was sold to Robert and Justine Bloomingdale, who offered the mural for sale at auction in 1991. The work was valued at between one and a half and two million dollars, and conditions of the sale included removal of the artwork at the buyer's expense. There were no takers. In 1998, the Bloomingdales offered the work as an anonymous donation to the Santa Barbara Museum of Art, which had just presented the well-received exhibition Portrait of a Decade: David Alfaro Siqueiros, 1930–1940. After four years of study, preparation, painting conservation, and a complicated stabilization process, the entire structure on which the mural was painted was moved to the museum, at a total project cost of just under a million dollars. Installed on the lawn near the museum entrance, *Portrait of Mexico Today* was unveiled in October 2002, almost precisely seventy years after it was completed.[32]

What, if anything, was the impact of *Portrait of Mexico Today* on Murphy and his work? Or of the time that Murphy had spent with Eisenstein and with Siqueiros, both articulate leftist theorists as well as eminent artists? While focused on attaining a comfortable berth in the film industry, Murphy had also sought out individuals with a radically different worldview, one that foregrounded political and economic analysis and privileged art over commerce. Spending time with one of the great directors of world cinema or coming home to a master of modern Mexican art at work in his backyard, Murphy grew discontent with projects like *Confessions of a Co-ed* and *The Sport Parade*. He'd achieved his goal of becoming a Hollywood feature film director but wanted more. Though part of an industry that was a vast, vertically integrated oligopoly, Murphy still saw himself— or more accurately, wanted to see himself—as an artist, successful both commercially and on his own aesthetic terms.

It was not something he was likely to accomplish as a middling director for RKO. The planned biography of Houdini vanished, in true Houdini fashion. Instead, Murphy struck out in a completely different direction. He'd long had a project of his own in mind, and in 1933 he went to New York, intent on producing it.

CHAPTER 8

STEPPING OUT OF
THE SYSTEM

The Making of *The Emperor Jones*

The property that Murphy hoped to bring to the screen was Eugene O'Neill's play *The Emperor Jones.* A one-act near-monologue, it recounts the final hours of Brutus Jones, an ambitious one-time Pullman porter who, through intelligence and cunning, became sovereign of a Caribbean island. His despotic rule has incited his subjects to rebellion; fleeing through the jungle, he confronts the specters of his own past and, in visions of himself aboard a slave ship and sold at auction, the African-American experience. Fueled by the relentless, escalating drumbeat of his pursuers, his vivid hallucinations drive Jones into a fearful, half-crazed frenzy, until he finally meets his end at the hands of his former subjects.[1]

The Emperor Jones was first presented in late 1920 by the Provincetown Players, a bohemian, semiprofessional theater company whose ranks intermittently included such Greenwich Village luminaries as socialist journalist John Reed and poet Edna St. Vincent Millay. O'Neill had fallen in with the group a few years before, during a summer in Provincetown at the tip of Cape Cod. Earlier in 1920, he had scored a major success with the company's production of *Beyond the Horizon,* which won him the first of four Pulitzer Prizes. As the sensation of the fall season, *The Emperor Jones* cemented the young dramatist's reputation.[2]

Today the play's racist assumptions are vividly apparent, but in the 1920s few mainstream critics saw it that way—quite the opposite, in fact. After decades of theatrical productions crudely lampooning African-American life, O'Neill's work was hailed as "the first serious psychological study of the Negro."[3] Others took it as a penetrating exploration of the human condition. "In itself *The Emperor Jones* is not particularly Negro," wrote film critic Harry Alan Potamkin. "One may question the thesis of atavism which runs through it, as one may easily deny the too patent psychology. But it is excellent theater."[4]

Despite critical acclaim, the play generated considerable controversy. At a time when segregation was the norm, discrimination rampant, and racialist thinking pervaded American culture, *The Emperor Jones* was a serious dramatic play featuring a powerful black man as its single major character. Some segments of the public were scandalized by the heights of grandeur to which O'Neill's protagonist ascended; others, by the barbarous, superstitious depths to which he ultimately fell. The African-American community found *The Emperor Jones* particularly problematic. While the play presented an African-American character of near-Shakespearean complexity, it also implied that blacks were easily overtaken by primitive impulses and incapable of enlightened self-government. O'Neill's writing reflected the racialized language of the time; liberally salted with racial epithets, the play's dialogue caused a furor in itself. A 1927 production at the Lincoln Theater in Harlem, for instance, closed on opening night amid vociferous rejection by its audience.[5]

Well into the 1920s, the minstrel show continued to reverberate in mainstream American theater. Even then, it was common for white actors to portray black characters—a practice carried over into film, most famously in *The Jazz Singer*. O'Neill had originally thought to cast a white actor in blackface as Jones. He himself had "blacked up" to portray "a West Indian Mulatto Sailor" in a 1916 production of his one-act play *Thirst* (1913). Years later, when Lawrence Tibbett, a white singer, portrayed Jones in an opera adaptation of the play, O'Neill wrote to his son, Eugene, Jr.: "I always knew any good actor, white or black, could make a hit in *Jones*. It's simply realistic superstition to think only a coon can play it. It's one of the surest fire parts in modern drama."[6]

Nevertheless, when the Provincetown Players premiered *The Emperor Jones* in New York in 1920, the role of Brutus Jones was originated by Charles Gilpin. A founder of the Lafayette Players, the African-American theater company based at Harlem's Lafayette Theater, Gilpin was one of the preeminent black actors of the day.[7] Middle-aged, wiry, and balding, his Jones was a wilier, more feral character than Robeson's robustly masculine later embodiment. Gilpin was an assertive, self-possessed actor, and he dealt with the play's problematic aspects on his own terms, particularly with regard to its language. Where O'Neill's script called for Jones to refer to himself as a "nigger" and to his subjects as "bush niggers," Gilpin substituted *Negro* or *colored man* and made other adjustments to the text as well. O'Neill, who expected his lines to be delivered precisely as written, found this maddening. "Yes, Gilpin is all ham and a yard wide!" he wrote to a friend. "Honestly, I've stood for more from him than from all the white actors I've ever known—simply because he was colored!"[8] After more than two hundred performances in New York, *Jones* toured nationally for two years. Away from O'Neill and the show's producers, Gilpin presumably made further modifications to the script.[9]

By the time *The Emperor Jones* was poised for its British premiere, O'Neill had had enough. "He played Emperor with author, play & everyone concerned," he wrote. "I'm 'off' him and the result is he will get no chance to do it in London." Instead, O'Neill chose Paul Robeson, "a young fellow with considerable experience, wonderful presence & voice, full of ambition and a damn fine man personally with real brains—not a 'ham.' . . . I'm sure he'll be bigger than Gilpin was even at the start."[10] Already embarked on a career as a concert singer, Robeson had been a legal scholar at Columbia University and an award-winning orator and all-star athlete at Rutgers. He first portrayed Jones in the play's 1924 New York revival, continuing in the Broadway production that opened in February 1925. That September, O'Neill tapped him for the London premiere. It closed in a quick five weeks; though Robeson's performance won critical acclaim, the play itself did not.[11]

"World Film Talking Rights": Bringing *Jones* to the Screen

Despite the problematic content of *The Emperor Jones*, Murphy's decision to adapt the play was in many ways a logical one. Years of acclaim had given it the aura of a classic, making it precisely the sort of property that Murphy, disillusioned with Hollywood, was eager to be involved with. It had terrific screen potential, as Harry Alan Potamkin shrewdly noted as early as 1929. "Here is your 'photogenic' opportunity! . . . The ominous and frightful shadows, the specters of the boy shot at craps, the phantom gallery—the cinema has long been well-prepared for these. And now the sounds," he wrote. "The sounds are part of the drama. The drumbeats, the bullet-shots, the clatter of the dice, the moan of the slaves, and the recurring voice of Jones, his prayer—what a composition these offer for a sound-sight-speech film!"[12]

Murphy first contacted O'Neill about *The Emperor Jones* in the mid-1920s. At the time, neither man had access to the requisite financing, and the project languished. But Murphy persisted. Though not on close terms, he and O'Neill were both part of the extended social group that gathered around Carl Van Vechten. In June 1929, while working on *St. Louis Blues*, Murphy sent O'Neill a four-page treatment outlining his ideas for *Jones*. In the accompanying letter, he made his case for directing the film.

> Several years ago, in your room at the Lafayette Hotel, I believe I told you of my enthusiasm for "Emperor Jones," and the tremendous desire I had to make a picture of it. Since that time, the idea has grown and grown with me. I have been to Hollywood to make some commercial pictures and several adventurous experiments in the use of this fascinating medium. Now that sound has entered the field, new possibilities have opened up, and if one realises [*sic*] the limitations of the medium, and does not try to imitate or photograph what is done on the stage, grand things can be done. The advent of sound, of course, makes "Jones" to my mind one of the greatest subjects for a truly great and dynamic film, and with my tremendous enthusiasm for it, I have been suggesting it for production, and have been in touch with [O'Neill's literary agent] Dick Madden. I have made a brief outline of some of my ideas for treatment, the main point being to establish a rhythmic note in the beginning of the picture, which constantly grows to the dynamic ending, which was one of the features of your play.

Fearful of developing the project only to see it assigned to another director, Murphy made a point of enlisting O'Neill's support.

> I am so vitally interested in "Emperor Jones" that it would nearly break my heart if I could not direct it myself. . . . I am so absolutely sure that I can make a great film out of "Emperor Jones," that I am willing to gamble or risk anything for the privilege of making it. If you have confidence in my ability, and if you feel that my enthusiasm and my experience and reputation for "avant garde" efforts in films is of value to "Emperor Jones," I wish you could feel that it would be to your advantage to make a stipulation in the sale contract for "Jones," that I direct or co-direct the production. If you could assure me of this, I would immediately close a deal for the production of "Jones," using Paul Robeson in the title role.

. . . I am at present finishing a picture of the St. Louis Blues, with an all colored cast, including Bessie Smith, and for the past six months have been experimenting and making pictures here with the best sound device on the market, and have accumulated a goodly amount of knowledge in the use of sound.[13]

Murphy's work on *St. Louis Blues* would have been a persuasive point for O'Neill, who was a jazz and blues fan.[14] And Murphy didn't stop there. In 1929 he purchased the rights to another O'Neill one-act play, *Before Break-fast* (1918). He proposed the property to RCA as a two-reeler that, like *St. Louis Blues* and *Black and Tan,* would demonstrate the company's sound system. "I was intrigued by the possibilities for showing offstage noises to note the action which is taking place," he wrote in the interdepartmental memo accompanying his film script adaptation. "This coupled with the exploitive possibilities of Eugene O'Neil's [*sic*] name . . . will make this a worthy experiment. It will be novel and powerful, possibly more of a pres-tige picture than a definite box-office undertaking."[15] At the time, most short sound films were still based on musical performances, with only the slightest of narrative hooks; *Before Breakfast* was a stark, two-person drama culminating in an offstage suicide. Not surprisingly, RCA passed on the project. For Murphy, though, O'Neill's work continued to signify "pres-tige." In 1933, fresh from his dismaying bout with Hollywood, he found *The Emperor Jones* more compelling than ever.

That year, Murphy met with O'Neill and presented his treatment for the film. The dramatist consented to a sixty-day option. Two days later, Murphy had lunch at the Algonquin. "Frank Case, the owner, who knew of my interest in *Emperor Jones,* introduced me to John Krimsky," he wrote.[16] Krimsky and his partner, Gifford Cochran, were Ivy League types with artistic ambitions and Cochran's family money behind them. At the time, they were fresh from an unexpected success with *Maedchen in Uni-form* (1931), a German film about goings-on at an upscale girls' boarding school. Purchasing the American distribution rights for eight thousand dollars, they'd ended up grossing four hundred thousand for the film's twenty-two-week run. Newly incorporated, they were looking for films to produce. The timing was right, Murphy's vision for the film was com-pelling, and his enthusiasm was infectious. Krimsky and Cochran bought the option on *Jones.*

DuBose Heyward was hired to develop a preliminary script. Like Marc Connelly, the Gershwins, and Murphy himself, Heyward was one of many whites who, in the 1920s and 1930s, attempted to interpret African-American subjects from a more enlightened perspective. Some aspired to change the prevailing norms of American racial politics; others simply recognized good material when they saw it. Heyward was one of the era's most successful white interpreters of black life in the South. He'd won acclaim for *Porgy* (1925), a novel set in the Gullah community of his native South Carolina, and with his wife, Dorothy Heyward, had adapted it into a successful Broadway play in 1927. He would go on to work with George and Ira Gershwin on the hit 1935 musical adaptation, *Porgy and Bess.*[17] *Mamba's Daughters* (1929), another of his novels of African-American life, won praise from the Harlem literary community before reaching the New York stage in 1939.[18]

With the major pieces falling into place, O'Neill was disposed to look favorably on the deal for *The Emperor Jones.* The motivation was largely financial. At the height of the Depression, he'd sunk a hundred thousand dollars into an estate on Sea Island, an exclusive resort off the Georgia coast. Sale of the film rights promised a welcome infusion of cash. Samuel Goldwyn was apparently after the rights as well, intending to star Lawrence Tibbett, the white singer who'd played Jones in the opera version.[19] O'Neill strongly preferred Robeson, as did Murphy. Moreover, O'Neill was no fan of Hollywood, having just seen his eight-hour play *Strange Interlude* compressed into a 110-minute star vehicle for Norma Shearer and Clark Gable. Again, money was the paramount consideration. "I don't really give a damn what they've done to it," he commented about the Shearer-Gable project. "Outside of money the films simply don't exist for me and nothing they do or don't do seems of the slightest importance."[20] For the price of thirty thousand dollars, O'Neill granted "world film talking rights" to *The Emperor Jones* to John Krimsky and Gifford Cochran, Inc.[21]

"I enjoyed immensely working with DuBose Heyward," Murphy noted in his memoir, and he evidently took an active role in the script's development. Expanding on passing allusions in the play or inventing completely new episodes, the film script opens Jones's story years before the action of O'Neill's play. Where the stage version begins with the emperor learning of the uprising against him, the film has a younger Jones leaving his small southern town for a career as a railway porter. From there it traces, in quick episodes, the events leading to his arrival on the Caribbean island, starting with his rapid acclimation to urban life, with its gambling and glamorous women; the rivalry between Jones and his friend Jeff,

ending with Jeff's murder over a pair of loaded dice; Jones's killing of a
prison guard and escape from the chain gang quarry; his getaway as a
stoker on a cargo steamer; and his arrival on the island after jumping ship.
Subsequent scenes sketch the clever tricks he uses to catapult himself from
castaway to emperor as well as his evident pleasure in royal life. At this
point, O'Neill's drama takes over, as the deposed emperor loses himself
in the jungle and succumbs to his fearful visions. Running madly, he falls
into the camp of his pursuers, where he's shot dead with a silver bullet—
the only thing, as he'd boasted earlier, that could kill him.

Heyward's script took its cue not only from O'Neill's play but from the
treatment Murphy had written in 1929. The rousing Baptist church service
that opens the film was an early scene in the treatment, though Murphy
placed it in Harlem rather than Heyward's South Carolina. The film's
nightclub scene, fatal craps game, and chain-gang killing were all outlined
in embryonic form. Murphy also sketched a scene in which Jones surveys,
"with imperial bearing his domain," a Pullman car. "In this sequence," he
wrote, "we get over through the conversation of some of the passengers,
that crooked deals, if done in a big way, are big business."[22] In the screenplay, this minimal notation plays out as a scene in which Jones, as porter
in the railroad president's private car, overhears talk of a corporate merger;
he deftly exploits the situation for his benefit, blackmailing the president
into cutting him in on the profits.

O'Neill may have professed complete indifference to what became of
his work on-screen, but before agreeing to the sale, he insisted on a presentation of the preliminary screenplay. Murphy, Heyward, and Krimsky
flew to Sea Island in a Lockheed Vega piloted by Russell Thorpe, a friend
of Murphy's who was, as he put it, "flying for Harold Vanderbilt," the
New York Central Railroad magnate; in fact, it was Vanderbilt's plane that
took them down to Georgia.[23] "We were shown into O'Neill's library,"
Murphy recalled. "He sat against a big plate glass window, with his handsome profile silhouetted against the sea and DuBose started reading our
manuscript." By Murphy's estimation, at least half the film involved the
new material that he and Heyward had created. "It was colorful, but it
had very little of O'Neill, with the exception of characters suggested in his
visions, when Jones is lost in the jungle. When we reached the point where
O'Neill's play started and he recognized his dialogue, he stopped us and
turning, he said, 'Gentlemen, if I had had what you have written, I would
have had a fine three-act play.'"[24]

A DECLARATION OF INDEPENDENCE

The satisfaction of finally plunging into his long-deferred project was, for Murphy, exhilarating. Living in New York again, earning plaudits from the likes of Eugene O'Neill, and working with producers who weren't answerable to a Mayer or a Zukor made his recent studio experiences all the more galling. Before filming had even begun, Murphy used *The Emperor Jones* as a means of publicly distancing himself from Hollywood. A crucial interview in the *New York Herald Tribune,* published soon after the production was announced, became his de facto declaration of independence. In it, he plainly laid out his dissatisfaction with commercial moviemaking and his desire for more fulfilling work. "'I went to Hollywood to prove that I could do the conservative type of thing, but with imaginative treatment,' he said. 'Now that I've made a number of pictures out there, doing just that—*Sport's Parade* [*sic*] was one of them—I feel it's misdirected energy; because it's a compromise. And that's the trouble with Hollywood: it's full of people, often brilliant, making compromises. Money and the greed of the place cause them to lose their perspective and gradually lose their integrity. I want to pull out before it's too late. I want to make pictures that total something, in my own estimation at least, when they are chalked up; pictures that I can believe in and believe have been worth the effort behind them.'"25

Not only was Murphy disillusioned with the film industry, he no longer had much faith in the moviegoing public. Abandoning his ambition to bring innovative, artful filmmaking to as wide an audience as possible, he instead envisioned his films as catering to the most discerning viewers. "And so he now proposes," wrote the *Herald Tribune,* "in that same spirit of pioneering which has marked his entire career in pictures, to become a producer himself. Not only to produce [films] individually, but to establish for them a new kind of audience—a segregated audience." Interestingly, Murphy chose to hinge his argument on a term that over time acquired overtly racial connotations. "'In every other field, literature, music, the theater, we have segregated the audience,' he said. 'Some music lovers prefer Tchaikovsky, others Gershwin, while in the theater there is room for both Shakespeare and *Abie's Irish Rose*. Yet motion pictures have found no distinctions in audiences here until recently. A dead level has been the rule among our producers, films being aimed at everybody's entertainment, with the result that they often please nobody."26

With *The Emperor Jones,* Murphy's filmmaking position shifted: he now aimed for "class" over "mass." But this was true only to a point. Even with an independent production like *The Emperor Jones,* Murphy still nurtured hopes of a major hit and the kind of box-office grosses that would establish him as a force to be reckoned with in the industry. Despite his disaffected stance, his goal remained the same: indisputable success on Hollywood's terms. He wanted to continue making films in New York, and a runaway box-office hit would allow him to do it.

In the context of Murphy's conflicted relationship with Hollywood, his dedication to *The Emperor Jones* reflects the state of his own career as well as his instincts for cinematic material. Focusing on an ambitious black protagonist, the project resonated with Murphy's perception of himself as an outsider in a rapidly changing, increasingly hostile industry. But his commitment to the film went beyond the ins and outs of Hollywood. The Roaring Twenties had come to a skidding halt with the stock market crash of 1929, and the deepening Depression prompted a surge in political activism through much of the nation. Murphy's time with Eisenstein and Siqueiros had provided provocative exposure to a leftist perspective. In New York, he found himself among a community of creative people who were generally leftist in their thinking, and the city's liberal political climate offered a refreshing change from the reactionary conservatism of Los Angeles.

With the notable exception of Marc Connelly's *The Green Pastures* (1936), the vogue for films about African-American life ended abruptly with the 1920s. At its most diverse, the industry had hardly been inclusive, but the bottom-line effects of the Depression, coupled with increasing censorship pressures, prompted all but the most mainstream characters to disappear from Hollywood films. The few African-American actors who appeared on-screen generally did so in the guise of maids, manservants, and easily frightened handymen. It was, without question, the wrong time to bring Brutus Jones—swaggering, murderous, and answerable to no one—to the American screen.

Beyond the political statement implicit in this choice of material, *The Emperor Jones* offered an exceptional opportunity to showcase Murphy's personal style. Despite repeated attempts at standard, narrative-focused films, he still preferred the musically inspired, visually emphatic style that he'd always worked with, which had come to such notable fruition with *Ballet mécanique.* His conflation of African-American musicality with a visually experimental, spectacle-based cinematic style, best demonstrated in *Black and Tan,* made *Jones* an obvious choice. In the *Herald Tribune* interview, he offered a self-serving, broadly revisionist overview of his career, revealing a certain unwitting condescension as he traced the connections from one film to the next. "'The very first thing I ever did was a short thing called *Ballet mécanique*. It cost $200 to make and the profits I gathered from it—I produced it myself—were enormous. It also won me considerable reputation both here and abroad. Eisenstein said it laid the foundation for the Russian montage idea, and it was supposed to be the first abstract film ever made. The next real fun I had was a few years later when I did two short Negro films called *St. Louis Blues* and *Black and Tan*. These proved to be box-office hits as well as artistic successes. They are one reason for my trying my hand at *Emperor Jones*,' he said. 'I like doing Negro things. You have a chance for mood and fantasy and camera angles. Then, too, the Negro music is always interesting.'"[27]

It is "mood and fantasy and camera angles"—in other words, visual spectacle and the pleasure of viewing it—that Murphy described as the link among these films. In discussing his filmmaking, he aligned himself (in the most flattering terms) with Eisenstein and his concept of montage, which involved intense manipulation of the cinematic image. But even as he was preparing to shoot a film in which narrative was paramount, he tellingly omitted any mention of story, plot, or character as essential elements of his style.

Just as he repudiated the standard Hollywood style, Murphy rejected the film industry's business model. As an alternative to the factorylike studio system, Murphy proposed a small-scale, low-budget approach that foregrounded the creative process, based on a cooperative arrangement among a core team of collaborators. Noting the difficulties facing the industry as the Depression deepened, he took an optimistic view of the potential for independent distribution, with characteristic disregard for the challenges it presented. "The ideal way of making pictures, he believes, is to make one at a time, with as little expense as possible, but with enough inspiration to bridge the gap of money. In short, his plan is to produce in partnership with his star and writer, each of them sharing in the profits," wrote the *Herald Tribune*. "'I'll have very little overhead so that I should be able to keep my expenses down and if necessary I'll peddle [the films] myself to exhibitors, for the theater chains are breaking up—thank Heaven!—and each theater owner is out to buy the thing he believes will satisfy his patrons. And look at the success of many of the foreign productions here, if you don't think there is already a specialized audience eager for artist pictures.'"[28]

Though he overshot considerably in predicting the demise of theater chains, Murphy's assessment of the moviegoing climate was in many ways on target. The industry's increasingly monolithic practices in production, distribution, and exhibition prompted a range of alternative approaches. As Murphy suggested, the art-house and ciné-club circuit fostered audiences for foreign and independent films; on the production side, even studio-system pillars like David Selznick and Walter Wanger eventually struck out on their own. Murphy's notion of independent production and distribution was inspired by several disparate models: his own experience in self-distributing his short films, including *Ballet mécanique;* the original concept behind United Artists, the independent company that took on distribution of *The Emperor Jones;* the enviable success of Krimsky and Cochran with *Maedchen in Uniform;* and the example of Rex Ingram, who had similarly attempted to establish himself apart from Hollywood with a core group of collaborators. The idea of an independent consortium of film professionals caught Murphy's imagination, and throughout his career he attempted to establish such an enterprise, the further from Hollywood the better.

At the time, though, New York was for him the logical place to make movies. "This is the only country where the film capital is not located in the theatrical capital," he pointed out some years later. "I'm not knocking Hollywood. . . . But with all the talent to be found in New York it strikes me as silly that no film producer has ever taken full advantage of it."[29] In the midst of filming, he declared, "The thing I consider important is bringing production here. I want to emphasize that pictures can be made in the East."[30]

THE EMPEROR OF ASTORIA

For Murphy, as for most filmmakers looking to produce outside Hollywood, "the East" meant the underutilized studios of New York City. Through the 1920s, several Hollywood studios had maintained New York facilities, including Paramount, which had occupied a large facility in Astoria, Queens, just over the Fifty-ninth Street Bridge. But as the economy worsened and production declined, little film work came East. *The Emperor Jones* was shot at the old Paramount facility (rechristened Eastern Service Studios), which had fallen into the hands of Western Electric, a subsidiary of AT&T. It was the first major project to be shot there since Paramount had left in 1931. According to Krimsky, Western Electric agreed to lend his company a substantial amount of money if *Jones* did its studio shooting there.

Murphy wasn't the first independent to attempt production in New York. Gloria Swanson, for instance, had shot several films there, choosing Cosmopolitan Studios in Harlem for her own first production, *The Love of Sunya*, on which Murphy had had such difficulty with the special effects. But Swanson quickly returned to Hollywood, unnerved by the challenges of New York's outmoded facilities and relatively inexperienced crews.[31] Krimsky acknowledged similar difficulties but gave them a positive spin. Even though Astoria "lacked the highly sophisticated technical facilities available in Hollywood, the film capital of the world," he wrote, "we recruited expert technicians who improvised many innovations in film-making."[32]

The production prompted a rustle of excitement in the New York entertainment world. Coverage in local papers began even before shooting started in May 1933, and reports from the set continued into July. "There is life again at the studio in Astoria, a busyness and cheerfulness that the film factory hasn't enjoyed in far too long," began one article. "Mr. Murphy, tall, slim, looking more blond than ever by contrast, spends his days now surrounded by the hundreds of Negroes who are finding sudden prosperity just over the bridge at Long Island City. He had a great time casting the film, selecting actors from the many capable colored players he found in Harlem."[33]

Though the cast numbered dozens, not hundreds (extras included), Murphy did have a great time finding actors for the film. His flamboyant approach bespoke an outsider's preconceptions but also an affinity for Brutus Jones's imperial tastes and his own delight in skewering conventional expectations. "I had always had a penchant for glamorous second-hand cars," he recalled, "and one day I saw a beautiful old Rolls Royce town car with a patent leather top and basket weave finish—a body which must have cost $10,000, for sale at Mr. Gilhooly's Foreign Car Salesroom. The car was for sale for $700. I was told that Tallulah Bankhead had been the former owner. As I was now casting extras and small parts for the picture, I would go back to Harlem, which I already knew, for types. I rented two suits of purple livery from the costume company and dressed two handsome Negroes, one as a chauffeur and the other as a footman to sit on the box and drive my Rolls to Harlem. Needless to say, I created quite an impression."[34]

Preproduction on *The Emperor Jones* was followed closely in the African-American press. The *Chicago Defender* reported in detail on Murphy's casting decisions, citing by name twenty of the actors he selected.[35] The

Afro-American wrote in March, two months before filming began, that
Robeson was to receive five thousand dollars per week for his work on the
film, considerably more than the roughly twenty-five hundred per week
he apparently did earn. A few months later, the paper reported that plans
for location shooting in Haiti had been scrapped, noting, "The necessary men for the picture are being recruited from Harlem's unemployed.
Already a number of tall men have been selected and are being taken to the
Astoria studio for two weeks' work."[36] In the *Pittsburgh Courier,* Chappy
Gardner reported enthusiastically on his visit to the set. "Right off the
start let me tell you that 'Emperor Jones' when finished will occupy a place
in the picture world decidedly different from any ever produced," he wrote.
"To begin with it marks the first time that American producers have
selected educated Negroes to do principal roles. It has a superior story
and packs a moral that one can't forget." Comparing the film favorably to
Hallelujah! and *Hearts in Dixie,* Gardner pointed out that "there is nothing so ridiculous in 'The Emperor Jones' as a minister stopping in the
midst of his services, running down the church aisle, gathering his sweetheart in his arms while fleeing with her to a bedroom," a plot turn that
occurs in *Hallelujah!*[37]

The budget for *The Emperor Jones* was publicly stated as $280,000.[38] But
as Scott MacQueen has pointed out, independent producers often inflate
such figures to enhance production value. He put the film's preliminary
estimating budget at just over $168,000, not including the producers' com-
bined salaries of $10,000. The largest outlay was the $30,000 to O'Neill
for the rights, followed by Robeson's fee of $18,000 for seven weeks of
shooting.[39] Murphy received $7,500 for his services as director; cinematog-
rapher Ernest Haller earned $300 per week, and William deMille earned
$6,000 as production supervisor.[40]

Just as O'Neill had specified Robeson for the title role, Robeson had
a stipulation of his own: no U.S. filming below the Mason-Dixon line.
The original estimating budget called for thirty-four shooting days, ten
of them on location in Haiti. But the entire film was shot in the New
York area in thirty-eight days, starting May 25, 1933. The chain-gang
scenes were filmed at a stone quarry in New Rochelle, and the future
emperor washed ashore not on a Caribbean island but on nearby Jones
Beach. A jungle and swamp were constructed in the studio, with heaters
in the water to prevent Robeson from catching cold. What Murphy had
termed "enough inspiration to bridge the gap of money" was abundantly
in evidence.

Not Quite Hollywood: A Film Style Emerges

In *The Emperor Jones,* key elements of Murphy's style took on more sustained expression. Foremost was the musicality of his short films. Structured as a series of virtually self-contained episodes—short films linked together—the movie is propelled by its music. Organized around four themes—African, South Carolina Gullah, Harlem jazz and blues, and Caribbean drums—J. Rosamond Johnson's score vividly evokes the African diaspora. Signature musical motifs were woven into the action. Reporting on the film in production, for instance, the *New York Times* noted a parallel between the snapping rhythm of a railway porter's shoeshine and the later beat of the island drums. Jones's discovery of the revolution is the least musical sequence in the film, its ominous silence effectively setting up the accelerating drumbeat that follows.

The film opens with an overhead shot of hands beating a circle of African drums and a high side-shot of generically feather-garbed Africans dancing in a circle and chanting to the drums. A match cut jumps the action to a southern Baptist church, where worshippers move, arms upraised, in a similar circle in the opposite direction. The ring shout leads into a spiritual ("Let Me Fly"), enthusiastically performed by the congregation, which immediately follows with a second song, "O, I Want Two Wings." About to embark on his career as a railway porter, Robeson as Jones appears in church to bid farewell. Giving one of only two brief musical performances in the film, he sings a reprise of "Let Me Fly," stopping abruptly as he hears the whistle of the approaching train. The congregation sends him off with another spiritual, "Same Train." As the story advances through scenes of a Harlem "buffet flat" whorehouse, elegant nightclub, pool hall, and prison quarry, the score ricochets from hot jazz to blues to spirituals again, giving the first half of the picture an almost nonstop musical dimension. "I packed the film with as much entertainment as possible," Murphy wrote, adding that the Hall Johnson Choir, which had appeared in *St. Louis Blues* and *Black and Tan,* performed in the church scenes and the Nicholas Brothers were among the tap dancers in the nightclub sequence.[41]

In *Jones,* Murphy most fully defines the visual vocabulary with which he'd been constructing, and would continue to construct, his interpretation of the African-American experience. The waiters with their spinning trays, who'd so captivated him on his early Harlem jaunts, appear here, years later, as a visual focus in the nightclub scene. (The tray motif, also seen in *St. Louis Blues,* surfaces again in *Lazybones,* one of the soundies

Murphy shot in 1941, long after Harlem ceased to be a nightlife destination for thrill-seeking Midtowners.) The scene in which Jones and his friend Jeff shine passengers' shoes is reprised in an inventive musical segment of the soundie *Alabamy Bound* (1941), which also recapitulates the train and railroad imagery in *Jones*. The juke joint of *St. Louis Blues* and the chic nightclub and silhouetted spiritual singers of *Black and Tan* all reappear, in modified form, in *The Emperor Jones*.

As in several of Murphy's previous films, the transitions between sequences offer a rich vein of visual play, usually linked to music. The opening cross-fade from African circle dance to African-American ring shout is one example, as is the diagonal screen wipe that visually rhymes with the unfurling of the emperor's red carpet, accompanied by a musical flourish of trumpets. The shoeshine scene on the train ends with a close-up of a shoe being shined; the rhythm of the polishing cloth is picked up by a piano riff (the opening bars of "St. Louis Blues") as the shot cross-fades to a close-up of the pianist in the buffet flat. Even when they don't involve music, the film's sound edits are often strikingly effective—for instance, the cut from the prison quarry, with the cacophony of dump trucks and blaring sirens cutting abruptly to the quiet of a South Carolina night and the fugitive Jones's stealthy rap on the window.

Although Murphy packed an enormous amount of music into the film and focused substantial attention on purely visual play, these elements work with, rather than against, the narrative flow. This is a significant departure from *The Sport Parade,* in which visual manipulations and the emphasis on spectacle at times impeded the narrative. In *Jones,* music and visual invention blend smoothly into the action, enriching the narrative. Similarly, Murphy's scene-to-scene transitions enhance the pleasure of spectatorship without pulling the viewer out of the story as forcefully as some of the visual strategies in *The Sport Parade*. Along with the compelling narrative arc of *The Emperor Jones,* Murphy's more restrained approach to visual play paradoxically brings the film closer to the classical Hollywood style than the studio film that preceded it.

Murphy handles Jones's hallucinations—the heart of O'Neill's drama—through an intrinsically cinematic technique, the double exposure. In another cinematic gesture, the entire final sequence depicting Jones's nocturnal flight through the jungle is tinted deep blue. By 1933, tinting had fallen out of fashion; though the blue is strikingly effective, at the time it was thought to give the film a dated look. Similarly, the double exposures were highly praised by some critics but dismissed as distracting by others—

another indication, perhaps, of the stark limitations that sound-film aesthetics continued to impose on the cinematic image during this period.[42]

On the film set, Murphy discovered that directorial strategies that worked well in smaller, more intimate productions did not necessarily transfer to a larger, more complicated one. Looking to create the sort of atmosphere that had given *St. Louis Blues* such an air of authenticity, he again served alcohol to the extras in the nightclub scene. In this case, though, they were given hard liquor, not beer; according to Krimsky, the result was a day's worth of useless footage.[43] And though Murphy was quick to praise Robeson ("He has a marvelous camera personality, as powerful in his own way as any of the few real stars"),[44] Robeson did not return the favor. Looking back a few years later, he thought Murphy had not directed him well, rushing him through sequences for fear he'd lose his focus and working from "the fool notion that negroes [sic] had moods" and could act effectively only when in the right one.[45]

At the time, this kind of thinking was disconcertingly common. Known for his sensitivity in working with actors, director King Vidor voiced similar views in a 1929 interview following the release of his film *Hallelujah!* As Vidor put it, "With the Negro it is best to allow full play to his emotions, getting the scene as well as you can. If you bother too much with the ordinary rules about cameras and microphones you may find you've lost the most valuable asset the Negro brings to the screen—his remarkable spontaneity of feeling." Whether working with experienced stage actors or field hands, Vidor found no difference: "They all showed the same reactions: naturalness, readiness to work just for the satisfaction of acting, and enthusiasm for singing and praying that often resulted in breaking the delicate light valves used on our sound sets."[46]

Despite the prevalence of such ideas, Murphy should have known better: Robeson was, after all, a Phi Beta Kappa with a degree in law from Columbia. But Murphy wasn't, and never had been, an actor's director. He was far more interested in camera work and visual play than in drawing a nuanced performance from his star. As filming progressed, Robeson became increasingly aware of the fact.

In an echo of Murphy's difficulties in asserting collaborative authorship of *Ballet mécanique*, the release of *The Emperor Jones* was accompanied by industry rumors that William deMille had taken a major uncredited role in directing the film.[47] The gossip might have originated with deMille himself. In a letter to his daughter, choreographer Agnes de Mille, he described himself as taking on not only directorial duties for the final jungle scenes but also heroically recutting the film himself—a version of events that side-steps any mention of the actual editor, Grant Whytock, a solid professional who by that point had cut a dozen Hollywood films and would go on to edit over fifty more.[48] In the off-the-record intimacy of a personal letter, deMille wrote in blistering terms of Murphy's incompetence and strongly implied Krimsky's as well. While it's likely that deMille contributed substantial expertise to the day-to-day running of the production, the letter gives an indication of his autocratic personal style (he was, remember, Cecil B. DeMille's older brother) and the type of problems he was capable of causing as well as solving.

"'Jones' has been a tough job," he wrote, "with an amateur producer and a director who hasn't the balmiest idea of what it's all about. It has been a constant battle." Not surprisingly, the greatest problems arose around Robeson's performance. "When we hit the O'Neill part of the picture, things were going so badly that they fired Murphy who wouldn't be guided by me—and asked me to shoot the picture myself. I reluctantly consented—then Murphy wept & wailed & said if they'd let him stay on as director I could take absolute charge & he'd obey orders. . . . I consented with the promise that he must leave the performance of Robeson *entirely* to me."[49]

It's unlikely that deMille, at the sputtering end of a lengthy career, was granted the kind of carte blanche that he described. Film historian Scott MacQueen, for one, has disputed the notion that deMille played more than a supportive role in the production, maintaining that he did not direct any portion of the film. Instead, MacQueen suggested, deMille may have found his way onto the production through DuBose Heyward, a personal friend.[50]

A review by Welford Beaton in the *Hollywood Spectator* tackled the rumor head-on. "How much Bill deMille had to do with it I have no way of knowing," Beaton wrote, "but in every reel there is ample evidence of the development of the tendency Dudley Murphy has always shown in his use of the camera. He realizes that the screen is a visual art and he gives his audience as much as possible to look at."[51]

DeMille's picture of a chaotic production on the edge of disaster stands in contrast to Krimsky's recollections several years later. "It seems to have been a happy set," he wrote. "In general, things went fairly well."[52] Though deMille's letter asserted that shooting went three weeks over schedule, the project appears to have stayed more or less on track.[53]

The Emperor Jones was the largest and most significant independent work that Murphy had made to date. It was only the second feature sound film, after *The Sport Parade,* on which he was the sole director. In bringing it to the screen as an independent production, he was looking to recreate the fluid, spontaneously creative environments of his earlier films, not the tightly organized, Hollywood production model that he'd so publicly rejected. With his improvisatory style and strong interest in music, rhythm, and visual impact, shaping actors' performances was not his greatest strength. In this regard it's likely that deMille, an experienced director, did have something to contribute. Coupled with a rookie producing team, Murphy's filmmaking approach may well have led to difficulties on the set—how much and of what nature, we can only speculate. On the other hand, it gave the film a distinctive style and self-assured vitality that reflected both his broadening cinematic vocabulary and ongoing aesthetic concerns.

RISKY BUSINESS

As Murphy and his producers soon realized, there were reasons why *The Emperor Jones* hadn't previously been made into a film. A decade earlier, it had been near-revolutionary for O'Neill to write a play dominated by a powerful black character and for the Provincetown Players to cast an African-American in the role instead of a white actor in blackface. In 1933, it was even more radical, by Hollywood standards at least, to market a feature film with a racially mixed cast, in which an African-American star received top billing over a white actor. "The question arose," Krimsky observed, "whether a major film distributor would contract to sell the finished picture," and if one did, whether any theaters would book it.[54]

Cross-currents of racial politics caught the film from the start. Although the Hays Office, the film industry's self-regulatory agency, wasn't formally empowered to censor films until 1934, by 1933 it could easily prevent a movie from being released if it didn't meet the Production Code standards.[55] Two days into the shooting, after some steamy scenes between Robeson and Fredi Washington as a buffet flat prostitute, the Hays Office insisted on screening the footage. Their verdict: the light-skinned Washington was too easily mistaken for a white woman, so the footage had to be reshot with her in dark makeup.

Once in the editing room, censorship began in earnest. Black-on-white violence was a Hays Office taboo, so the shot in which Jones kills the sadistic white prison guard was cut, leaving a disconcerting jump in the action. The scene in which the fugitive Jones, back in South Carolina, almost murders a white sheriff, then sends his dog out to lay a false trail for his pursuers, was also pulled.[56] A shot of a woman smoking was cut, and in some markets, the shot in which Smithers, the island's white trader, lights a cigarette for the new emperor was deleted as well. Other cuts ranged from suggestive moves by nightclub dancers to a close-up of Washington's character tucking money into her garter. Most significant was the removal of two crucial jungle hallucinations in which Jones envisions himself on a slave ship and sold at auction. These last deletions compromised the film's dramatic resonance, doing a real injustice to the concept of O'Neill's play.[57]

Viewing *The Emperor Jones* today, audiences may find it difficult to grasp the social climate in which the film debuted. In 1933, the United States was still deeply mired in the Depression. Having taken office in March, Franklin Delano Roosevelt was just assembling the early building blocks of the New Deal, and unemployed millions roamed the country in search of work. The nation was politically polarized, with labor and grass-roots leftist groups enjoying significant popular support. In the first three decades of the century, the Great Migration had sent more than a million blacks northward. Between 1920 and 1930 alone, the South lost 10 percent of its African-American population and, in the 1930s, 5 percent more.[58] Blacks fled not only poor living conditions but also the violence and intimidation ingrained in southern race relations. What one historian cat-aloged as "the degrading racial etiquette . . . the dehumanizing caricatures, the ritualized subservience, the verbal and physical harassment, the savage public murders, and the quiet murders" were intrinsic to southern life.[59] The North was no paradise—segregation, discrimination, and unemploy-ment were pervasive there, too—but for thousands of African Americans, ongoing coercion and violence made the South intolerable.

Though the number of lynchings began to decline in the mid-1920s, partly in response to black flight, white terrorism remained a potent tool for political and social domination. In October 1933, as *The Emperor Jones* began to open around the country, the *Afro-American* tallied more than thirty-one lynchings nationally since that January, "the largest number in the past five years."[60] A month later, the *Chicago Defender* documented additional fatalities in Arcadia, Florida. "The lynch orgy that has swept the country during the past few months arrived here this week and left four more persons—three women and a man—in its wake. . . . So badly were they mutilated by burns about their faces and bodies that complete recognition and identification have not yet been established."[61] In the courtrooms of Alabama, the ongoing legal lynching of the "Scottsboro Boys" (nine young African Americans charged with raping two white prostitutes on a freight train two years earlier) continued to draw national attention. Small wonder that Robeson insisted on no filming below the Mason-Dixon line.

Despite Murphy's yearnings, it seemed unlikely that *The Emperor Jones* would sweep the national box office. While advance word on the picture was good, the film industry kept a wary eye on its moneymaking potential. With typical bottom-line pragmatism, *Variety* predicted that "the south is entirely lost to it for consumption by whites, while in the colored theatres down in Dixie some question arises as to whether it will not meet opposition. It is understood already that colored operators below the Mason-Dixon line are objecting to the use of the term 'nigger,' which may have to be cut where occurring if exhibition is wanted for the Ethiopian trade."[62]

The film premiered in New York on Tuesday, September 19, 1933, at two theaters: Murphy's Broadway standby, the Rivoli, and the Roosevelt in Harlem. While the mood was celebratory, neither Murphy nor his friends could deny the challenges facing the picture. "The premiere at the Rivoli was a gala occasion," Murphy recalled. "I gave a dinner party beforehand at 21 and Harrity, a practical joking friend of mine, had delivered to me a handsomely gift-wrapped package during dinner. I opened it and inside was an ostrich egg with a note saying, 'This is nothing to the egg your film will lay tonight.'"[63]

The uptown opening was also a gala event, with Harlem dignitaries turning out in force. Scheduled as a single showing, it drew such crowds that a second screening was added, and the theater completely filled again. "In keeping with the occasion," reported the *New York Amsterdam News*, "the Roosevelt Theatre, where it is on view, threw forth orange-colored lights, was specially decorated, and a number of prominent Harlemites attended,"[64] among them pugilist Jack Johnson, dancer Bill Robinson, and two of the film's costars, Fredi Washington and Frank Wilson.

In the mainstream press, *The Emperor Jones* was a critical success. *Time* magazine considered it "ably directed by Dudley Murphy," while Mordaunt Hall in the *New York Times* called it an "immensely satisfactory version" of the play. "It is a distinguished offering, resolute and firm, with a most compelling portrayal by Paul Robeson," he wrote, adding a compliment that Murphy must have found both heartening and a trifle chilling: "Dudley Murphy, the director, and DuBose Heyward, the author of the script, have attacked their respective tasks without any idea of catering to the box office. . . . The telling of the story is just what one might expect from such competent and experienced persons."[65]

In the trade press, the response was generally enthusiastic. The *Hollywood Reporter* singled out Murphy for special praise. "It took Dudley Murphy ten years to sell this idea. . . . The screen is now indebted to [him] for an unusually fine production that will certainly place him in the top ranks of directors . . . there is no lack of action and plenty of drama in every moment of the picture."[66] Despite its concerns about commercial viability, *Variety* gave the film a lengthy, largely positive review. "Artistically, 'Emperor Jones' ranks high in cinematic achievement," the reviewer wrote, adding, "The budget obviously was not encumbered to the detriment of production value. The settings themselves are imposing, notably of the emperor's island and the forest. Robeson is the entire picture, but in Dudley Digges, as a white trash Cockney trader, he has chief of support that is excellent."[67]

Whatever directorial contretemps might have occurred during the filming, Robeson's performance earned enthusiastic praise. "Playing his first cinema role with effortless honesty," wrote *Time*, Robeson "made the Emperor Jones a person so plainly and completely real."[68] The *New York American* referred to him as "Paul Robeson, the mighty, the magnificent," who "overshadows this starring vehicle of his with a characterization that ranks with the finest acting ever seen on either stage or screen."[69] The *Chicago Daily Tribune* called it "a privilege . . . to have seen Mr. Robeson. He is a great, natural actor."[70] And *Variety* wrote that "Robeson's performance of a madman, shooting at apparitions which appear in the darkness until crawling into the hands of his followers to receive the silver bullet, is one of the best things ever contributed to the screen."[71] Dissenting critics generally faulted his casting, finding him too refined for Jones's barbarity.

Riding a wave of positive reviews, the film did strong business in New York. According to Krimsky, opening day at the Rivoli broke the theater record for that year, and by 3:00 p.m. the following day, business had increased by a third.[72] On September 26, *Variety* reported the Rivoli's first-week grosses for *Jones* at "$37,500, big."[73] Uptown, the box office was also booming. To draw Harlem audiences to the Roosevelt rather than the Rivoli, the theater offered reduced admission for the film's run: twenty-five cents in the afternoon, thirty-five cents at night.[74] Even at those prices, the theater grossed ten thousand dollars the first week and continued to draw crowds for a holdover second week. On the strength of that success, Krimsky and Cochran cautiously undertook distribution in the South.

A Losing Proposition

The South posed enormous problems for *The Emperor Jones*. Aside from the obvious challenges, the region loomed large in Hollywood's bottom-line sensibilities, possibly more so than its actual box-office figures may have warranted. In the decades between the world wars, industry trade papers regarded the South as a culturally conservative but powerful bellwether market that could make or break a picture. As Thomas Cripps has pointed out, this was something of a misconception.[75] Compared with other parts of the country, the South did not generate particularly strong box-office receipts; in fact, it often placed near the bottom of regional revenue tallies. Even so, industry publications such as *Variety* generally predicted dire economic outcomes for films that dared to depict black characters as anything but comic, deferential "Hollywood Negroes."

Variety certainly predicted a dire outcome for *The Emperor Jones*. "As a commercial property, it is doubtful," the reviewer wrote. "Picture's circulation will be greatly limited, not only in appeal but in exhibitor acceptance." The problem, as *Variety* saw it, wasn't simply racial. It had to do with the very quality that had drawn Murphy to the project in the first place. "The O'Neill play always enjoyed a class rather than a mass appeal," the paper pointed out, "and thus its best grossing possibilities are limited to the larger urban centers of the U.S. In the medium-sized and smaller localities, it is not regulation screen fare. . . . the picture is still a character study of a Negro whose audience acceptance will either be sympathetic or unsympathetic, according to viewpoint."[76]

In some cities, the film defied the gloomy predictions. According to Krimsky, it did eleven thousand dollars worth of business in its first week in Washington, D.C., which was a thousand dollars more than its first-week receipts in Harlem.[77] And in the unlikely locale of Portland, Oregon, it performed particularly well, thanks to a skillful promoter. "J. J. Parker launched a terrific campaign on 'Emperor Jones' (UA), now into the United Artists [theater]," *Variety* reported. "Figured that pic warranted exploitation on a magnificent scale, or otherwise hard to sell. 'Emperor Jones' got going at the UA from the start and looks like this week's top gross."[78] In Los Angeles, the film was held over for at least a week at the Filmarte, where it had a gala opening in November. In other markets, though, the film did not fare as well. Despite "great critical notices" for its Philadelphia opening, the run there didn't show "much promise for big box office activity. Picture will probably be held in for a second week, but that will be forcing. Between $5,000 and $6,000 indicated." It was a disappointing figure compared with the top-grossing pictures in the city that week, which pulled in from $12,000 to $19,500.[79]

In Murphy's opinion, *The Emperor Jones* was given short shrift by United Artists, which promoted it badly and hustled it out of the theaters before positive word of mouth could have any effect. He was particularly stung that, after only two weeks, the film was forced out of the Rivoli, where it was doing top business—bumped by an inconsequential Wallace Beery vehicle that United Artists had produced itself (as opposed to *Jones,* which it was merely distributing).[80] In Murphy's estimation, the company saw *The Emperor Jones* as nothing more than a stepchild, and an expendable one at that.

The African-American press understood how much was riding on the film's success. In an *Afro-American* article entitled "Will 'The Emperor Jones' Restore Our Lost Place in the Movies?" Ralph Matthews wrote, "If the picture is successful, it is believed that other outstanding Negro dramas will be forthcoming and that the door to this great industry will be opened to stay."[81] A week into the film's New York run, the *Chicago Defender* observed that it was, fortunately, making money. "People are crowding the theaters," the paper reported. "The Race audiences find the O'Neill play a little rough in spots upon the sensibilities, due to the realistic dialogue and to the type of character of Jones. However, as Frank Wilson, the actor, said on the opening night, there should be a spirit of tolerance because herein was opened up a new field of activity for Race actors and actresses which will afford new opportunities to portray different types of Race members. And then it is a work of art, the conjuring of a melancholy genius—O'Neill—and not an indictment of an entire people."[82] Black entertainment journalists were acutely aware of the challenges facing the picture. "If, as they say, films starring Race players must show whites in power in order to gain sales in the South," wrote Rob Roy, "we fear for 'The Emperor Jones' going over below the Mason-Dixon line."[83]

Despite the hopes attached to the film's success and calls for a spirit of tolerance, the African-American community was painfully divided in its response to the film. The racist assumptions and epithets of O'Neill's play loomed even larger on the screen, and the film provoked anger and outrage.

At the same time, Robeson was an admired figure, and his portrayal of a self-possessed black man was exceptionally strong. With intelligence, ambition, and complete lack of servility, his Jones definitively broke many of the screen stereotypes of African Americans prevalent in the 1920s and 1930s while, some contended, it reinforced others. "Not only is it far-fetched, but it ended in a welter of nonsense and confusion at which I found myself yawning and the audience snickering," wrote J. A. Rogers.[84]

An article by T. R. Poston in the September 27, 1933, issue of the *New York Amsterdam News* reflected the community's ambivalence. Headlined "Harlem Dislikes 'Nigger' in Emperor Jones but Flocks to See Picture at Uptown House," it reported that the film "has aroused more heated discussion, and in some quarters more indignation, than any other incident of the last decade. . . . In view of the almost unanimous criticism, it is interesting to note that the Roosevelt Theatre has played to 'standing room only' houses daily since the premiere of the photoplay last Tuesday evening." Discussing viewers' responses, Poston noted, "Despite the fact that Brutus Jones was a killer, despite the fact that he was unscrupulous, despite the fact that he exploited his Negro subjects far more ruthlessly than the white man who preceded him, the audience—or the major part of it—fairly worshipped him. Worshipped him with continuous applause even after he had done the unforgivable thing—said to a white man, 'We niggers understand each other.' Every utterance of the banned epithet brought a chorus of 'tch-tch-tch-tches,' of course, but this didn't dampen the fans' ardor for the next step upward of the Emperor Jones." Once viewers left the theater, however, the verdict was different. Poston noted, "The recent cheers seemed to have been forgotten, and only one thought apparently remained in the minds of those who had momentarily ridden to a vicarious triumph with the Emperor Jones a few minutes before. This thought was expressed by the argument of a little short man who was escorting a tall woman from the theatre. He said: 'I got my opinion of a nigger who would stoop that low and use that word on the screen for white folks.'"[85]

In the same issue of the *New York Amsterdam News,* under the headline "Takes a Poke at 'The Emperor Jones,'" J. A. Rogers decried the film's commercialism in the guise of art and its characterization of black life: "Nearly all the old stock-in-trade as crap shooting, gin-guzzling, immorality, cutting, killing, fear of ghosts and other supposed Negro characteristics are dragged in in heavier quantities than usual, not to mention the refrain of 'Nigger, nigger, nigger,' which runs through the whole piece from beginning to end."[86]

Objections were particularly strong in the Washington-Baltimore area, where the *Afro-American* spearheaded a campaign to remove offending language from the sound track, and not only on the southern circuit. "The word 'n——r' will be eliminated from all prints of the film, 'The Emperor Jones,' to be released by United Artists, A. E. Lichtman, managing director of the Lichtman Theatres, announced here [in Washington, D.C.] last week," the paper reported. Thirty-three deletions, "eliminating all use of the objectionable words," were made, said to total almost two hundred feet of cuts. "The new version, minus the epithets, is a production of artistic excellence," the paper affirmed—then reversed itself the following week.[87] "Purged of its indecent language, Eugene O'Neill's 'Emperor Jones,' with Paul Robeson in the star role, still lacks universal approval," it wrote, noting that aside from his willingness to work, Brutus Jones "has no regard for the Ten Commandments or the Sermon on the Mount."[88] Nor did Robeson himself escape negative comment. While hesitating to attack him openly, the black press found ways to indicate its disapproval. "Robeson was bitterly denounced by his formerly best friends and supporters for his appearance in the film," wrote the *Afro-American*. The *Chicago Defender* ran a large photograph of the performer seated at a piano, under the headline "Attacked by Film Fans." The caption informed readers that the star "is being severely criticized by movie fans for having accepted the lead role" in the film.[89]

Despite the critical firestorm, some African-American commentators were steadfast in their praise. "Yes, I liked 'The Emperor Jones,'" wrote Rob Roy on the occasion of the film's Chicago premiere. "You'll see many worse films and few better."[90] Robeson "is holding audiences spellbound by the brilliant and dazzling performance he is giving" in "one of the few pictures in which Negroes are really starred," wrote Romeo L. Dougherty.[91] Even J. A. Rogers conceded that "Paul Robeson deserves every whit of the praise showered on him by the white critics for his acting in this film."[92] In Pittsburgh, two versions of the film were shown: one with an intact sound track, which opened at a downtown theater in October, and another with the offending words deleted, which opened a month later. "It's a picture you might not like," wrote William G. Nunn in the African-American *Pittsburgh Courier,* "but you'll come away from the theater with that inferiority complex, so many of you have, knocked into a cocked hat." Though its review of the film coincided with the October opening, the *Courier* encouraged its readers to wait for the expurgated version the following month. "The Roosevelt [movie theater] is . . . urging you to see it at this theater, where you can maintain your race pride and self-respect without being insulted or offended. You'll see it minus the use of the word 'Nigger,' and if that means anything, we'd advise you to wait."[93]

Hoping to counter negative coverage in the African-American press, Murphy made a personal appeal to Walter White, director of the NAACP. In a letter dated October 6, 1933, two weeks before the film's New York opening, he invited White to screen the film with him, asking White, if he saw fit, to recommend *The Emperor Jones* to the black community as "a sincere work of art." Some two weeks earlier, White had encouraged NAACP staff member Roy Wilkins to report favorably on the film's strong box-office showing in New York and to support the effort to break into the southern distribution market. But with the NAACP already embroiled in a controversy over the handling of the Scottsboro Boys case, White was reluctant to plunge into the debate over *Jones*. Replying to Murphy a few days later, he begged off, citing an upcoming trip to Washington and promising to phone on his return.[94] *The Emperor Jones* faced American moviegoers, black and white, on its own.

Between the cuts mandated by censors and the footage lost in clipping objectionable language, postproduction edits to *The Emperor Jones* made for a jumpy, discontinuous, and at times unintelligible viewing experience. On top of the film's already controversial profile, the editorial hatchet job further discouraged positive word of mouth. It also left *The Emperor Jones* in terrible shape for posterity. Restorations were attempted in the 1970s by the American Film Institute, the National Film Board of Canada, and Janus Films, among others. Despite these efforts, for many years the film remained fragmentary and disjointed—a historical relic rather than a work of cinema.

In a two-year project completed in 2002, the Library of Congress undertook a thorough restoration and preservation of the film. The primary source material was a 35mm nitrate negative acquired in 1977. The Museum of Modern Art, the National Archives of Canada, and other organizations also contributed footage. As late as 1933, many movie theaters around the country still used the old Vitaphone sound-on-disc system, and much of the missing sound track was recovered from one such set of discs for the film. (In the fatal crap-game scene, the word *nits* is noticeably substituted for *nigger*.) The original blue tinting in the jungle sequence was re-created, but the deleted hallucination scenes—Jones envisioning himself on a slave ship and sold at auction—unfortunately remain missing.[95] Even so, the Library of Congress restoration is as close to Murphy's original vision for

The Emperor Jones as any version that has existed since the finished film was first screened for the Hays Office in August 1933.[96]

Gains and Losses

Despite the immense difficulties facing *The Emperor Jones* in production, distribution, and exhibition, the film appears to have made back most of its budget. According to Krimsky, it lost "a small amount of money" in its domestic run.[97] But the numbers were disappointing and certainly not what anyone on the production was hoping for.

For Murphy, *The Emperor Jones* was a watershed. He started the project as a disgruntled cadet in the ranks of Hollywood studio directors. He finished as a self-declared independent, committed to turning out quality productions for the most discerning segment of the moviegoing audience, a segment that he paradoxically hoped would take on mass-market proportions. Even more unrealistically, he hoped that the film's success would win him acclaim and status in Hollywood, which, despite everything, remained his primary frame of reference.

With such exorbitant expectations riding on the film, its tepid bottom-line performance was a bitter disappointment, not only to Murphy, but to Krimsky and Cochran, whose partnership soon dissolved. "In spite of its glowing notices, it was not an important financial success," Murphy wrote with wistful regret. "Had it been as successful financially as it was critically, I would have been one of the most successful motion picture directors."[98] Pinned to the anticipated triumph of *The Emperor Jones,* Murphy's vision of New York as a filmmaking hub quickly collapsed. So did the hope of the African-American community that, with *Jones,* "the door to this great industry will be opened to stay."[99] Murphy had taken an enormous gamble—on the taste of the moviegoing public, the state of the film industry, and his own talent—and lost.

Among the most poignant of the many magazine and newspaper articles about *The Emperor Jones* is a clipping from the *Boston Traveler,* dated September 23, 1933. The headline reads "Director of Film 'Emperor Jones' Is the Son of Winchester Artist." A large photo shows Hermann Dudley Murphy seated on a sofa, flanked by Murphy and his sister, Carlene Murphy Samoiloff. It's a group portrait of tension and discomfort that gives lie to the article's cheery home-boy-makes-good narrative. Attired in professorial tweeds, Hermann stares stiffly at the camera while Carlene watches the two men with a look of guarded concern. Knee to knee with his father, Murphy's pose is more casual than Hermann's but no less tense. Having introduced Murphy as the film's director, the article confided that "he breathed much easier today, for his father, H. Dudley Murphy, noted artist of Winchester and his sister, Carlene Bowles Murphy, both attended the first performance today at Keith's, where the picture is playing, and they pronounced it good. That was quite a hurdle for Murphy to face, for he wasn't so sure about their verdict." Speaking off the record, "Father Murphy could have criticized the composition of a couple of shots, but by and large he agreed with Sister Murphy that it was a wonderful job. And between Father Murphy all but bursting with pride and Sister Murphy's own radiant happiness, it was easy to understand the sigh of relief that escaped from the heart of Director Murphy."[100]

Since his start in the film industry, Murphy had used his identity as Hermann's son as a means of shaping his own creative persona. In the early years, he'd exploited Hermann's reputation and connections and drawn on his own artistic background as an element in his filmmaking style. Murphy was proud of *The Emperor Jones* and eager for Hermann to see it. As a feature-length sound film in national distribution, adapted from a prestigious source, it was a work that Hermann could appreciate far more easily than some of Murphy's previous projects. According to his daughters, Murphy remained financially dependent on his father, at least intermittently, for most of Hermann's life; and while he increasingly valued Hermann's esteem as he got older, he rarely seemed to receive it. Preserved by his family long after Murphy's death, the *Boston Traveler* article attests to a rare if grudging nod of approval from "Big Man" for his son.

The Emperor Jones did not do for Murphy anything close to what he'd hoped. It didn't win him his Hollywood triumph or jump-start his vision of an alternative filmmaking center in New York. The film's success, such as it was, lay in another direction: as a compelling and well-crafted challenge to the deliberate exclusion of African-American subjects from Hollywood films and to the near-universal stereotyping of black characters as comical buffoons. In Paul Robeson, the film presented a sexualized and charismatic African-American actor at a time when black male sexuality was not only invisible on screen but still capable, in its mere suggestion, of eliciting violent reprisal in daily life. The film preserves what is arguably the greatest performance by one of the twentieth century's most remarkable actors, offering an eloquent reminder of how much was lost in the tremendous waste of Robeson's stunted film career. With *The Emperor*

Jones, Murphy achieved what he'd set out to do, as the prime mover behind a project he'd been trying to bring to the screen for years. "I want to make pictures that total something, in my own estimation," he had declared, "pictures that I believe in and believe have been worth the effort behind them."[101] With *The Emperor Jones,* he did; but the price of that achievement, as it turned out, was high.

CHAPTER 9

AN EQUIVOCAL
INDEPENDENCE

In the weeks and months following the release of *The Emperor Jones,* Hollywood left Murphy conspicuously alone. At the end of 1932, he'd been preparing to direct the Houdini picture with Adolphe Menjou. He'd reportedly been awarded the medal of honor by the Screen Society of Europe "for the most unusual technique in his picture, 'Ballet Mechanique'" and planned to accept in person at the society's meeting in Vienna the following May.[1] As late as June 1933, while *Jones* was in production, he'd been mentioned as the probable director for *Sitting Pretty,* a film version of the stage hit *Broadway Parade.*[2] But now, with disappointing grosses for *Jones* reported around the country, no offers—directing, writing, or otherwise—materialized. The film's poor showing at the box office marked the first in a succession of turning points that, by the end of the 1930s, pushed Murphy from Hollywood's top studios to its poverty-row periphery.

For his part, Murphy stubbornly blamed the lack of post-*Jones* interest on his agent. "Had he been devoting his attention to placing me [he] could have made a good deal for me with one of the majors," Murphy wrote, "but he was so busy moving his offices from Hollywood to Beverly Hills that he let the grass grow under his feet."[3] This may have been true, but it conveniently overlooked the inflammatory, antagonistic statements that Murphy had made to the press just months before, damning Hollywood for its "cheap and tawdry work" done from a "misguided deference to the box office" and the perpetual greed and compromise that prevented good work from ever being done there.[4]

Nor did Murphy acknowledge the depth of the challenge that *The Emperor Jones* represented. It was a complex and ambiguous work that dealt with loaded racial issues in a manner that defied easy resolution from any perspective. Eliciting a profoundly ambivalent but ultimately negative response in the African-American community, it was a difficult film for many white audiences as well. The nation was only starting to come to terms with the mass exodus of blacks from the South, and racial politics, like everything else, was greatly affected by the social and economic dislocations of the Depression. With its troubling ambiguities and knack for unsettling a broad spectrum of audiences, *The Emperor Jones* found no ready niche in the cultural terrain of 1930s America. Had it been a runaway box-office hit, Hollywood would have found a way to deal with it. As a marginally break-even project, the industry felt free to ignore it, and did.

Unwilling to return to the West Coast, Murphy tried producing independently in New York. Twelve years before, he'd charmed the Long Island social set into financing *High Speed Lee,* but the Depression had depleted many of the private cash reserves that might have been coaxed into such ventures. With the film industry now immovably centered in Hollywood and the studios' integrated monopolies holding firm, there was far less maneuvering room for independent producers, especially those, like Murphy, who preferred small-scale projects.

Still he kept trying. On September 18, 1933, the day before *The Emperor Jones* premiered in New York, the *New York Morning Telegraph* carried a short article headlined "Murphy Takes Film Partner." The partner was Jefferson Machamer, "illustrator and revue author," with whom Murphy planned to produce a film at the studio in Astoria. But the project was little more than smoke. "Murphy and Machamer are burning the midnight oil preparing a suitable script," wrote the *Morning Telegraph,* "and as soon as such necessary details as financing can be arranged the film will get under way."[5] Predictably, no picture resulted. The projects that Murphy had hopefully floated in press interviews before and during production on *Jones*—from *The Sun Also Rises* to *Alice in Wonderland*—also came to naught.

Reluctantly, ignominiously, Murphy went back to Hollywood. His timing was as bad as it could be. In early 1933, the film industry had hit its lowest point since the stock-market crash more than three years earlier. By midyear, the Roosevelt administration came to the rescue with the National Industrial Recovery Act (NIRA).[6] One of the earliest New Deal programs, it sanctioned specific monopolistic practices, along with labor organizing and collective bargaining. The studios' integrated monopolies were safe for the time being, but Hollywood was at last a union town. The cinematic division of labor became more rigidly defined, and the atmosphere even more factorylike than it had been when Murphy left.

Through 1933, a mounting religious and political backlash struck at the sex and violence that Hollywood had so cheerfully purveyed throughout the 1920s and early 1930s. In 1934, the Hays Office established the Production Code Administration to enforce rigorous censorship standards. Along with unpunished criminality and explicit sexuality, the PCA swept away any sense of ethnic, racial, religious, or sexual inclusiveness. Post-Code movies were almost entirely white, gentile, and heterosexual. Where race or ethnicity was unavoidable, characters were innocuous, subservient, and, if possible, minor. It was, as Richard Barrios put it, "the bleak golden age of Hollywood's racial insensitivity."[7] There was little motivation to welcome back a renegade director like Murphy, especially one with such a marked partiality for African-American subjects.

Arriving in Los Angeles, Murphy promptly fired his ineffectual agent. He signed with Myron Selznick, a powerful industry figure whose clients included Carole Lombard, Katharine Hepburn, and other stars favored by his younger brother, producer David O. Selznick. Murphy had worked with David Selznick at Paramount and RKO; in early 1933, Selznick had left RKO to become a vice president at MGM, where he was one of four top executives to head his own production unit. This was a major innovation at the tightly run studio, where the ailing Irving Thalberg was being eased out of his crucial position as central production head.[8] Not surprisingly, the first directing job that Myron Selznick secured for Murphy was at MGM: a musical called *The Night Is Young* (1935).

It was not a felicitous assignment. For one thing, Murphy detested the music. An old-fashioned operetta by Sigmund Romberg with libretto by Oscar Hammerstein II, it was a far cry from the muscular jazz, blues, and spirituals that had powered *The Emperor Jones*. And while the return to Hollywood-style film production would have been difficult under any circumstances, for Murphy the project came with an exasperating cross to bear: producer Harry Rapf.

In the late 1910s and early 1920s, Rapf had worked for Lewis J. Selznick, father of Myron and David, who'd been a top distributor of independent films before going bankrupt in 1923. As a producer and assistant to studio head Louis B. Mayer, Rapf had helped David Selznick get his start at MGM in 1926. Over the course of the 1930s, Rapf produced some thirty movies for the studio, none of them particularly distinguished. Like Mayer, he favored the predictable and conventional, with an eye toward the bottom line. After Thalberg died in 1936, Rapf became a member of Mayer's eight-person Executive Committee, which steered the studio into an increasingly conservative approach.[9] David O. Selznick had an almost predatory intelligence toward filmmaking and a keen, if guarded, appreciation of innovation. Rapf was in every respect his opposite, and Murphy bristled under his supervision. "This was the type of man who had made the name 'producer' anathema to creative directors," he fumed.[10]

The Night Is Young starred Ramon Novarro opposite Evelyn Laye, an English musical comedy actress little known in the United States. It was a thinly veiled, sound-film remake of *The Student Prince,* a 1927 silent hit by Ernst Lubitsch. Murphy was not happy with his two leads. He thought Laye, in her midthirties, too old to play opposite Novarro, even though he was a year her senior—a judgment evident in the heavy gauze filters used in several of her close-ups. But Laye was a creditable rival to reigning musical romance star Jeanette MacDonald. She had a light comedic touch, charming screen presence, and a pleasing way with Romberg and Hammerstein's forgettable score.[11]

The supporting cast included such stalwarts as Edward Everett Horton, Una Merkel, and a luminous young Rosalind Russell. Together, they gave the film a fluent if familiar comedic style. Though not a high-budget production, it had a polished look, with sets by famed MGM art director Cedric Gibbons, for whom Murphy had worked at Goldwyn some fifteen years earlier. Designed by Dolly Tree, the frothy gowns were the sartorial equivalent of Viennese whipped cream.

Novarro, however, was jarringly miscast. One of Rex Ingram's early 1920s discoveries, he'd found stardom in such heroic roles as Ben-Hur and the swashbuckling André-Louis Moreau in *Scaramouche* (1923). He had already played the lead in Lubitsch's silent version of *The Student Prince,* from which *The Night Is Young* was so liberally adapted. But sound film brought out another side of his screen persona. Novarro was, in real life, unequivocally gay. Portraying a young Austrian archduke indulging in an improbable affair with a ballerina, his obvious lack of chemistry with Laye transformed the film from a flirtatious sexual romp into the equivalent of a children's slumber party. *The Night Is Young* more or less outed him, and MGM released him from his contract as soon as it was completed. The tension over his performance badly affected his working relationship with Murphy. An item in the *Hollywood Reporter* hinted at trouble on the set, including an episode in which Murphy purportedly left Novarro stranded on the ferris wheel where most of the day's filming took place.[12]

Murphy's difficulties with the project, however, ran deeper than problematic actors, insipid music, or a ham-handed producer. By its nature, studio filmmaking of the time favored simple plot lines, straightforward narrative style, and budgetary efficiency. The constraints of a closely monitored, studio-style production ran counter to his directorial approach, which continued to incorporate the kind of visual play that was rapidly disappearing from Hollywood films. Murphy was one of a handful of filmmakers attempting to counter the rising tide of realism; among his fellow holdouts were European-born directors such as Josef von Sternberg and Rouben Mamoulian. (Even Fritz Lang inserted an expressionistic shot of clucking chickens into the gossip sequence of his 1936 film, *Fury*.) But midway through the 1930s, with the Depression showing no signs of lifting, Frank Capra seemed to have gotten it right: American movie audiences wanted to be enfolded in stories and remain there, uninterrupted, until the lights went up. "Not a single thing must be done to take your audience's attention" from story or character, Capra wrote. "The success of your picture depends upon the story."[13]

But some degree of visual embellishment was generally expected in operetta-style musicals, and Murphy was as lavish as a closely watched budget would allow. After introducing the cast in a series of opening-credit cameos, the film fades up on a close-up of a music-box ballerina twirling in arabesque. As the tinkling music cross-fades to the pounding piano of a studio rehearsal, the image cross-fades to a group of ballerinas dressed like the music-box figure, all turning in arabesque. The camera picks out the one in the center, her position in the frame perfectly matched to that of the fading music-box figure. In another playful visual transition later in the film, a glossy carriage with a pair of handsome, smartly trotting horses is wiped off the screen by a single, slowly plodding black horse pulling a streetcar, neatly pointing up the class distinction between the film's characters.

The songs in *The Night Is Young* enhance the narrative, advancing the story rather than simply embellishing it. "There's a Riot in Havana," for instance, is a duet between the archduke and the ballet dancer with whom he is, at that point, only pretending to have an affair. Engagingly and economically, it signals their growing mutual attraction. As reported in one of the trade papers, the action of *The Night Is Young* was so wedded to the music that "the entire script was mimeographed on special music paper, with the action and dialogue inserted between the staves and timed to each measure." This was not unlike the approach used by Mamoulian in *Love Me Tonight* (1932), in which the songs and rhyming dialogue were recorded to the beat of a metronome to better coincide with the action.[14]

It's unclear whether Murphy had seen *Love Me Tonight* or known of the techniques used in making it, but his integration of music into the film is reminiscent of Mamoulian's work. In both films, for instance, a song begun in one locale is seamlessly carried forward into several others, as in the "wiener schnitzel" sequence in *The Night Is Young*. In this musically motivated montage, simple lyrics about the dinner menu are passed, line by line, among the four lead characters as they cluster around a beer-garden table. The lines are then sung in turn by the maître d', waiter, and chef and pastry chef in the kitchen. Close-ups of the singers are intercut with shots of food being dished out and delivered to the table. Tightly edited to the music, with a lively pace and some wry framing (the pastry chef gets a particularly heroic low-angle shot), it's one brief sequence, running less than a minute, in which Murphy clearly enjoys himself.

The Night Is Young was a polished, professional piece of work, exactly what one would expect from an MGM production. But it had a studio assembly-line air and lacked the passionate spark of Murphy's most creative projects. Too, by the time it was released in early 1935, critics and movie-goers were wearying of the operetta-style musical. As a result, Murphy was put in the odd position of being chastised for his proficiency. "Month by month the unbelievable sameness of musical films becomes a more terrifying phenomenon," wrote Andre Sennwald in the *New York Times*. "According to the current standards of costumed musical romances, 'The Night Is Young' is invincibly correct. If you want to be rude about it, you can add that it is likewise without any single distinguishing virtue except for its appalling competence in every department of its manufacture."[15]

"THE HIERARCHY OF HOLLYWOOD"

The MGM deal that Myron Selznick had arranged for Murphy had been for a single film with option to renew. Despite mixed reviews, *The Night Is Young* "turned out pretty well," as Murphy put it, and his option came due. "It called for a raise in salary," he wrote, "but the powers that be at Metro wanted me to stay on at the same salary without the boost." As an agent, Myron Selznick was known for hard bargaining with the studios, his brother's included. "I was talked to by [MGM general manager] Eddie Mannix, Irving Thalberg, and by Mayer himself," Murphy recalled, "but my agent, Selznick, and his assistant, George Volk, felt that we should hold out for the option boost. Metro refused and I was out of a job."[16]

The loss left Murphy profoundly shaken. No longer the cocksure independent of *The Emperor Jones,* he now feared that he'd irretrievably damaged his standing in the industry he'd savaged less than two years before. Too late, he realized that this Goliath was not likely to fall. He understood the power wielded by the producers and studio heads he'd disparaged so freely and saw that with this small, unsuccessful negotiating maneuver, he'd crossed a line he'd never overstepped in all his anti-Hollywood tirades. "I was out of a job, and worse than that, I had not gone along with the hierarchy of Hollywood," he wrote. "Most of the producers played poker together and discussed various Hollywood personalities. Unless one was very important, you didn't cross Metro or Mayer."[17] Or, he might have added, Harry Rapf. Murphy had undoubtedly underestimated the influence of a figure whose talent he didn't respect. Rapf may have been a second-string producer, but he was one of Mayer's confidantes, and for all Murphy knew, a poker player, too.

Murphy's assessment of that influential gathering was seconded by another industry outsider, his old *Emperor Jones* colleague William C. deMille. "There is a Hollywood legend about a certain poker game which occurs from time to time among a selected group of overlords," deMille wrote in 1939. "During this game, it is said, various personalities are weighed and discussed, not only in regard to their work, but also as to their politics and their willingness to conform or, as the industry naively puts it, to 'co-operate.' It is believed that these six or eight men virtually determine, over the green cloth, who shall or shall not work in pictures."[18]

In his day, Rex Ingram had been important enough to cross Mayer with impunity. Murphy, chastened by the poor financial showing of *The Emperor Jones,* all but admitted that he was not. In a memoir studded with self-aggrandizing anecdotes, it's a humbling moment. The price of going against the industry is chillingly clear.

Momentarily at a loss, Murphy again fell back on screenwriting. Irish author and playwright Liam O'Flaherty was in California at the time, trying for a foothold in Hollywood while his cousin, director John Ford, brought his novel *The Informer* to the screen. Together, O'Flaherty and Murphy wrote *Dust over Kansas,* a film script about the dustbowl conditions that were ravaging the Great Plains. According to reports in the

Los Angeles Times, Alfred Green would "probably direct" the project "for Warner Brothers when he finishes the Nino Martini production, *Here's to Romance,* for Jesse Lasky."[19] There's no indication, however, that the project was produced.

Eventually Murphy found directing work again, though not with a major studio. The film was *Don't Gamble with Love* (1936), produced by Columbia Pictures. A former poverty-row studio, Columbia had grown into an industry player with such films as Frank Capra's *It Happened One Night* (1934) and John Ford's *The Whole Town's Talking* (1936). With Universal, it was one of the "little two"—feisty contenders nowhere near the size or strength of the "big five," MGM, RKO, Fox, Warner Bros., and Paramount. Columbia was a big step down from MGM, the top major, but it was still respectable.

Like *Twenty-four Hours, Don't Gamble with Love* is a domestic drama about a flawed husband. Jerry (Bruce Cabot) runs an honest gambling den, but his wife, Ann (Ann Sothern), persuades him to give it up after she spots him teaching card tricks to their toddler. Jerry begins working with one of his customers, an investment banker who soon skips the country, leaving him to take the rap on embezzlement charges. Though acquitted, he's embittered and returns to the gambling business. Ann leaves him, establishing a successful dress shop. "Baby meanwhile," noted the *New York Times,* "does not grow an inch." Going for rigged gambling this time, Jerry arouses the ire of a crooked competitor, who plans to kill him. Learning of this, Ann rushes to the club and exposes Jerry's shady tricks. She ruins his business but saves his life, as his rivals have no need to kill a discredited competitor. For her pains, Ann is shot by a compulsive gambler who'd lost big on the rigged deals, but the wound is minor. The couple are reunited, "but baby still seems a little backward. He still hasn't grown an inch."

Despite the sly commentary, the *Times* review was generally if not extravagantly favorable, calling it "a mildly amusing little program number, ideally suited for the neighborhoods." But it also described the film as "one of those pictures-without-a-purpose, unless it be to glorify simple home virtues, such as parenthood and not running gambling hells."[20] *Variety* concurred, calling it "fairly well produced, backgrounded and photographed" but noting that the stars "aren't more than moderate lure at the ticket window."[21]

As he struggled to get his career back on track, Murphy's personal life took a few hairpin turns as well. He and Jo-Jo were divorced in 1934. In a small *Los Angeles Times* item headlined "She Divorces 'Late' Husband," Johnson Murphy reportedly charged that Murphy had "stayed out late, and on many occasions he did not return home at all."[22] By the following year, the gossip columns were linking him to a series of attractive companions. In March 1935, Ed Sullivan reported actress Alice White "bending an attentive ear" to him. In June of that year, he was implicated in a nasty custody battle between actress Ann Harding and her former husband; facing jail for contempt, Harding steadfastly refused to answer questions about her relationship with Murphy.[23] A few months later, in September 1935, he was back in the tabloids, reportedly engaged to debutante Polly Peabody. "The Big Moment is Dudley Murphy, tall, blonde playboy, whose rise to a movie directorship shortly after his arrival in Hollywood five years ago from Paris, had everybody amazed," wrote the *New York Daily Mirror,* giving Murphy's career a convenient nip and tuck. But the death-by-pearls episode continued to dog him. "He's Dudley Murphy who has been irresistible to the women of two continents and in whose futuristic penthouse here in January, 1930, Mrs. Harriet Adler, 38, died of acute alcoholism, bringing Murphy unpleasant notoriety."[24] Murphy had already passed up marriage with a Santa Barbara socialite, Geraldine Graham Dabney, whom he'd begun seeing while working on *The Sport Parade.* Six months after its announcement, the engagement to Polly Peabody met a similar fate, and he went on to fresh conquests.

INDEPENDENCE, TAKE TWO

Murphy had had a difficult enough time enduring factory-style movie-making at the top majors. With his Hollywood star on the wane, he faced working for smaller studios on even tighter budgets and schedules. The prospect left him itching for independent production. "I felt again that my best work had always been done when I was my own boss," he wrote.[25] He became acquainted with actor Leslie Howard, and the two decided to form a production company.

Howard was a well-established screen actor who'd made more than a dozen films since his 1930 debut, including such hits as *Berkeley Square* (1931), *The Scarlet Pimpernel* (1934), and *Of Human Bondage* (1934). On Broadway, he'd played the lead in Robert E. Sherwood's play *The Petrified Forest,* re-creating the role in the 1936 Warner Bros. version. As part of his agreement on the film, he secured the role of the villain for his young

Broadway costar, Humphrey Bogart, usurping the studio's choice, the more bankable Edward G. Robinson. Though he won that battle, the experience may have left Howard, like Murphy, hungry for nonstudio production.

Though under contract to Warner Bros., Howard assumed he was free to pursue independent projects outside the United States. "So we drew up an agreement to form our company," wrote Murphy, "and I followed him to London. There we formed our company, which we called Associated Artists, Ltd. We took offices on St. James Street."[26] Writer Hugh Walpole, who'd done screen adaptations for *David Copperfield* (1934), *A Tale of Two Cities* (1935), and *Little Lord Fauntleroy* (1936), was the third principal in the venture. As outlined in a September 1936 article in the British trade journal *Today's Cinema,* the company's plans called for fifteen pictures in the first two years, with Howard starring in a picture a year. Already in development were *Bonnie Prince Charlie,* starring Howard, directed by Murphy, with a script by Walpole; *King for a Day,* from a story by Dashiell Hammett; and *The Martyr,* with a script by Liam O'Flaherty, Murphy's collaborator on the *Dust over Kansas* screenplay.[27]

Murphy returned to the States to drum up interest. An undated, untitled newspaper clipping in his personal collection, attributed to the motion picture editor of the *New York American,* updated the plans outlined in *Today's Cinema.*[28] Associated Artists had acquired screen rights to the Crime Club series of stories and was planning to release its films in the States through United Artists. Murphy was purportedly on the hunt for four additional stars, possibly including Kitty Carlisle, as well as two writers and four directors. James Cagney had been approached to take the title role in *The Martyr.*

But the film industry wasn't about to let valuable talent go veering off into private enterprise. Before long, Associated Artists ran into trouble from an entirely predictable source. "I received a phone call," Murphy recalled, "from [Warner Bros. president] Harry Warner, who asked me to come see him at the Dorchester Hotel." There, Warner informed Murphy in no uncertain terms that "Leslie Howard had an exclusive contract with them and had no right whatsoever to make an independent picture. This was a bombshell," Murphy recalled, "and I now had to enter a period of legal consultations to see if we could not have the right to make our independent picture." By the time lawyers in London, Hollywood, and New York succeeded in extricating Howard from the contractual thicket, the damage had been done. "All our money had gone for legal fees and we were never able to make the picture."[29]

Had Associated Artists succeeded, Murphy would have accomplished one of his greatest professional goals: an independent production center removed from Hollywood but successful on Hollywood's terms. Along with other moves toward independent production that occurred around this time (such as David O. Selznick's company, Selznick International Pictures), a thriving, London-based cooperative venture would have helped to loosen Hollywood's chokehold on the industry. Even allowing for the exaggerations of the trade press, the slate of projects that Associated Artists was proposing, the amount of capital that it had reportedly accumulated (close to seven hundred thousand pounds), and the caliber of talent involved were considerable. Had the venture moved forward, it would have posed a provocative model for independent filmmaking at the height of the studio system's power and influence.

But it didn't. Perhaps the company's capital was eaten up by legal fees, as Murphy claimed, or it could be that when Harry Warner started saber rattling, Leslie Howard thought better of the venture. In any case, Howard's career suffered no setback from the failure of Associated Artists. Thanks to the company's costly legal wrangling, his right to appear in independent productions was secured. He starred in and received codirecting credit on *Pygmalion* (1939), shot in Great Britain for independent producer Gabriel Pascal, then immediately went on to make *Gone with the Wind* (1939) for Selznick International Pictures. Initially Howard had no interest in the film; as an inducement, Selznick offered him the chance to produce a second film for the company. Howard made *Intermezzo* (1939), in which he starred opposite Ingrid Bergman and for which he received associate producer credit.

Murphy's fortunes took no such spectacular turn. In 1938, he dramatized the Horace McCoy novel *They Shoot Horses, Don't They?* with the idea of bringing it to Broadway. Producer George Abbott passed on the project but thought enough of it to mention it in a newspaper interview; in 1939, George Jessel was reportedly planning to produce it, but it never reached the stage.[30] Instead, Murphy brought another theatrical project to the screen. *One Third of a Nation* (1939) marked a return to the familiar realm of small-scale, New York–based independent production. It was shot at Eastern Service Studios, Inc., the same Astoria facility where Murphy had filmed *The Emperor Jones*. Veteran Broadway producer Harold Orlob is credited as producer, but so, in a way, is Murphy: the film's opening title frame bears the line "A Dudley Murphy Production."

As a play, *One Third of a Nation* was staged in New York by the Federal

Theatre Project of the Works Project Administration and was the first WPA play to become a commercial film. A forceful argument for slum clearance and new housing for the poor, the play utilized the Federal Theatre Project's "Living Newspaper" format, embedding a substantial dose of law, statistics, and housing regulations in a dramatic framework. It was a politically progressive and challenging subject that undoubtedly appealed to Murphy. He did the initial adaptation himself; it's likely his hand that moderated the play's vehement tone, jettisoned most of the didacticism, and overlaid the experimental drama with a crowd-pleasing, rich boy–poor girl romance between stars Leif Erikson and Sylvia Sidney.[31] The plot of the film, like the play, centers on a run-down "old law" tenement—so called because it was built before the tenement laws of 1901, exempting it from the safety and living standards imposed on newer buildings. Driving through the city with a friend, wealthy New Yorker Peter Cortlant (Erikson) spots a distant fire. As an amusing diversion, he instructs his chauffeur to head toward it. They come to the slums of the Lower East Side, where the brutal blaze has claimed several lives, and a boy is badly injured in a fall from a defective fire escape. Mary Rogers (Sidney), the boy's distraught sister, commandeers Peter's car to take Joey for help; Peter insists on taking them to an expensive private hospital and paying for the boy's treatment.

After a month, Joey (played by director Sidney Lumet in his only screen role) returns home on crutches, no longer able to walk.[32] Meanwhile, Peter has discovered to his shock that he himself owns the wretched building and that most of the Cortlant wealth is derived from slum housing. He resolves to tear it all down and put up more livable housing, but his sister (Muriel Hutchison), a cool, callous socialite, vows to remove him as administrator of the family trust if he proceeds. His hands tied, Peter breaks the news to a disappointed Mary, spoiling a romantic dinner aboard his yacht. When Joey hears that the hated old building will not, in fact, be torn down, he takes matters into his own hands, setting fire to the property and perishing in the blaze. His death convinces Peter to move ahead with his plan, and the film closes with a shot of him dressed in work clothes, directing the demolition of several buildings with Mary at his side.

One Third of a Nation displays what one British journal called "a genuine Wellman-like regard for proletarian America."[33] Unlike several of Murphy's previous films, the opening sequence is not a site for visual play. Instead, the film fades up on a straightforward shot of the New York skyline that tilts down to, then quickly fades in on, crowded neighborhood streets far from the skyscrapers of Midtown. The opening sequence is a

The Sport Parade (1932): (above) Joel McCrea at right; (below) McCrea, Marian Marsh, and William Gargan. Photographs courtesy of the Margaret Herrick Library, The Academy of Motion Picture Arts and Sciences.

Portrait of Mexico Today (1932), painted by muralist David Alfaro Siqueiros on the walls of the backyard patio at Murphy's Amalfi Drive home. The mural is now in the collection of the Santa Barbara Museum of Art. Photograph courtesy of the Santa Barbara Museum of Art. Photograph by Anthony Peres, 2001. Copyright Estate of David Alfaro Siqueiros/SOMAAP, Mexico/VAGA, New York.

Ruby Elzy (Dolly), Paul Robeson (Jones), and Dudley Murphy on the set of *The Emperor Jones,* 1933.

The Emperor Jones: Brutus Jones prepares to leave his sweetheart, Dolly, and the small-town South for a career as a Pullman porter. Photograph courtesy of the Library of Congress/Motion Picture Conservation Center.

The Emperor Jones: the fatal dice game between Jones and his friend Jeff (Frank Wilson), in dark suit and fedora. Photograph courtesy of the Library of Congress/Motion Picture Conservation Center.

Newly arrived on the Caribbean island, Jones is taken on by the white trader, Smithers (Dudley Digges). Photograph courtesy of the Library of Congress/Motion Picture Conservation Center.

Robeson as Emperor Jones. Photograph courtesy of the Library of Congress/
Motion Picture Conservation Center.

Fleeing through the jungle, Jones falls into a panicked delirium. In the
original film and 2002 Library of Congress restoration, this footage is tinted
blue. Photograph courtesy of the Library of Congress/Motion Picture
Conservation Center.

The sister and father of Dudley Murphy, director of "Emperor Jones." His sister is Carlene Bowles Murphy, his father is H. Dudley Murphy, noted Winchester painter. The young man (at the right) is the director.

From the *Boston Traveler*, after the local premiere of *The Emperor Jones*. Clippings courtesy of the Murphy Family Collection.

A WINCHESTER MURPHY MAKES GOOD

Dudley Murphy is in Boston, as a movie director. He bossed the taking of "Emperor Jones," that Boston folk will see at RKO Keith's. You see the former movie critic and his father. M. Dud'ey Murphy and sister, Mrs.

Alexander Samorloff, as they dined in town. The 35-year-old director is in Boston for the first time in 10 years. Read story of the Winchester boy making good, on another page, in this edition. *Story on Page 3*

A staged recording session for *The Night Is Young* (1935). Murphy, standing under the arm of the microphone at left, looks toward stars Evelyn Laye and Ramon Novarro.

The Night Is Young: Ramon Novarro and Evelyn Laye, center, with Charles Butterworth and Una Merkel at right. Photograph courtesy of the Margaret Herrick Library, The Academy of Motion Picture Arts and Sciences.

One Third of a Nation: Muriel Hutchison (Ethel Cortlant), Leif Erikson (Peter Cortlant), and Horace Sinclair (John, the butler). Photograph courtesy of the Library of Congress/Motion Picture, Broadcasting, and Recorded Sound Division.

Murphy with son, Michael "Pat" Murphy, and father, Hermann Dudley Murphy, on a sailing canoe trip to Sugar Island, Canada, in the mid-1930s.

Murphy (center) with Hermann Dudley Murphy and nephews Alexander Samoiloff (rear) and Dudley Samoiloff in the late 1930s or early 1940s.

Tijuana, 1949: Murphy (center), with (from left) former wife Katharine Hawley, daughter Poco Murphy, wife Ginny Bellondi Murphy, daughter Christopher "Kit" Murphy, and son, Michael "Pat" Murphy.

Murphy and daughter
Poco Murphy at her
home, mid-1950s.

Alabamy Bound (1941):
(above) Four members of the Five
Spirits of Rhythm as a Pullman porter
percussion section; (left) a naturally
segmented film frame in the
sleeping-car sequence, reminiscent
of the kaleidoscopic imagery in
Ballet mécanique and *Black and Tan.*
Photographs courtesy of the Library
of Congress/Motion Picture,
Broadcasting, and Recorded
Sound Division.

Dorothy Dandridge (center),
singing in *Easy Street* (1941).
Photograph courtesy of the
Library of Congress/Motion
Picture, Broadcasting, and
Recorded Sound Division.

Yes, Indeed! (1941): (top) Dorothy Dandridge shaking hands with the congregation in *Yes, Indeed!* (1941); (right) the silhouetted shadows at right recall the deathbed scene in *Black and Tan.* Photographs courtesy of the Library of Congress/Motion Picture, Broadcasting, and Recorded Sound Division.

Easy Street (1941): Dorothy Dandridge sings. Photograph courtesy of the Library of Congress/Motion Picture, Broadcasting, and Recorded Sound Division.

The original Holiday House accommodations, designed by Richard Neutra and built in 1948. Photographs by Julius Shulman. Copyright J. Paul Getty Trust; used with permission. Julius Shulman Photography Archive, Research Library at the Getty Research Institute (2004.R.10).

Murphy in the 1960s: At the Holiday House restaurant (above) and at right. The woman in both photographs is actress Olga San Juan, wife of actor Edmond O'Brien.

Murphy with actors from the television series *Malibu Run* (1961), which frequently filmed location scenes at Holiday House.

lively montage of kids' street games, reminiscent of Helen Levitt's 1930s photographs. A fast-paced round of hide-and-seek introduces Joey and his pals. The Irish cop on the beat comes by to chase away boys playing at an open hydrant, while upstairs, a married couple quarrel at the window, and two women exchange insults on the tenement stairs. Deftly and economically, the opening establishes the film's mise-en-scène and lays the groundwork for the melodrama to follow. No more than a minute and a half elapse before the fire, ignited by a carelessly tossed cigar, bursts into flames.

While the film is well shot, it lacks Murphy's customary visual finesse. This may have been a function of budget but might also reflect the challenges he faced in recasting an experimental, stridently propagandizing play into a commercially viable film—a case of moderating the innovations of others rather than adding his own. In the play, the old tenement is a central character, a villainous presence that speaks to Joey in the voice of a flinty old man. The film includes only two such dialogues, in which Joey stands dwarfed before the overpowering façade. The loudspeaker, which was one of the play's focal points, is also gone from the film. Overt didacticism is largely confined to a municipal hearing about the first fire, in which a succession of city inspectors instruct an absurdly astonished official in the intricacies of New York City housing law.[34] In the film's closing sequence, the image of a smiling Joey is superimposed on a shot of spacious new housing and grounds, while the final shot features even larger images of Mary's and Peter's faces in profile, gazing up and out— not at each other—like heroic workers in a socialist realist painting.

With its fervent social-interest plot, *One Third of a Nation* would never be mistaken for a classical Hollywood film. But it wasn't far from one. "As 'One Third' shapes up it's no worse and—considering the reported very moderate production investment—rather better than a commensurate modest-budgeter essayed on the Coast," wrote *Variety*.[35] "The film is less truculent than the play," noted the *New York Times*. "For all that, it has a point of view. . . . We will not say it is a film that should be seen, merely one that you probably will want to see."[36]

As a write-up in the *Los Angeles Times* suggests, *One Third of a Nation* is an early example of the "social-problem film," a genre that reached its peak in the 1940s. "'One Third of a Nation' is yet another answer to the New York critics' prayer for realistic films, and they're particularly interested because it comes from the Long Island studios instead of Hollywood," the reviewer wrote. "The revival of eastern production is thought here to portend a new freedom of subject matter for the movies, and the hopes of the social-minded have largely been based on this film version of the Federal theater play." With a hometown partiality for Hollywood product, the Los Angeles paper was reserved in its appraisal. "Its approach to the subject of housing greatly resembles the realistic Warner films to which we're accustomed," the reviewer wrote, "and it is inferior to many of them."[37]

Seizing the promotional opportunities presented by the film's New York opening, Murphy floated another idea for turning the city into a filmmaking center. His plan called for producing plays that, while running on Broadway, would be filmed simultaneously during the day; by the time a play ended its run, the film version would be ready for national release. The first project in the scheme was his adaptation of *They Shoot Horses, Don't They?* In a *New York Times* interview headlined "A Noble Experiment," Murphy asserted that he'd already signed actress Miriam Hopkins, his paramour of years past, for the lead in a play and film based on the novel. "If the idea works out, Miriam and the rest of the cast will be seen at night on Broadway in the legitimate version and during the day they'll be completing the movie in Astoria," he explained.[38] He went on to discuss two other projects he was working on: a "swing picture," inspired by the pop music that was sweeping the country, and an exposé of the "glamour" phenomenon, which turned New York debutantes into overnight media celebrities. The latter project in particular caused a stir in the gossip columns. "Mary Anita Loos, press agent for Fefe's Monte Carlo, will portray the press-agent role in Dudley Murphy's film, *Glamour Girl*," wrote one columnist. "In addition, she's been hired to press agent the picture."[39]

But neither Hollywood nor Broadway was biting. Like Murphy's previous attempts to incubate East Coast film production, the film-theater plan floundered, presumably for lack of investors, and no more was heard of *Glamour Girl*. By the end of the year, a news item in the *New York Times* "Gossip of the Rialto" column mentioned that Murphy's script for *They Shoot Horses, Don't They?*—the cornerstone of his Broadway-to-film plan—had been sold to actor Wallace Ford.[40] With no New York work in the offing, Murphy had no choice but to head West once again.

DRIFTING AWAY

Murphy's second 1939 release was made for Republic Pictures. A latecomer among Hollywood studios, Republic was founded in 1935 by film-processing laboratory mogul Herbert Yates. It was a small, low-budget operation, the antithesis of MGM and a sobering indication of Murphy's sinking industry status. "I felt that I must now play the Hollywood game and compromise," he wrote. But this newfound flexibility came too late to do his career any real good. His finances in precarious shape, he "accepted an assignment with the production head of the studio on a story which [he] had very little faith in."[41]

Murphy's success in overlaying a commercial gloss on a social-interest film like *One Third of a Nation* may have won him the Republic project, a melodramatic tale of politics, parental sacrifice, and redemption called *Main Street Lawyer* (1939). Abraham Lincoln Boggs, a small-town attorney with a reputation for decency, is blackmailed into throwing an important racketeering case to prevent his adopted daughter's dark secret from coming to light. (She's the child of a convicted murderess.) When the daughter is framed for murder, Boggs undertakes her defense, cleverly tricking the real murderer into firing at him. The bullet is found to match the one in the victim, the daughter is exonerated, and the murdering racketeer is brought to justice.

Murphy's lack of faith in the project was borne out by the critics, who praised the performances and direction but knocked both script and story. Bosley Crowther called it a "rickety little horse-and-buggy opera,"[42] while *Variety* noted that "Dudley Murphy's direction gives this small-town yarn considerable lustre, but the story itself has been too frequently done in revised form. But better." The paper's "Miniature Review" ruled: "Good cast and direction, but story relegates it to the duals."[43]

"The duals"—second-rate movies shown on double-bills in neighborhood theaters—were hardly what Murphy had had in mind when he first broke into film twenty years earlier. In that time, though, Hollywood had changed more rapidly and thoroughly than he had. He'd done badly at adapting to the system as it evolved and at exploiting it to his benefit. *Main Street Lawyer* was Murphy's last feature for a Hollywood studio. As a valedictory, it wasn't the high note he might have hoped for. But it was a fair indication of where his career had taken him. Almost despite himself, he'd become a seasoned professional, singled out in reviews for the quality of his directing work. But he'd reached a point where his talent was superior to the material he could expect to be offered.

Murphy and Hollywood were tremendous disappointments to each other. Had he been even slightly more flexible, more politic, or more astute, he might have parlayed his artistic reputation into a solid position within a studio hierarchy. Instead, he moved in the opposite direction. With

The Emperor Jones, he declared his separation from Hollywood in such incendiary terms and with such a controversial project that few bridges, personal or professional, were left standing. From the outset, Murphy had never been great film-factory material; he was too impulsive, too extemporaneous, and had too strong a preference for cinematic experimentation. For its part, the Hollywood of that era couldn't have been less hospitable to a filmmaker of his talents and inclinations. Nor could it abide a director who didn't, as William C. deMille put it, "co-operate."[44]

The manuscript of Murphy's memoir ends abruptly with the late 1930s, and the chronology after his dismissal from MGM is vague. But his career continued. Drifting out of the industry, he continued to find quirky, unexpected niches for his style of filmmaking, further and further from the mainstream. After his Broadway-to-film scheme fizzled, he was no longer interested in pursuing independent production in New York or elsewhere. When he did work again, two years later, it wasn't in features but in short films—the shortest and most musical films a wartime entertainment industry could devise.

CHAPTER 10

CHANGING DIRECTION

Though he no longer worked for a studio, Murphy continued to think of himself as a filmmaker. He never considered himself lost to Hollywood. Eventually, he assumed, he'd hit upon a project that would restore him to the industry's good graces. Meanwhile, he was careful to speak respectfully of the studios.

Even as he drifted out of the industry, though, Murphy remained a member of the Hollywood community. He continued to appear in local gossip and social columns: mentioned as one of the guests at a dinner party hosted by B. P. Schulberg, for instance, attending a cocktail party given by European royalty, and inaugurating the new steam room at Chasen's. In early 1940, Hedda Hopper mentioned *Hollywoodland,* a screenplay he'd written with scriptwriter Dudley Nicholls; two studios were reportedly bidding on it.[1]

His time in London with Associated Artists had left Murphy with a heightened awareness of England's wartime struggles, and in mid-1940 he looked for ways to mobilize support in Hollywood. Working with British-born actor Alan Mowbray, he quickly came up with one: an evening of short Noel Coward plays, to be presented as a benefit for British war relief. Typically, the project advanced several of his interests: not only did it raise money, it made a case for legitimate theater in Los Angeles. "Hollywood has finally awakened to the need for better theater," wrote Louella Parsons of the project. "Dudley Murphy and Alan Mowbray, president and vice president of the [newly established] Theater Guild of Southern California, are largely responsible for this new consciousness which has aroused our movie folk from their lethargy."[2]

Not coincidentally, the project, called Tonight at 8:30, brought Murphy into working relationships with the kind of A-list actors who were otherwise inaccessible to him now. "The plan had an enthusiastic response from the British film colony and we signed run-of-the-play contracts for scale with Greer Garson, Olivia de Haviland, Joan Fontaine, etc. at $25 a week," he wrote. "Several of the top directors offered their services. . . . The project snowballed and one afternoon I found myself having to tell Mary Pickford, who had called to play in one of the plays, that we were all cast."[3] He directed the last of the evening's three presentations; opening night found "practically every celeb in town in attendance," as Louella Parsons reported, with Murphy accompanying Katharine Hepburn, Marlene Dietrich, and Coward himself.[4] Within days, Murphy announced additional Theater Guild productions: Vivien Leigh and Charles Boyer in Henri Bernstein's *Melo* and possibly a collaboration with Charlie Chaplin on *Charlot's Review of 1940*. "There is a good chance that Murphy will also present John Barrymore in 'Hamlet,'" the *Los Angeles Times* wrote.[5] Despite the immense goodwill generated by Tonight at 8:30, none of these productions appears to have gotten off the ground.

Murphy had always enjoyed the technical side of filmmaking, from early synchronization systems for silent film to the prismatic lenses used in *Ballet mécanique* and *Black and Tan*. But the industry's lengthy learning curve with sound and the static, narrative-heavy films that went with it sent his technological interests into eclipse for most of the 1930s. They reemerged in 1941 with a film format known as soundies.

In the late 1930s, a Los Angeles dentist and tinkerer named Gordon Keith Woodard successfully crossed a film projector with a jukebox. His invention, an early antecedent to the music video and pay-per-view, was a coin-operated machine he called the Cinematone. Tested in taverns around L.A., it was an immediate hit. But Woodard was undercapitalized and lacked connections in the already entrenched jukebox industry, leaving him poorly positioned to move ahead with his product. That distinction fell to a leading jukebox manufacturer, the Mills Novelty Company, and its eventual subsidiaries. Joining forces with businessman James Roosevelt, a son of President Franklin Roosevelt, the company launched its version of the movie jukebox, the Mills Panoram. In September 1940, Roosevelt and company chief Fred Mills hosted a Hollywood reception to present their new apparatus and the product it played: short musical films they called soundies.

Placed like jukeboxes in bars and restaurants, the Panoram machines each held eight hundred feet of film: enough for eight soundies, which were rear-projected by mirrors onto a ground-glass screen.[6] At a dime a shot, patrons could summon up the likes of Louis Armstrong, Fats Waller, Jimmy Dorsey, Gene Krupa, and Duke Ellington, along with such lesser lights as the Skating Continentals and Pansy the Wonder Horse. The ten-cent price, however, applied only if a patron's selection were next on the reel. Access to a specific film was impossible; users were obliged to watch whatever was cued to play next or invest the time and dimes to reach the soundie of their choice.

With the Panoram screen variously estimated at sixteen by twenty inches or eighteen by twenty-two, the viewing experience was much closer to television than to an old-fashioned nickelodeon.[7] The film reels in each machine were changed anywhere from once a month to once or twice weekly. An estimated 450 film prints per week went into circulation in roughly 4,500 Panoram projectors around the country. The demand for new soundies was intense, and a small stable of production units (in Los Angeles, New York, and the Mills Company's home base of Chicago) worked furiously to keep pace.

In late 1941, Murphy joined RCM Productions as a director. RCM was the Mills Company's production unit in Los Angeles; Roosevelt and Mills were the *R* and *M* of the name. The *C* belonged to Sam Coslow, a veteran songwriter who'd supplied the tunes for some twenty minor Hollywood films, from *Why Bring That Up?* (1929) to *Dreaming Out Loud* (1940). Coincidentally, Coslow had also written "Just One More Chance," the number that an unknown Bing Crosby had sung in Murphy's *Confessions of a Co-ed,* released ten years earlier.[8]

Like the jukebox, soundies were unpretentious popular entertainment. The musical menu featured a mix of jazz and swing dance tunes, dreamy ballads, and novelty acts. In terms of budget and production values, they made even the most bare-bones poverty-row studio seem like MGM. Coslow estimated that between 1941 and 1943, he churned out soundies at the rate of five or six per week.[9] The music was rarely filmed live but rather lip-synced to a prerecorded playback. Each production usually took a day, with music recording in the morning and filming in the afternoon.

Even so, many soundies had an undeniable appeal, which sprang in part from the form itself, the vivacity (and in some cases the oddity) of the performances, and the abundant good humor that many of them conveyed. Like musical time capsules, they're concentrated, occasionally loopy expressions of American culture and social attitudes in the early 1940s. Given the constraints of low-budget production, brief running times, and the assumptions implicit in their lyrics, soundies often resorted to ethnic stereotypes, naively blatant but not necessarily mean-spirited. Tambourine-rattling gypsies, Latin spitfires and caballeros, kilted Scotsmen, hula dancers, Russian babushkas, and double-talking Swedes all made their appearances on soundie screens. *The Pennsylvania Polka* (1942) was performed by a cast of coal miners, and in *Mountain Dew* (1941), Murphy himself may have elaborated on the theme of drunken, moonshining hillbillies.[10] In *I'm an Old Cowhand* (1941), veteran vaudevillian Gus Van heaped stereotype upon stereotype to comic effect, repeating the lyrics of the cowboy pop tune in the guise of a Russian cossack, an Irishman, an Italian, and other ethnic figures.

As a cinematic form, the soundies appealed to many of Murphy's film-making interests: new technology, the visual interpretation of music, and in some instances the depiction of African Americans on screen. It's diffi-cult to ascertain his complete soundie filmography, as credits don't always survive on existing prints. Film scholar William Moritz attributed ten to him, including such titles as *Abercrombie Had a Zombie* and *Jazzy Joe,* on which soundie historian Maurice Terenzio and his colleagues did not identify a director. Even without directorial credits, however, Murphy's filmmaking style is clearly identifiable in such works as *Easy Street* and *Alabamy Bound.*

In several of Murphy's soundies, themes and visual motifs from his fea-ture films appear in synoptic form. Featuring African-American singer and actress Dorothy Dandridge—barely twenty years old and just breaking into films—*Yes, Indeed!* recalls the spirited prayer service that opened *The Emperor Jones,* situating it in a stark, deeply shadowed setting reminiscent of the deathbed scene in *Black and Tan.*[11] Wearing a strapless dress and fluffy black boa, Dandridge leads the shouting, rolling congregation in a swing-ing call and response, backed by the Spirits of Rhythm as church deacons.

Easy Street is Murphy's version of utopia from an urban black perspective, with a wry, stylish approach to mainstream clichés about African-American life. Here, a concentrated shorthand of dancing, drinking, gambling, and flamboyant fashion blend in a languid, dreamlike fantasy. Bearing little resemblance to an actual urban locale, the set of Easy Street is spotlessly clean and sunnily bright, with barely a hint of shadow. The piece opens with a shot of a street sweeper with his wheeled cart and broom, resting next to a sign reading "No Horses Allowed on This Street." Seated with her male companion in an open-air pedicab, Dandridge is beautifully decked out in a low-cut dress, furs, glittering jewelry, and a hat with long, swooping feathers. She begins singing as her carriage pulls up to a building from which another stylish black couple is leaving. A sign near the entrance reads, "Rest Awhile Café / Free Eggs / Free Gin / Free Lunch / Free Music / FREE EVERYTHING." As Dandridge and her friend cruise slowly up the street, their pedaling attendant occasionally sprays them with "Love's Dream." The film cuts to a shot of men shooting dice on the sidewalk. A black policeman greets them cordially and keeps walking. He passes a crate of chickens bearing a sign that reads "Help Yourself"; another man does so while the cop beams in approval. He passes out of frame right as Dandridge and her carriage enter frame left. She alights and saunters past the musicians on the sidewalk, who play backup for her. As couples begin to jitterbug slowly behind her, she continues to sing, then resumes her seat in the pedicab, wheeling away with the last line of the song. As the film ends, they roll out of frame past a man sleeping against a lamppost, near a sign that reads "Danger—Man at Rest."

Like all soundies, *Easy Street* is a hundred feet long, roughly three minutes' running time. But unlike most of them, which were little more than documented performances, *Easy Street* is a short movie, densely packed with vignettes, sight gags, and telling visual details. Starting from the mainstream stereotype of African Americans' supposed laziness, the film overlays its clichés of black life with an urbane sophistication grounded in Dandridge's poised and self-possessed performance. With the offhand elegance of a Fred Astaire musical, the film spins a visual story that's determinedly at odds with its ostensible content, acknowledging and stylishly tweaking depictions of African Americans that had been the norm for Hollywood in the 1930s. On a more material level, the film features an all-black cast at a time when Hollywood had lost interest in such productions, and African Americans made up little more than 2 percent of the actors in Los Angeles.[12] With its focus on African Americans and their depiction in the culture, the film reflects Murphy's urban sensibility transplanted to L.A.'s less cosmopolitan milieu.

By late 1941, when Murphy was working on his soundies, Europe had already been engulfed in World War II for two years. The United States stood ready to enter the conflict, and the African-American community soon knew the irony of fighting against fascism overseas while facing insufferable racism at home. The comic and condescending stereotypes in Hollywood films of the 1920s and 1930s began to seem out of step with the times. As early as 1937, for instance, David O. Selznick advised his writer on *Gone with the Wind,* "I, for one, have no desire to produce any anti-Negro film. . . . In our picture, I think we have to be awfully careful that the Negroes come out decidedly on the right side of the ledger . . . in these fascist-ridden times."[13]

Given the changing political climate and the sophisticated tone of *Easy Street,* one of Murphy's other 1941 soundies, *Lazybones,* is a jarring throwback. Here, composer Hoagy Carmichael sings an admonishment to a lazy figure who'd rather sleep in the sun than do his work. Nothing in the lyrics intrinsically references African Americans, but the inference is present nonetheless, and the film's action makes the connection clear. While Carmichael drawls out the tune at the piano, attended by two admiring white women, a black manservant (Peter Ray), accompanied by a maid (Dandridge), brings in an elaborate silver coffee service on a tray.

That's the sum total of the action. But it's done as a slow-motion dance from the kitchen door to the grand piano, with Ray precariously balancing the entire silver service on his head. Dressed in a sexy version of a maid's uniform with a short, tutulike skirt, Dandridge can do little but eye his progress with alarm, in reactions that don't always appear feigned. As the song winds down, she helps him transfer the tray to the piano top with undisguised relief. That action coincides with a line in the lyrics about sleeping all day, at which point Ray yawns and leans sleepily against Dandridge, who shakes her head in disapproval. It's an absurd moment, even within the film's own logic, as it completely denies the achievement (surreal as it is) of Ray's having made it to the piano with his burden intact—the feat that constitutes the film's central spectacle, or "work." For Murphy, dancing waiters spinning trays on their fingertips were an unforgettable aspect of 1920s Harlem, and he included them in nightclub scenes in several of his films. But balancing a full coffee service on one's head was probably not a variation he spotted at Small's Paradise. For his part, Carmichael spends his time at the piano swatting the women's hands away from his cigarettes and keyboard. With the contextualized racism of the lyrics, the stereotyped absurdity of Ray's choreographed task, and the latent tensions between Carmichael and his female companions, *Lazy Bones* is a roiling brew of racial and sexual politics in the guise of a simple pop-hit soundie.

Murphy's work with RCM did produce at least one small gem: *Alabamy Bound.* Here, the brevity of the form works in its favor, distilling the movie musical to its essence. The film opens with the Santa Fe Railroad logo superimposed over the image of a fast-moving train, followed by a montage of train wheels at high speed—motifs used in *The Emperor Jones,* here given added speed and fluency. The action cuts to the train's bar car, where the star, Jackie Greene (an Eddie Cantor look-alike), converses with an attractive woman as a smiling African-American bartender looks on. Greene is tapped on the shoulder by the conductor, who says, in rhyme, "Change at Kansas City for Atlanta. Are you by any chance Eddie Cantor?" To that, Greene rolls his eyes in a plausible Cantor imitation and launches into song. He finishes the verse with a prancing, Cantor-ish dance, waving a large white handkerchief. In a typical Murphy transition, the film quickly cross-fades from Greene's handkerchief to a close-up of a white shoeshine cloth. Attired in porters' jackets, the Five Spirits of Rhythm perform a tightly edited interlude of shoe buffing and polishing.[14] In their hands, the snapping cloths are percussion instruments, and Murphy treats them as musicians, giving them playful close-up solos.

As the music changes key, a quick locomotive wheel-and-piston montage bridges into the next sequence, a dance routine set in a sleeping car. Framed by the black curtains of their berths, four white female dancers (two above, two below) roll down their stockings in unison and break into a seated dance, flashing their legs in one direction, then another. Visually, the berths divide the screen into quadrants; it's as though Murphy were filming a kaleidoscopic shot for *Ballet mécanique* or *Black and Tan* but without the prismatic lens. The sequence also evokes the stop-action, mannequin-leg Charleston of *Ballet mécanique*. The routine goes on to feature close-up shots of the individual women and extreme close-ups of their dancing legs. The women poke their heads out from the black curtains, re-creating the quadrant motif. The conductor enters and starts singing a repeat of the opening verse as he pats and pinches their cheeks good night. Up in the locomotive, the engineer picks up the next line of the song, in a pass-along of the lyrics reminiscent of the "wiener schnitzel" sequence in *The Night Is Young*. Greene picks up the closing lines; it's now daylight, and as the train pulls into the station, the porters brush off the debarking passengers. Greene is last; the film closes with a close-up of him wreathed by five outstretched hands waiting for tips. He rolls his eyes, the music wraps with a flourish, and the film ends.

As marginal and low-budget as they were, the soundies were for Murphy a close to perfect film form, tapping his strengths as no film had since *The Emperor Jones*. In such pieces as *Alabamy Bound* and *Easy Street,* he created a dense, musically driven cinematic style in which narrative is subjugated to elements that he himself valued more highly: rhythm, texture, and visual wit. Even his more mundane soundies, such as *I Don't Want to Set the World on Fire,* are sparked by inventive touches: a yearbook photo that starts singing, for instance, or a visually complex, overhead tracking shot along malt-shop booths filled with cuddling couples.

Murphy's work with soundies suggests an interesting point: though the narrative feature film isn't inherently at odds with a musically driven approach, it's not necessarily the form best suited to it. This may be one reason why Murphy's short films, from *St. Louis Blues* to *Alabamy Bound,* display a fluidity not evident in most of his features. But given how decisively the narrative feature has dominated both the industry and film history, a flair for short films didn't get him very far. Had Murphy made an equally impressive showing in his feature films, most likely his reputation would have been assured. As it was, his affinity for the short-film form resulted in some of his strongest works and some of his most obscure. In formal terms, Murphy's soundies are most closely related to his early silent films, such as *Soul of the Cypress,* which were similarly structured around music, rhythm, and visual imagery rather than the demands of narrativity or the construction of filmic space. At the same time, *Alabamy Bound* and *Easy Street* suggest modern music videos transplanted to the swing era. Seeing them, one can't help thinking that Murphy would have been a virtuoso of that late twentieth-century form and the rapid-fire, visually rich film style that it fostered.

Regardless of his accomplishments in the genre, it's impossible to deny that, for Murphy, the soundies represented a vertiginous step down the commercial filmmaking ladder. It was grueling work—literally a film a day—and the pay was negligible. To accept such a position, he'd have had to be highly motivated, and he probably was. In August 1941, he'd married for the fourth time. His new wife, Virginia "Ginny" Bellondi, was an aspiring actress some fifteen years his junior, whom he'd met in New York; a baby was due at the end of the year.[15] Other than the soundies assignments, Murphy apparently produced no films during this time.

Although soundies historian Maurice Terenzio and his colleagues wrote that Murphy remained with RCM until the company moved to Chicago in April 1942, the last soundies they listed Murphy as making were shot in December 1941.[16] It could be that the intense schedule and chronic low budgets were too much for Murphy, especially with a new baby in the house. Or it's possible that his most elaborate productions, utter extravaganzas by soundies standards, were more than RCM wanted or needed.

The soundies barely outlasted Murphy's involvement with them. In December 1941, the month he filmed his final projects, Pearl Harbor was attacked. Once the United States entered World War II, the tons of metal and rubber that went into making movie jukeboxes were earmarked for the war effort, cutting off the possibility of new markets. With the country at war, the public lost its enthusiasm for soundies almost overnight. In the spring of 1942, for example, Panoram machines in New England were doing roughly one-sixth the business they'd averaged over the previous fifteen months.[17] By 1943, the craze was all but over. The films themselves went on to a limited second life as compilation reels for the home movie market, but the soundies remain, for the most part, a footnote to mid-twentieth-century American film history.

From Associated Artists to Artistas Asociados

Murphy's career soon took another interesting bounce. Nine months after he finished his last soundie, he was again directing a feature—not in Hollywood, but some sixteen hundred miles south in Mexico City. The film was *Yolanda,* aka *Brindis de amor* (*Toast to Love,* 1942), the romantic tale of a Russian ballerina on tour in Mexico City. No prints of this film or of the second film Murphy made in Mexico are known to exist in the United States. They did, however, generate substantial comment in the Mexican press at the time and among later Mexican film historians.

How Murphy came to direct films in Mexico is not entirely clear. He'd made his first trip there in the early 1930s with Pasadena socialite Geri Dabney, one of several women he'd considered marrying at one time or another. Though he was a frequent visitor after the early 1940s and, according to family members, owned an apartment in Acapulco for several years, there's no indication of his having been in Mexico City between that first visit in the 1930s and the filming of *Yolanda.*

Murphy could have come to the Mexican film industry through several different routes. Norman Foster, one of the lead actors in *Confessions of a Co-ed,* later became a writer and director, turning out several "Charlie Chan" and "Mr. Moto" pictures in the late 1930s. He was the nominal director of Orson Welles's *Journey into Fear* (1943), and Welles tapped him for "My Friend Bonito," the Mexican segment of his aborted South American anthology film, *It's All True.* By the early 1940s, Foster was directing features in Mexico City, including a well-received remake of the 1931 film *Santa* (1943) and *La fuga* (The Escape, 1943). It's conceivable that he and Murphy had remained in touch over the years and that Foster matched him with the *Yolanda* project.

Another possible connection was Miguel Covarrubias, Murphy's boon companion from his Harlem nightclubbing days. At the height of his success as a caricaturist and illustrator, Covarrubias conceived an interest in anthropology and in 1933 was awarded a Guggenheim fellowship to pursue field studies in Bali. He received a second Guggenheim in 1940 for a book on the indigenous cultures of the Isthmus of Tehuantepec. In 1942, he returned to Mexico permanently and began conducting research through the National Institute of Anthropology and History.[18] A well-known figure, he presumably had contacts in the Mexican film industry and may have exploited them on Murphy's behalf.

Finally, it may have been the film's producer, Manuel Reachi, who brought Murphy to *Yolanda*. In the 1930s, Reachi had worked in Hollywood as a producer and musical arranger on films for the Spanish-speaking market, notably *La buenaventura* (1934) and *El cantante de Napoles* (1935). *Yolanda* was his first Mexican production. According to Mexican film historian Emilio García Riera, Reachi started out directing the film himself but handed it over to Murphy for the necessary "cosmopolitan touch."[19] It was something of a ghost-directing assignment. As García Riera noted, "The name of Murphy did not figure either in the credits or in the publicity for the film, which was shown in Mexico as though it had been directed by no one."[20] Once again, for reasons that aren't entirely clear, Murphy's cinematic contribution was marginalized.[21]

Set in the late nineteenth century, the plot of *Yolanda* centers on a Russian ballerina, Yolanda Petrova (played by prima ballerina Irina Baranova of the Ballet Theatre), on tour in Mexico City.[22] She falls into an amorous triangle with a handsome young army officer, Julio (David Silva), and a powerful older politician, don Carlos (Miguel Arenas). To force Yolanda to marry him, the influential don Carlos arranges for her parents to be arrested in Russia and threatened with exile to Siberia. Though she loves Julio, Yolanda reluctantly agrees to marry don Carlos. Eventually, she discovers that her nightmare literally *is* a nightmare, a bad dream caused by a letter from home. All ends well, with Yolanda happily settling with Julio. Laced with excerpts from classical ballets, the film also features appearances by noted Mexican soprano Fanny Anitúa and the "orquesta de cien profesores" (orchestra of a hundred professors)—what García Riera referred to as "injections of culture" catering to "the tastes of the fat ladies" among the Mexican nouveau riche.[23]

Murphy may have had personal reasons for preferring Mexico City over Los Angeles at this time. According to an unidentified clipping in the

archives of the Academy of Motion Picture Arts and Sciences, Murphy
and his wife had separated in December 1942, a year after the birth of
their daughter Kit.[24] Much younger than her husband, Virginia Bellondi
Murphy was a Boston native whose hometown naïveté and sense of pro-
priety (by Hollywood standards, at least) charmed and amused him. She
in turn had been dazzled by the celebrity-studded parties at the Amalfi
Drive house, where Charlie Chaplin entertained with comic pantomimes,
or John Barrymore might be found in the garden declaiming Shakespeare
in the nude.[25] But the late 1930s and early 1940s had been a struggle for
Murphy financially, and at times he'd been forced to rent out the house
for income. In March 1943, Bellondi Murphy sued for divorce, citing cruelty. The pair eventually reconciled and ultimately remained together until
Murphy's death in 1968.[26] It's ironic, though not altogether unexpected, that
the one marriage of Murphy's that endured, lasting more than twenty-five
years, was to a Bostonian. In the early 1940s, though, the relationship was
foundering. For Murphy at that time, directing in Mexico City, whether
credited or not, may have held a certain appeal.

In its preproduction phase, *Yolanda* attracted a modest amount of interest from the Mexican press. Shortly before shooting began, the magazine
Tiempo published a lengthy article about Murphy and the film, empha-
sizing his connection to writer Budd Schulberg (son of studio executive
B. P. Schulberg), who'd recently set Hollywood abuzz with his scathing 1941
novel, *What Makes Sammy Run?* According to *Tiempo*, Schulberg was in
Mexico with Murphy, working on a screen adaptation of the Jack London
story "The Mexican" and a film about Zapata—Murphy's next productions for Reachi's company, Promesa Films.[27]

Once *Yolanda* was completed, however, Murphy returned to Los Angeles without making either film.[28] In L.A. in 1943, he crossed paths with
William Faulkner, who'd first come to Hollywood as a screenwriter in the
early 1930s. Over the years, Faulkner periodically returned for scriptwriting
stints, for which he earned enough to support his literary endeavors and
an extended family of remarkable breadth and number. Together, he and
Murphy undertook a film treatment of his 1936 novel, *Absalom! Absalom!*
They called their version *Revolt in the Earth.* By this time Murphy had all
but slipped off the Hollywood radar, but the film gave him a compelling
reason to start knocking on studio doors again. When it came to personal
projects, safe and easy had never been his style; controversial "prestige" pictures were more like it, and Faulkner's novel promised that. *Revolt in the
Earth* would have been the most complex and ambitious film of Murphy's

career. A multigenerational saga of family, southern history, and race told
in a shifting montage of voices, *Absalom! Absalom!* was innately musical
in its structure, with an unorthodox approach to language and poetically
cadenced prose. Faulkner grappled with issues of race on a level that
Murphy's African-American films had never approached. It was in every
way a project that resonated with Murphy, and he pitched the treatment
with skill and enthusiasm. There was some interest among the studios,
most seriously from Warner Bros., where Faulkner was under contract.
Nothing, however, came of it. As writer Tom Dardis commented, "1943
was not the year for Hollywood to undertake a miscegenation film."[29]

Hollywood may not have been interested in what Murphy was pitching, but Mexico still offered possibilities, if not for the Faulkner project,
then for something else. In any case, Murphy's resourcefulness was by no
means exhausted. In 1944, he succeeded in creating a place for himself
in the rapidly expanding Mexican film industry. Associated Artists, the
aborted venture with Leslie Howard, resurfaced as Artistas Asociados, a
similar enterprise launched with the head of Mexico City's Azteca Studio.
With Hollywood film production diminished by the war, the new company received generous press coverage in the States. The *New York Times*
devoted a hefty article to it, focusing on the implications for international
commerce. "Another link in the Hollywood-Mexico movie chain was
forged last week when United Artists closed a distribution deal with Artistas Asociados, S.A., newly formed Mexican producing company. Dudley
Murphy, the Hollywood director, organized the new company of which
José Calderon is president. . . . Artistas Asociados will make four films
for U.A. release next season, with Mr. Murphy, its chief producer as well
as general manager and treasurer, personally directing the first two."[30]

Murphy's first project for the company was the one collaboration with
Schulberg that did go into production. *Alma de bronce* (Soul of Bronze,
1944) was an adaptation of "The Bell of Tarchova," a short story Schulberg
had written for the *Saturday Evening Post*. In its original form, it was a tale
of heroic resistance in the face of Nazi oppression. Adapting it for Latin
American audiences, Murphy and Schulberg set the story against the French
invasion of Mexico in the 1860s. The cast was headed by top stars Gloria
Marín, Andrés Soler, and Pedro Armendáriz, a screen idol of the 1940s
often described in the North American press as the Mexican Clark Gable.
They were supported by such solid character actors as Narciso Busquets,
Emma Roldán, and Carlos Orellana.

Filled with outsized, archetypal characters and melodramatic action, the plot of *Alma de bronce* is worthy of grand opera.[31] In the small village of San Juan, the impoverished hero and heroine (Armendáriz and Marín) are in love, but a devious wealthy older man (Soler) schemes to make the heroine his wife. No sooner do the young lovers manage to wed than word comes that the French have invaded. Arriving in the village, they're quartered at the home of the rich villain. The villagers refuse to assist the French troops, and as punishment, the French commandeer the church bell, the pride of the town, intending to smelt it for cannons. Renowned for his physical strength, the hero manages to steal the bell away and hide it up in the mountains. From there, he and the other villagers defiantly ring it, confident the French cannot find it. The villain suggests that the French retaliate by kidnapping the hero's wife and infant son. They grab the heroine, but the villagers hide the baby, narrowly saving him from capture. The heroine is taken to the home of the villain, but before he can have his way with her, the hero appears. The villain shoots him, inflicting what appears to be a minor wound. It doesn't stop the hero from killing the villain with a hatchet blow. He and his wife head to the mountain hideaway, where the gunshot wound proves fatal. Surrounded by wife, son, and the precious bell, the hero dies.

Once production was completed on *Alma de bronce*, Murphy went to Los Angeles to promote the film, Artistas Asociados, and his larger plans, which extended beyond film production or even international film distribution. In an unidentified, undated interview in what appears to be a Los Angeles newspaper, he advanced another version of the alternative film production center that he'd been trying to establish for more than a decade.[32] This time, he specifically cited the low production costs at the Mexico City studios as an opportunity to try less-commercial filmmaking approaches. As usual, it wasn't only Hollywood's system for making films that Murphy questioned but the films themselves. But he was no longer the hotheaded independent, and even as he proposed an experimental alternative to the industry, he was careful not to slam any doors. "Dudley Murphy has an idea that Mexico City can become the Paris of the Americas—cinematically speaking," wrote Los Angeles film reporter Virginia Wright. Calling Artistas Asociados "a kind of laboratory for film experiments," he positioned it as "a workshop for craftsmen who want to try out new ideas but who can't afford to experiment under the costly Hollywood setup." He spoke of his next picture for the company: *Acapulco,* a musical comedy to be shot in both Spanish and English, with an American actress starring opposite Armendáriz. "Murphy's interest in Mexican production doesn't indicate any renunciation of Hollywood, however," wrote Wright. "One picture he would like to do here is 'Swing Family Robinson,' an all Negro revue he wrote with Sid Kuller, and for which Duke Ellington will write the score."[33]

But Murphy didn't make *Swing Family Robinson,* or *Acapulco* for that matter. Though a hit for Armendáriz, *Alma de bronce* was not well received by Mexican critics or movie audiences. "If [Norman] Foster managed to make films of sufficient quality to shut the mouths of certain xenophobes," wrote García Riera, "Murphy was the object of all kinds of sarcasms and criticisms."[34] One critic of the time called it "a magnificent picture for tourists, made by a tourist."[35] Writing in the Mexican publication *Cinema Reporter,* Alfonso de Icaza complained about the implausibilities of the plot, pointing out that the bronze bell that Armendáriz supposedly carried up the mountain probably weighed close to a ton. For Icaza, such incon- sistencies weren't the film's only flaws. "Decidedly, the North American elements that work in our cinema display a marked preference for a theme that we, the Mexicans, would prefer to forget: our already distant civil war that gave pretext to French intervention," he wrote. "Here, in *Alma de bronce,* as is becoming customary, the 'liberal' is a young man who is gen- teel, friendly, honest and noble, while the 'conservative' is an avaricious old man, hypocritical and perverse. An admirable system of constructing history!"[36]

Though Hollywood watched Murphy's venture with guarded interest, the Mexican film industry had little need for his American-style filmmak- ing. With the United States enmeshed in World War II, American films no longer overwhelmed the Mexican market, and local studios made the most of the opportunity. The 1940s are widely regarded as a golden age of Mexican cinema, in which a generation of talented directors, including Julio Bracho, "El Indio" Emilio Fernández, and Roberto Gavaldón (who served as Murphy's assistant director on *Yolanda*), made dozens of power- ful films that spoke directly to Mexican audiences and to Latin America as a whole.

Murphy himself may have arranged the screening of *Alma de bronce* that took place in Los Angeles in 1945; there's no indication that the film was released nationally in the States. A review in the *Los Angeles Times* makes two things clear: despite everything, Murphy was still a hometown favor- ite; and regardless of its dual-audience, Mexican-and-American concept, the film was a solidly north-of-the-border affair. "Probably adapted from an old tradition," the review read, "'Alma De Bronce' (liberally translated

as 'Soul of the Bell'), while a Mexican patriotic saga, is nevertheless so
bedecked with romance, joyous fiestas, beautiful church ceremonials and
other pleasant embellishments, that it is not the deadly serious picture
it might otherwise have been. . . . Dudley Murphy directed for Artistas
Asociadas and he has done a fine job."[37] But Mexico, not Hollywood,
was where the money—or at least the production studio—was. With its
single completed film doing poorly at the Mexican box office and apparently never released nationally in the United States, Artistas Asociados met
the same fate as Associated Artists. No further directing assignments
awaited Murphy in Mexico, and in 1945 he returned home.

A Shack on the Beach

Murphy found no directing jobs in Los Angeles either and was unable to
drum up interest in independent projects. *Alma de bronce* was the last picture he made. At the age of forty-seven, he was out of the film business.
    On April 16, 1945, around the time that Murphy returned from Mex-
ico, Hermann Dudley Murphy—"Big Man"—died. He'd lived to the age
of seventy-seven and had survived his second wife by almost four years.
Murphy and his sister, Carlene, inherited the bulk of their father's estate.
    Through most of his adult life in Los Angeles, Murphy had turned to
Malibu as a cheap place to live in lean times. Empty and undeveloped, for
decades it was considered little more than a summer getaway. It virtually
closed down in the winter, making off-season rents especially low. Since
the 1920s, Murphy had often retreated to Malibu when finances were dire.
He was living there with Ginny and their daughter when Hermann died.
According to family lore, one of the Murphys' summer neighbors at Malibu
was Donald Douglas, a fellow aviator, MIT graduate, and founder of the
Douglas Aircraft Corporation (which eventually merged into McDonnell
Douglas). He urged Murphy to invest his inheritance in Malibu land,
which at the time was going for next to nothing. Murphy took the advice.
He bought a swath of acreage overlooking the beach and continued to
increase his holdings over the years. Griswold Raetze, a designer who'd
worked with Charles and Ray Eames, drew up plans for a cottage tailored
to Murphy's specifications: minimal maintenance, easy indoor-outdoor
living, and expansive ocean views. The house was built in early 1946, with
Murphy acting as his own contractor and carpenter. According to one
article, he even gathered, hauled, and laid the flagstone for the patio.[38] A

feature in the June 1948 issue of *House and Garden* showed off the sunny living room, with its floor-to-ceiling, ocean-facing picture windows, and pointed out details ranging from the built-in patio barbecue to a convenient outside entrance to one of the bathrooms.

With their sleek, magazine-ready beach house, the Murphys were early exemplars of California living, the informal lifestyle that breezed through the American social landscape in the years after World War II. The emphasis on clean lines, uncluttered interiors, and natural materials was not unlike the Arts and Crafts aesthetic that Murphy had grown up with at Carrig-Rohane, but the casual elegance, minimal maintenance, and delight in outdoor living were pure Southern California. The late 1940s saw studio couches and buffet-style dinners sweep away ornate furnishings and formal entertaining in many American homes, as decks, patios, and barbecue grills took over the nation's backyards. Murphy had always had an eye for design (the decor of his 1930s bachelor-pad penthouse had been described as "futuristic"),[39] but Malibu vaulted him into a new lifestyle vanguard. He'd originally gone there for an inexpensive shack on the beach, where he could write, stare at the ocean, and contemplate what came next. Now it seemed the next career move was Malibu itself.

Murphy envisioned a resort hotel on the water. The idea was to support his family and a writer's lifestyle with a small, casual business hosting friends and old colleagues eager for a few days' oceanside getaway. To design it, he hired architect Richard Neutra. Active in Southern California since the 1920s, Neutra had already done several important projects, including an internationally acclaimed house for Josef von Sternberg in the mid-1930s.[40] Given Murphy's and Sternberg's overlapping social circles and shared interest in art, Murphy may have visited Sternberg's house and other homes that Neutra built for the film-industry elite. In the early days, they might have run into each other at Jake Zeitlin's bookstore or the home of Murphy's friend Paul Jordan Smith.

Holiday House was one of the first small, motel-style resorts to be designed by a major modernist architect, and its clean, almost stark lines influenced generations of motels that followed. The distinctive spider-leg outrigging that Neutra developed for the building became a stylistic signature on several of his residential projects of the 1950s. Scholarly surveys of his career almost invariably include Holiday House; at the time, it was showcased in several architecture journals and was one of three Neutra projects in 1948 to win citations from the American Institute of Architects.[41] Again, Murphy did the general contracting on the project as well as part of the construction. "Careful and pleasant relationship between various elements and materials gives this building unique distinction," pronounced the *New York Times* in 1950.[42]

From the start, Holiday House was a hit with the film crowd, who delighted in the mix of pampered luxury, exclusivity, beachside informality, and seclusion. Murphy's understanding of film people, his cosmopolitan tastes, and easy sociability created an appealing atmosphere. Ginny Bellondi Murphy proved a vivacious and well-organized cohost, and the couple's two daughters, Kit and Erin, offered an appealing touch of family life.[43] Murphy found other ways of fitting into the burgeoning beachfront community as well; in an echo of his early sailing canoe trips with Hermann, he piloted his sailing dinghy, *Kit Wit,* to victory in the 1948–49 autumn and winter races at the Malibu Yacht Club.[44]

Holiday House quickly became an industry haven. Movie stars and studio executives relished the opportunity to relax with fellow insiders in script sessions, romantic trysts, and drunken benders, along with the occasional suicide attempt. A feature in the July 1949 issue of *Architectural Forum* gave an indication of the establishment's appeal. "In this small, swankily furnished resort," it read, "the owner, a film director, caters successfully to Hollywood notables and provides 'quickie' vacations, complete with swimming, cabanas, barbecues, *prix fixe* dinners, Continental breakfasts and built-in bars. Holiday House, 35 minutes from Beverly Hills, is a resort that is satisfied to keep its vacation guests no more than a week or two, and depends upon overnight transients for half its occupancy."[45]

By the early 1950s, Murphy had built the Holiday House restaurant into an equally thriving concern: an exclusive spot where guests dined on Continental specialties prepared by a Parisian chef while admiring the vista from open-air terraces. It quickly became a celebrity watering hole in its own right, attracting the likes of Frank Sinatra and Ava Gardner, Marilyn Monroe, and other stars. Murphy was back in the gossip columns, this time as jovial host to other celebrities' minor scandals and imbroglios. Patricia Neal and Gary Cooper went public as a couple dining at Holiday House in 1951. Ten years later, Louella Parsons reported a gleeful Liz Taylor and Eddie Fisher calling from their getaway there. In the early 1960s, the television series *Aquanauts* (later known as *Malibu Run*) regularly shot location scenes at Holiday House. By then, Murphy's resort had acquired the patina of L.A. legend, even as his own filmmaking career faded into obscurity. In his role as restauranteur, he made a cameo appearance in William Saroyan's 1961 short story, "Take Her to Vegas"—a vivid walk-on with a barely fictional air. "The fact is, he had run into Fred at Dudley Murphy's Holiday House only three nights ago," Saroyan wrote. "Dudley himself had introduced them, saying, 'Writer, meet Movies.' Later Dudley introduced them to Aircraft, Real Estate, Fish and Money. Everybody got a little acquainted, and after about an hour, Van drove down the road six miles to his shack."[46]

During the later years of his self-imposed Hollywood exile, which lasted from 1940 to 1951, Man Ray was a regular at Holiday House. In *Self Portrait,* he blithely dismissed the career of his erstwhile collaborator. "Dudley took [*Ballet mécanique*] back to Hollywood and got some work on big films as a result, made some money, and opened a charming restaurant and motel on the Pacific coast, which I myself frequented during my *séjour* in Hollywood in the Forties," Man Ray wrote. "He was a charming and generous host, but never referred to the movies again."[47] This is probably true. With Holiday House awash in industry insiders, Man Ray was hardly the person with whom Murphy would have chatted about movies; Man Ray was a renowned and influential artist, but he'd made his last film in 1929. Murphy was still immersed in the film industry and had never fully abandoned his dream of directing again. In 1948, he was reportedly planning an independent production adapted from a Craig Rice crime story, "Murder-Go-Round"; a year later, he'd packaged it as *Innocent Bystander* "for production at a major studio."[48] In 1950, he was "readying a series of TV vehicles on experiences of [his] guests. . . . Tentative title is 'Holiday House.'"[49] The following year, he was trying once again to produce *Acapulco* (with Fernando Lamas in the lead) and shopping *Innocent Bystander* as a television show.[50] According to an item in a Mexico City newspaper, he was pitching the Faulkner project to at least one major Mexican studio as late as 1960.[51]

Another *Ballet mécanique* associate took Murphy's filmmaking more seriously than Man Ray did. In the early 1950s, composer George Antheil proposed to Virgil Thomson the idea of making a series of musically inspired films. "The producer I had in mind for the shorts is Dudley Murphy," he wrote to Thomson. "I personally like Dudley. He has changed very little since 1924, is the one legitimate producer in Hollywood who, with very few exceptions, has not been slowly and inevitably corrupted by commercialism; and has heard of, if not actually heard—say, for instance, Boulez. Yet he knows the field, here, utterly. . . . He is anxious to make a comeback, and show everybody what. Nothing could be too wild for his taste." Antheil knew of Murphy's Hollywood reputation but was untroubled by it. "If you inquire about him you will find that a great many people 'in the industry' think he is crazy; it is true that he has been responsible for several atrocities. But, on the other hand, he commands respect in many other quarters here. . . . With proper artistic supervision, I would say that he is our man."[52] The project never materialized, but Murphy and Antheil remained on cordial terms. According to Murphy, they discussed collaborating on a sound version of *Ballet mécanique,* incorporating an adaptation of Antheil's score, before the composer's death in 1959.[53]

As the 1950s progressed, Murphy turned his attention to real estate. His various transactions included the 1955 purchase, with Cornelius Vanderbilt Whitney, of the celebrated Garden of Allah apartments on Sunset Boulevard. In the late 1950s, he added at least one structure to the Holiday House complex: a three-story apartment building on the beach, connected to the rest of the development by a funicular railway. But the demands of running the enterprise began to tell on him. He was in his sixties, and his health started to fail. In early 1965, a local newspaper reported that "two young 'good life' pioneers" had taken over the three-quarter-million-dollar option on Holiday House.[54] As a film director, Murphy had gone to Malibu seeking refuge in tough times; as a hotelier and restauranteur, he ended up a comparatively wealthy man. Increasingly debilitated by arthritis and a lung ailment, he died three years later, in February 1968.[55]

Murphy's film career was no triumphant upward climb. It wasn't even a gracefully arched parabola. It was as sputtering and disjointed on the way up as it was on the way down, producing films that were at times exhilarating, at times ghastly, and sometimes maddeningly both. Even so, his relationship to Hollywood was as evocative and densely textured as any enjoyed by his more successful colleagues. It was, in all respects, a relationship shaped by absence and implication. In the films he made—and, more significantly, in the films he didn't make, the production companies that failed, and the schemes that never caught on—one can discern, in negative contour, the outlines of the film industry as it grew and solidified. At the same time, Murphy's vision of cinema—inclusive, improvisational, and intrinsically musical—stands in contrast to both classical Hollywood film form and the actual films that the studios produced. In his own productions and in stealthy, intermittent insertions into his studio films, Murphy offered glimpses of another direction in which film might have evolved, a cinematic road not taken. That concept of a freely visual, less narratively driven cinema is crucial to understanding his career. And while it may not be his most significant contribution to film history, it's certainly the most provocative.

Holiday House survived Murphy. With a buttressed managerial staff, Ginny Bellondi Murphy continued to run the restaurant until 1974, when she sold the property to a real estate partnership headed by talent agent Charles Stern. In 1979, the original Neutra-designed motel units were packaged as luxury condominiums, and the apartment building was demolished a few years later. The restaurant, known since the mid-1980s as Geoffrey's, continues to flourish as a casual but exclusive dining establishment, with a Continental menu reminiscent of the one served at Holiday House. Murphy's eye for location and his flair for setting a scene were superb. If, as some contend, Los Angeles is the geographic and psychological edge of America, the Pacific coast is the golden edge of Los Angeles. And on that stretch of stunning, costly shoreline, even today there's no more convivial spot for sipping a glass of wine, gazing out over the ocean, and watching the sun go down.

ACKNOWLEDGMENTS

Working on this book has brought many unexpected pleasures. Principal among them was discovering the network of family and friends that Dudley Murphy left behind, as well as a small but gratifyingly obsessed band of scholars who added their research, knowledge, and in some cases their voices to the telling of his story.

Chief among the contributors are Dudley Murphy's children: the late Michael Murphy, Poco Murphy, and Erin Murphy O'Hara. All three were warmly supportive of this project from its inception. They unstintingly shared their recollections about their father and family and generously opened their personal archives to me. I'm especially indebted to Erin Murphy O'Hara for sharing the manuscript of her father's unpublished memoir, which has been crucial to this work; and to Poco Murphy and her son Sebastian Li for numerous family letters, documents, and photographs. I'm also grateful to Murphy's nephew, the late Dudley Samoiloff, who contributed personal recollections as well as papers left by his maternal great-grandfather, John Bowles. Jerry Herendeen Moderwell, a nephew of Murphy's first wife, Chase Herendeen, generously shared family documents, photographs, and memories.

Among scholars, the late William Moritz looms large over this project. At the time I began my research, Bill was, to my knowledge, the only one to have examined Murphy's career in any depth. He welcomed my inquiries and offered carte-blanche access to his files when I was in Los Angeles. Our correspondence was minimal—he was teaching at Cal Arts and battling cancer at that time—but every so often a videocassette would turn up in the mail, yet another obscure Murphy film he had found somewhere. In many ways, his writing and research provided the starting point for this book, and I am indebted and deeply grateful to him. My thanks as well to Cindy Keefer of the Center for Visual Music for facilitating access to Bill's files.

Much has been written about *Ballet mécanique,* and undoubtedly more will be. The chapter in this book was shaped to a great extent by lively conversation, vociferous opinion, and contentious debate (otherwise known as "dialogue") with independent curator Bruce Posner, who is researching the film and its variant prints. Bruce is another individual who graciously shared his research and knowledge, and when it comes to *Ballet mécanique* I regard him as a true coconspirator, above and beyond our differences. I also appreciate his introducing me to other toilers in the *Ballet mécanique* vineyard, including music scholar Mauro Piccinini of Trieste, Italy, who is writing a biography of composer George Antheil. In addition to providing information and myriad clarifications about Antheil and his music, Mauro directed me to correspondence that was crucial in gaining a fuller picture of *Ballet mécanique.* I am very grateful.

Thanks to David James of the University of Southern California, who shared an early partial draft of his essay on Murphy's film *Soul of the Cypress.* I enjoyed discussing the film in some detail with him. Eric Schaeffer of Emerson College and independent curator David Shepard helped to clarify potentially confusing points regarding the Library of Congress prints of *Soul of the Cypress.*

This book was researched at many institutions; at all of them, capable staff members made the process far easier and more enjoyable than it could have been, almost to the point of prolonging it past its natural lifespan. New York University's Bobst Library was home base, and much is owed to Pamela Bloom and the other research librarians there. At the Library of Congress, special thanks to Zoran Sinobad and Rosemary C. Hanes of the Motion Picture, Broadcasting, and Recorded Sound Division, and to Kenneth Weissman, Jennie Saxena, and James Cozart of the Motion Picture Conservation Center. A tip of the hat to Monica Mosely of the New York Public Library for the Performing Arts, who brought William C. deMille's personal correspondence to my attention, and to Ned Comstock of the University of Southern California for his timely assistance. Thanks, as always, to Robert Haller and Anthology Film Archives. Long may they wave.

Other institutions where this book was researched include the Beinecke Rare Book and Manuscript Library at Yale University; the Irving S. Gilmore Music Library at Yale University; the Margaret Herrick Library at the

Academy of Motion Picture Arts and Sciences, Los Angeles; the Film Study Center at the Museum of Modern Art; the New York Public Library Schomburg Center for Research in Black Culture; the New York Public Library—Humanities and Social Sciences; the UCLA Film Archive; the University of Southern California Cinema and Television Library; and the University of Virginia Library at Charlottesville. My thanks to all these institutions and their staffs. Thanks as well to the institutions that generously supplied images, including Anthology Film Archives, the Getty Research Institute, the Library of Congress, and the Santa Barbara Museum of Art.

The path from initial research to finished book is riddled with potential pitfalls. If this project has escaped them, credit is due several people. Chief among them is Douglas Armato, my editor at the University of Minnesota Press, with whom I have greatly enjoyed collaborating. I am deeply grateful to Daniell Cornell and to Beth Kracklauer—friends, colleagues, and exceptionally attentive readers—whose manifold insights have greatly enriched the manuscript. Thanks as well to Michele Wallace, who brought Murphy into focus for me in a fresh context, and to William Boddy, who offered thoughtful assessments and encouragement in the project's early stages, even as it wore out its welcome. Peter Agree was immensely helpful in getting the ball rolling, and I'm grateful to Ellen Chandler for pointing me in his direction. Thanks to Missy Sullivan for spot-brainstorming where it was needed most.

Nadine Covert provided invaluable assistance in readying the manuscript for publication, as did Amy Capuano with the images. Kudos to the staff of Cameron Graphics, Inc., who worked magic with several precious but aged photographs. Many hands at the University of Minnesota Press sped the book on its way from copyediting to design and production, and their consummate professionalism is deeply appreciated. Countless other individuals contributed in small but significant ways. My thanks to them all.

When a project takes years to complete, it's virtually impossible to quantify the support that is offered, day in and day out, by that member of the household who is *not* writing a book (or at least not at the time). Authors generally claim that the work would not have been possible without the loving support of a spouse or partner, and generally it's true. It certainly is in my case. Without the humor, intelligence, companionship, and loving support of my husband, Jeffrey Ehrlich, it's unlikely that Murphy's saga would have seen the light of day in book form. When it comes to Jeff, whatever gratitude I have expressed thus far should be moved many, many decimal places to the right. And then some.

NOTES

INTRODUCTION: AT THE EDGE OF THE FRAME

1. Dudley Murphy, "Murphy by Murphy," memoir, 1966, 22–23, Murphy Family Collection.

1. ROOTED IN ART

1. Murphy, "Murphy by Murphy," 1.

2. Ibid., 1.

3. Trevor J. Fairbrother, *The Bostonians: Painters of an Elegant Age, 1870–1930* (Boston: Museum of Fine Arts, Boston, 1986), 67.

4. During the early 1900s, when Maurice Prendergast wasn't in Europe, he lived with his brother, Charles, in Winchester. Until Maurice's art started selling, the frame-making business was the main source of income for them both. Patterson Sims, *Whitney Museum of American Art: Selected Works from the Permanent Collection* (New York: Whitney Museum of American Art in association with W. W. Norton, 1985), 242.

5. Reviewing a 1999 exhibition of frames at the Addison Gallery of American Art in Andover, MA, the *Boston Globe* wrote of Carrig-Rohane: "The firm's signature is carving that is sumptuous but also worn-looking, as if from great age, and obviously done by the human hand rather than a machine." Christine Temin, "Frames of Reference: Addison Show Treats Frames with the Respect Given Art," *Boston Globe,* February 11, 1999, sec. D, 1.

6. Decades later, Hermann's frame designs continued to set the standard in framing American impressionist works. See Suzanne Smeaton, "American Picture Frames of the Arts and Crafts Period, 1870–1920," *Magazine Antiques* 136 (November 1989): 1124–37.

7. Murphy, "Murphy by Murphy," 1.

8. Ibid., 2.

9. Kevin Starr, "Los Angeles 1900–1930: The Great Gatsby of American Cities," in Sarah Vure, *Circles of Influence: Impressionism to Modernism in Southern California Art 1910–1930* (Newport Beach, CA: Orange County Museum of Art, 2000), 13.

10. From the tables "Population Growth in Selected Cities, 1890–1930" and "Nonwhite Population as a Percentage of Total Population, Selected Cities, 1890–1930," in Robert M. Fogelson, *The Fragmented Metropolis: Los Angeles, 1850–1930,* Classics in Urban History (Berkeley: University of California Press, 1993), 78, 82.

11. From the table "Negro Population and Nativity of Foreign Born in Los Angeles, 1890–1930," ibid., 76.

12. Carey McWilliams, *Southern California Country: An Island on the Land,* American Folkways Series (New York: Duell, Sloan and Pearce, 1946), 324.

13. Perley Poore Sheehan, *Hollywood as a World Center* (Hollywood: Hollywood Citizen Press, 1924), 35 and 41.

14. Kevin Starr, *Material Dreams: Southern California through the 1920s* (New York: Oxford University Press, 1990), 133. Starr quotes Willard Huntington Wright, who left the *Los Angeles Times,* where he was literary editor, to become editor of *The Smart Set.*

15. See Vure, *Circles of Influence,* 31–37. Carmel's history as an artistic outpost for Los Angeles dates back at least to 1903, when a group of real estate developers established Carmel-by-the-Sea as an artists' colony. See Derrick R. Cartwright, "Appendix: A Chronology of Institutions, Events, and Individuals," in *On the Edge of America: California Modernist Art 1900–1950,* ed. Paul J. Karlstrom (Berkeley: University of California Press in association with the Archives of American Art, Smithsonian Institution, and the Fine Arts Museums of San Francisco, 1996), 273–87.

16. It still does, as the organization's quarterly newsletter attests.

17. Cited in Vure, *Circles of Influence,* 27.

18. In an August 9, 1920, letter to Murphy, for instance, Caroline noted that she and Carlene were spending the evening with the Sinclairs. Murphy Family Collection.

19. Murphy, "Murphy by Murphy," 4.

20. Ibid., 5.

21. Letter from Hermann Dudley Murphy to Dudley Murphy, June 18, 1918, Murphy Family Collection. Potatoes were a staple crop in the region, but Murphy landed in a field of wet grass, which allowed the seaplane's pontoons to skid on the slick surface. Had it been a potato field, he would have crashed. See Murphy, "Murphy by Murphy," 8.

22. Ibid., 15.

23. Despite the rapid growth of Southern California during World War I, trolley car patronage fell between 1914 and 1918. By contrast, between 1914 and 1919, automobile registration quadrupled to sixty thousand in Los Angeles proper and doubled in Los Angeles County to more than one hundred thousand. See Fogelson, *The Fragmented Metropolis,* 167–70.

24. Kevin Brownlow, *The Parade's Gone By . . .* (Berkeley: University of California Press, 1968), 34.

25. Kevin Starr, "Carey McWilliams's California: The Light and the Dark," in *Reading California: Art, Image, and Identity, 1900–2000,* ed. Stephanie Barron, Sheri

Bernstein, and Ilene Susan Fort (Berkeley: Los Angeles County Museum of Art and University of California Press, 2000), 18.

26. In addition to overseeing the construction of several Los Angeles residences designed by his father, Lloyd Wright designed his own projects, including the Oasis Hotel in Palm Springs, the second shell at the Hollywood Bowl, and a number of private residences. A member of Jake Zeitlin's literary circle, Lloyd Wright designed the interiors for Zeitlin's first two bookstores, including the original Sign of the Grasshopper. See Starr, *Material Dreams,* 222–25.

27. McWilliams, *Southern California Country,* 376.

28. See Bruce T. Torrence, *Hollywood: The First Hundred Years* (New York: New York Zoetrope, 1982), 87–89. According to Torrence, from 1910 to 1920, Hollywood's population exploded by some 720 percent, virtually all of it newcomers trying to break into the film industry.

29. Kevin Starr has noted that during this period, the editor of *Touring Topics* was "the resident spokesman and arbiter of establishment Southern California, for in Southern California the automobile and its club stood as the very center of organizational life." Starr, *Material Dreams,* 314.

30. Murphy, "Murphy by Murphy," 19.

31. After Goldwyn merged into MGM in 1924, Gibbons set the standard for screen glamour as art director for hundreds of productions, including *Greed* (1924), *Grand Hotel* (1932), *Dinner at Eight* (1933), and *The Philadelphia Story* (1940)—work that, over the course of his career, earned him ten Oscars. He served as art director on *The Night Is Young,* which Murphy directed for MGM in 1935.

32. St. Clair went on to direct such hits as *The Grand Duchess and the Waiter* (1926) and *Gentlemen Prefer Blondes* (1928). He continued to direct into the 1940s.

33. Murphy, "Murphy by Murphy," 20.

34. See Ilene Susan Fort, "Altered State(s): California, Art and the Inner World," in *Reading California,* ed. Barron, Bernstein, and Fort, 31–49.

35. Presented in the 1901 Theosophical publication, *Thought Forms;* cited in Fort, "Altered State(s)," 38. See also William Moritz, "The Dream of Color Music, and Machines That Made It Possible," *Animation World* 2, no. 1 (April 1997): 1–5.

36. Caroline Bowles, undated handwritten notes, Murphy Family Collection.

37. Letter from Caroline Bowles to Dudley Murphy, dated June 17, 1918, Murphy Family Collection. That day, Bowles had gone to Krotona with Carlene, who appeared there in a pageant presented by Ruth St. Denis.

38. Murphy's memoir incorrectly identifies Chase's last name as Harringdine.

39. Murphy, "Murphy by Murphy," 22, 23, 24.

40. Ibid., 24.

41. Herendeen's birth certificate appears to have been altered from 1901 to 1904, possibly later in life. Family documents refer to her as being eighteen at the time of the marriage.

42. According to Murphy's daughter Erin, Chase's mother, Ada Herendeen Dudley, extracted a promise from the couple that they would not consummate the marriage for a year. Were they both ready for a sexual relationship, it's unlikely that such a promise would have deterred them. Correspondence with author, August 8, 2005.

43. Murphy, "Murphy by Murphy," 22.

44. Ibid., 19.

2. GREEK GODDESSES FOR THE MOVIEGOING PUBLIC

1. Hermann Dudley Murphy mentioned the company by name in a February 24, 1920, letter to Murphy, who had evidently sent him a prospectus. Murphy Family Collection.

2. William Moritz, "Americans in Paris: Man Ray and Dudley Murphy," in *Lovers of Cinema: The First American Film Avant-Garde 1919–1945,* ed. Jan-Christopher Horak, Wisconsin Studies in Film (Madison: University of Wisconsin Press, 1995), 121.

3. Horak, "Introduction," *Lovers of Cinema,* 4, 6. This definition of avant-garde cinema dates the existence of an American avant-garde to the 1910s or earlier, as opposed to the 1940s.

4. Brian Taves, "Robert Florey and the Hollywood Avant-Garde," in *Lovers of Cinema,* ed. Horak, 94. Taves is referring primarily to Florey (1900–1979), who made several short avant-garde films while advancing within the film industry. As a young director, Florey caught Hollywood's eye with the experimental short film *The Life and Death of 9413—a Hollywood Extra* (1928), made with special-effects artist Slavko Vorkapich, who also went on to enjoy a lengthy career in the industry. Florey codirected the Marx Brothers in *The Cocoanuts* (1929) and made such films as *God Is My Co-pilot* (1945) and *The Beast with Five Fingers* (1946). In later years he was a successful television director; his credits include episodes of *The Untouchables, The Twilight Zone, The Outer Limits,* and other series.

5. Murphy, "Murphy by Murphy," 31.

6. "At Broadway Theaters," *Wid's Daily,* July 29, 1921, 4.

7. Experiments in visual-musical equivalents were not limited to film. See Judith Zilczer, "Music for the Eyes: Abstract Painting and Light Art," in *Visual Music: Synesthesia in Art and Music since 1900,* ed. Kerry Brougher et al. (New York: Thames and Hudson, 2005); also Moritz, "The Dream of Color Music, and Machines That Made It Possible," 1–5.

8. Murphy, "Murphy by Murphy," 25.

9. Brigman was the first (and by some counts, the only) California member of Alfred Stieglitz's prestigious Photo-Secession group. In 1909, 1912, and 1913, her images were published as photogravures in Stieglitz's quarterly, *Camera Work.* A mock-religious photograph entitled *Anne of the Crooked Halo* (1917–23) depicts Brigman as a figure of adoration surrounded by a bevy of worshipful young photographers, including Edward Weston, Dorothea Lange, and Imogen Cunningham (who avowedly detested Brigman's work). See Susan Ehrens, *A Poetic Vision: The Photographs of Anne Brigman* (Santa Barbara, CA: Santa Barbara Museum of Art, 1995). See also David James, "*Soul of the Cypress:* The First Postmodernist Film?" *Film Quarterly* 56, no. 3 (Spring 2003): 25–31; James discusses Brigman's photography specifically in the context of Murphy's work.

10. See Richard Koszarski, *An Evening's Entertainment: The Age of the Silent Feature Picture, 1915–1928,* vol. 3 of *History of the American Cinema* (New York: Charles

Scribner's Sons, 1990), 127–30. For the 2001 film series Unseen Cinema: Early American Avant-Garde Cinema 1893–1941, curator Bruce Posner struck a new print of *Soul of the Cypress* from Library of Congress materials, reconstructing Murphy's original tinting from notes taken by the library's film technicians before the original, badly deteriorated print was destroyed. Telephone conversation with the author, August 2, 2001. A DVD version of the Unseen Cinema series was released in October 2005.

11. The 180-degree rule is a constant of classical film form. To maintain consistency in the cinematic construction of space, within each scene the camera remains positioned along, and never crosses, a 180-degree axis.

12. Letter to the author from Jerry Herendeen Moderwell, October 24, 2003.

13. Murphy, "Murphy by Murphy," 25.

14. Ibid., 26.

15. Ibid., 26.

16. Ibid., 26. It's possible that Herendeen did appear nude in the film. While Hollywood wrestled with issues of censorship and self-censorship throughout the 1920s, the Production Code, with its stringent rules regarding sexuality on-screen, wasn't put into place until 1930 and not rigorously enforced until 1934. On the other hand, the film was shown (at a private screening) in 1920 in Boston, which at the time was still aggressively banning material found offensive to public morals.

17. "The Fine Arts: Art in the Movies," *Boston Transcript,* August 30, 1920, Murphy Family Collection.

18. Lesser went on to a lengthy producing career, becoming involved with Sergei Eisenstein's *Thunder over Mexico* project, producing critical successes such as *Our Town* (1940), and turning out a string of lucrative Tarzan pictures in the 1940s and 1950s.

19. Murphy, "Murphy by Murphy," 26.

20. *Boston Evening Transcript,* August 30, 1920.

21. Sidney Woodward, "Colored Films Shown by Dudley Murphy," *Boston Post,* September 2, 1920, 13.

22. Agreement between Community Motion Picture Bureau and Dudley Murphy, October 11, 1920, Murphy Family Collection.

23. Murphy, "Murphy by Murphy," 27.

24. "In the Courts," *Wid's Daily,* July 2, 1921, 2.

25. "In the Courts," *Wid's Daily,* December 21, 1921, 2.

26. See letters from Hermann Dudley Murphy to Dudley Murphy, January 11, 1922, February 6, 1922, and August 30, 1922; and letter from Dudley Murphy to Hermann Dudley Murphy, February 10, 1922; Murphy Family Collection.

27. Letter from Hermann Dudley Murphy to Dudley Murphy, dated "May 17, Sunday eve," Murphy Family Collection.

28. Undated letter from Dudley Murphy to Hermann Dudley Murphy, Murphy Family Collection.

29. "On Broadway," *Wid's Daily,* July 11, 1921, 2.

30. "The Screen," *New York Times,* July 11, 1921, 9.

31. "Screen: The Year in Pictures," *New York Times,* January 1, 1922, sec. 6, 2.

32. "Newspaper Opinions," *Wid's Daily,* July 12, 1921, 4.

33. "Some Short Reels," *Wid's Daily,* July 24, 1921, 18. At the time, the film industry classified films by the number of standard-sized reels they filled. Each reel ran

approximately ten minutes, depending on projection speed. For industry purposes, films were known as one-reelers, two-reelers, and so on. See Koszarski, *An Evening's Entertainment*, 48.

34. Murphy, "Murphy by Murphy," 25.

35. "Murphy Working on Camera," *Wid's Daily,* August 6, 1921, 3.

36. In a letter to Murphy dated June 23, 1921, Hermann noted that he was "writing to Mr. Ames regarding [the position], and hope you will hear from him soon." He also mentioned Ames and "the Dartmouth job" in letters of June 29, 1921, and July 1, 1921. Correspondence indicates that Murphy had begun work with Ames by late July and was back in New York by late September 1921.

37. See Moritz, "Americans in Paris," 122. For more on Ames and his work, see Hermann M. Burian, M.D., "The History of the Dartmouth Eye Institute," *Archives of Ophthalmology* 40 (August 1948).

38. According to David Shepard, George T. Post was a White Russian émigré who never learned much English. He collected silent films to entertain his friends in San Francisco's Russian-speaking community, who had trouble following the dialogue in American sound films. E-mail message to author, February 5, 2003.

39. No safety or screening prints were made from the Blackhawk nitrate print.

40. Shepard is convinced that Post never would have inserted the pornographic footage himself and must have acquired his prints in their reedited form. E-mail message to author, February 5, 2003.

41. I am indebted to David James for the concise description of the pornographic footage in his essay, "*Soul of the Cypress:* The First Postmodernist Film?" which he generously shared in early draft form.

42. E-mail message to author, March 8, 2002. Schaefer notes that one Educational Pictures short from the 1930s had some nudist camp footage spliced in, probably without the studio's consent; it was shown on the exploitation circuit.

43. Telephone conversation with the author, August 2, 2001.

44. Eric Schaefer, "*Bold! Daring! Shocking! True!" A History of Exploitation Films, 1919–1959* (Durham, NC: Duke University Press, 1999), 8.

45. James, "*Soul of the Cypress:* The First Postmodernist Film?" 30.

46. "Show Synchronized Film," *Wid's Daily,* July 11, 1921, 1.

47. "Murphy and Macgowan Making One Reel 'Visual Symphonies,'" *Motion Picture News,* January 21, 1922, 606.

48. "Films from Music," *Wid's Daily,* December 23, 1921, 2.

49. Murphy, "Murphy by Murphy," 27.

50. See "Offers Film to Supplant Prologue," *Exhibitors Herald,* January 28, 1922, 46; and *Motion Picture News,* January 21, 1922.

51. "Murphy and Macgowan Making One Reel 'Visual Symphonies,'" 606.

52. Murphy's sister studied with Bolm in New York around this time and may have been the catalyst for the collaboration. See obituary for Carlene Bowles Samoiloff, *Boston Globe,* November 9, 1985, 14.

53. In *Der müde Tod,* a pair of young lovers arrives at a small German town, where a mysterious stranger (Death) takes the young man into his walled estate. The young woman pleads for his return; instead, Death shows her three exotic tales with the same moral: it's impossible to reclaim a doomed life. At the end, the woman accepts her

own death, and the lovers are reunited in the hereafter. See Patrick McGilligan, *Fritz Lang: The Nature of the Beast* (New York: St. Martin's Press, 1997), 70–73.

54. Bruguière went on to make at least two well-regarded experimental films: *The Way* (1923) and *Light Rhythms* (1929–31), done in collaboration with Oswell Blakeston. In 1915, he had collaborated with Anne W. Brigman in mounting an exhibition of Pictorial photography for the Panama-Pacific International Exposition in San Francisco. See Moritz, "Americans in Paris"; and Ehrens, *A Poetic Vision.*

55. Moritz, "Americans in Paris," 124. The animation is credited to F. A. A. Dahme.

56. Also known as Olin Howlin. A durable Hollywood character actor, he appeared in such films as *Zander the Great* (1925), *Brother Rat* (1938), *The Paleface* (1948), and *The Blob* (1958).

57. The Society of Motion Picture Engineers estimated that in 1920, some 80 to 90 percent of all films included at least some tinted sequences. By 1921, Eastman Kodak had begun supplying pretinted stock for release prints, eliminating the cost of treating each print individually. See Koszarski, *An Evening's Entertainment,* 127.

58. *New York Herald,* July 23, 1922, sec. 2, 7; "Motion Picture Theatres," *New York Evening Post,* July 22, 1922, 8.

59. "Screen: Film Circulation," *New York Times,* August 6, 1922.

60. For Horak, the film's use of animation and its multiple-exposure treatment of Death were enough to place it in experimental territory. Moritz conceded that insofar as it records a staged dance performance, "it may be hard to see the film as extremely avant-garde," but averred that "*Danse Macabre* must be seen as an unusual, adventurous 'art film.'" See Jan-Christopher Horak, "The First American Film Avant-Garde, 1919–1945," in *Lovers of Cinema,* ed. Horak, 43; and Moritz, "Americans in Paris," 125.

61. "'Visual Symphonies' Find Recognition: New Short Subjects Replace Prologues," *Moving Picture World,* January 28, 1922, 387.

62. *Motion Picture News,* January 21, 1922, 606.

63. Murphy, "Murphy by Murphy," 28.

64. Undated letter from Dudley Murphy to Hermann Dudley Murphy, probably written in early February 1922, Murphy Family Collection.

65. Ibid.

66. Nothing further is known about this production. Powers (1869–1948) had been producing films since 1909 and was noted for introducing silent film stars Mary Miles Minter and Pearl White to the screen. In 1912, Powers Picture Plays was incorporated into Carl Laemmle's Universal Pictures. Powers continued to produce films, primarily Westerns, and was the first to distribute Walt Disney's animations. See Gene Fernett, *American Film Studios: An Historical Encyclopedia* (Jefferson, NC: McFarland and Company, 1988), 171–74. According to Moritz, at the time Powers hired Murphy, Powers would have been running the Film Booking Office.

67. Murphy, "Murphy by Murphy," 28–29.

68. Ibid., 29.

69. Ibid., 29–30. In the early 1930s, Herendeen found a measure of show-business success under the name Chase Herendon, becoming, as the *New York Daily Mirror* described her, "one of Broadway's most charming showgirls." She married several times and had one son; according to her nephew, she died in a Vermont rest home in the 1980s at the age of eighty-two. See "'Pol' Peabody to Wed Actor," *New York Daily*

Mirror, September 2, 1935; also letter to author from Jerry Herendeen Moderwell, October 24, 2003.

70. Letter from Hermann Dudley Murphy to Dudley Murphy, May 10, 1921, Murphy Family Collection.

71. Letter from Hermann Dudley Murphy to Dudley Murphy, June 23, 1921, Murphy Family Collection.

72. See Moritz, "The Dream of Color Music"; also Zilczer, "Music for the Eyes," 70–82.

73. Wilfred later denied any relationship between lumia and music: "The two arts are so different in nature that attempts to design lumia instruments in imitation of musical ones will prove as futile as attempts to write lumia compositions by following the conventional rules laid down for music." Thomas Wilfred, "Composing in the Art of Lumia," *Journal of Aesthetics and Art Criticism* 7, no. 2 (December 1948): 90; cited in Zilczer, "Music for the Eyes," 76.

74. Stark Young, "The Color Organ," *Theatre Arts Magazine* 6 (January 1922): 30–31. See also Zilczer, "Music for the Eyes," 76.

75. Murphy, "Murphy by Murphy," 30.

76. A version of a clavilux performance was re-created for the exhibition Visual Music, shown at the Museum of Contemporary Art in Los Angeles and the Hirshhorn Museum and Sculpture Garden, Smithsonian Institution, in 2005. In Washington, the clavilux performances were shown on flat screens, not as three-dimensional projections, leading one critic to compare them to "lava lamps and Hubble space photos before the fact." Michael Kimmelman, "With Music for the Eye and Colors for the Ear," *New York Times,* July 1, 2005, sec. E, 33.

77. Bruguière's response to the clavilux was similar to Murphy's. According to Moritz, Bruguière was "so impressed . . . that he began planning to make moving pictures that would extend his own photography into the realm of time." The immediate result was *The Way* (1923), which Moritz described as an "unfinished 'surrealistic' film." Moritz, "Americans in Paris," 118.

78. Murphy, "Murphy by Murphy," 31.

79. Marquand (1893–1960) went on to win a 1938 Pulitzer Prize for his novel *The Late George Apley.*

80. Hitchcock (1900–1944) was a world-class polo player who achieved a ten-goal rating, the highest possible, every year from 1922 to 1940. As an aviator, he served in the Army Air Corps in both World War I and World War II. He was killed in the crash of a test plane in 1944.

81. Murphy, "Murphy by Murphy," 31–32.

82. "Picture Plays and People," *New York Times,* July 30, 1922, 81.

83. *Bioscope,* May 19, 1927, 43.

84. Murphy, "Murphy by Murphy," 32.

85. Ibid., 32.

86. "Independents and Exhibitors Need Agreement, and Quickly," *Variety,* December 13, 1923, 18.

87. The 1927 review in the British trade publication *Bioscope* indicates that the film was offered for theatrical distribution there. See note 83.

88. Murphy, "Murphy by Murphy," 33.

89. Ibid., 33.

90. In discussing the disastrous shift to the gold mark standard a year later, *Variety* noted, "It was the worst thing that could have happened to Germany that she could make films so much cheaper than the rest of the world that even though she made them inefficiently, they could still be sold for a fourth of what the same film cost to make in any other country. This naturally led to carelessness in the handling of money and many incompetent directors have gotten positions which they never could have obtained under normal conditions." "German-Made Cheap Films Have Seen Their Last Day," *Variety,* September 20, 1923, 2.

91. Blanke made a successful transition to Hollywood, eventually producing such films as *Jezebel* (1938), *The Maltese Falcon* (1941), and *The Treasure of Sierra Madre* (1947).

92. Murphy, "Murphy by Murphy," 43–44. Fersen was known in Capri, Murphy wrote, "as the man who had been expelled from Paris and who had himself married by a Catholic priest to a handsome young man." His exploits were immortalized in Roger Peyrefitte's 1959 novel, *The Exile of Capri.*

93. Murphy, "Murphy by Murphy," 39.

94. Ibid., 44. According to a newspaper notice of their 1931 divorce, the couple married on December 5, 1923. "Seeking Reno Divorces," *New York Times,* July 26, 1931, 23.

95. Murphy, "Murphy by Murphy," 34.

96. Ibid., 45.

3. VEXED AND DISPUTED: THE MULTIPLE HISTORIES OF *BALLET MÉCANIQUE*

1. Léger did design work on Marcel L'Herbier's *L'inhumaine* (1924) and developed ideas for additional films of his own, but none of them was produced. He contributed a scenario to Hans Richter's *Dreams That Money Can Buy* (1947), as did Man Ray.

2. This description is based on the print of *Ballet mécanique* held by Anthology Film Archives, also known as the Kiesler print. At least three other distinct versions of the film are known to exist.

3. Richard Watts, Jr., "Apprehensive Glances at the Mechanization of the Screen," *New York Herald Tribune,* March 28, 1926, sec. 5, 3.

4. William J. Reilly, "When Is It a Moving Picture? Dudley Murphy Helps to Answer the Question," *Moving Picture World,* May 15, 1926.

5. An English translation of the notes, under the title "Film by Fernand Léger and Dudley Murphy Musical Synchronism by George Antheil," was published in the *Little Review,* Autumn 1924–Winter 1925, 42–44. It was published in the original French in *L'Esprit Nouveau* 28, undated (most likely November or December 1924).

6. In *The Cubist Cinema,* for instance, Standish Lawder draws many of Léger's comments about *Ballet mécanique* from the artist's 1954 interview with Dora Vallier, "La vie dans l'oeuvre de Léger," published in *Cahiers d'art* 2. See Standish D. Lawder, *The Cubist Cinema* (New York: New York University Press, 1975).

7. See Moritz, "Americans in Paris."

8. By the time he started work on *Ballet mécanique,* Antheil had fallen out with Stravinsky, who apparently thought the brash young American had exploited and exaggerated their relationship. Antheil in turn decried Stravinsky's "cramped Slavic modes" and "neoclassicism" and resented his success. See undated letter from George Antheil to Ezra Pound, written from 12 rue de l'Odéon, Paris, and others in the Ezra Pound Papers, Yale Collection of American Literature, Beinecke Rare Book and Manuscript Library, Yale University; see also Linda Whitesitt, *The Life and Music of George Antheil 1900–1959,* Studies in Musicology no. 70 (Ann Arbor, MI: UMI Research Press, 1981).

9. Murphy, "Murphy by Murphy," 41.

10. Ibid., 41–42.

11. Man Ray later described Murphy's equipment as "an old Pathé camera on its tripod, the kind used in the comic shorts of the day." Man Ray, *Self Portrait,* reprint (1963, Boston: Little, Brown and Company, 1988), 218.

12. The agreement, if it existed, was likely verbal. Léger apparently made no written mention of it.

13. Murphy, "Murphy by Murphy," 41.

14. Léger observed some of the filming on *La roue,* wrote about it, and designed a poster for it, but did not himself work on the film. See Judi Freeman, "Bridging Purism and Surrealism: The Origins and Production of Fernand Léger's *Ballet mécanique,*" in *Dada and Surrealist Film,* ed. Rudolf E. Kuenzli (New York: Willis Locker and Owens, 1987), 29.

15. Fernand Léger, quoted in Lawder, *The Cubist Cinema,* 89.

16. Léger, 1924 notes on *Ballet mécanique,* as translated and quoted in Lawder, *The Cubist Cinema,* 131.

17. "Film by Fernand Léger," 43. Despite its precision, the structure that Léger outlines in these notes does not match any known version of the edited film. See Lawder, *The Cubist Cinema,* 131; and Posner, conversation with author, July 10, 2005.

18. See Lawder, *The Cubist Cinema,* 130 and 256 n. 65. See also Freeman, "Bridging Purism and Surrealism," 32. In unpublished, undated errata deleted from "Americans in Paris," William Moritz noted that "Henri Langlois complained that Léger to his dying day still never mastered the simplest elements of film technology." Dudley Murphy files, Moritz Collection, at the Center for Visual Music, Los Angeles.

19. Lawder, *The Cubist Cinema,* 123. In his written text, Léger notes only that the screen is divided into equal parts. However, the accompanying sketch of the screen shows nine squares.

20. Judi Freeman, "Léger Reexamined," book review, *Art History* 7, no. 3 (September 1984): 352.

21. Murphy apparently described the film in these terms in a letter to his father. See Freeman, "Bridging Purism and Surrealism," 32 and 43 n. 12.

22. During World War I, the ranks of the 369th Infantry Regiment, the highly decorated "Harlem Hellfighters," were filled with African-American jazz musicians, recruited by the head of its military band, orchestra leader James Reese Europe. Songwriter and orchestra leader Noble Sissle had been the regimental drum major, and the band's members included drummer Buddy Gilmore, trumpeter Arthur Briggs, and dancer Bill "Bojangles" Robinson, who strutted at the head of its marching unit. Sent

on a lengthy goodwill tour of French towns and villages in 1918, the band met with a wildly enthusiastic response. France's comparative acceptance of African Americans and its embrace of jazz encouraged several musicians to remain there after the war and others, dismayed at the conditions at home, to quickly return. See Tyler Stovall, *Paris Noir: African Americans in the City of Light* (Boston: Houghton Mifflin Company, 1996).

23. Kristen Erickson, "Chronology," in Carolyn Lanchner, *Fernand Léger* (New York: Museum of Modern Art, 1998), 269; also William A. Shack, *Harlem in Montmartre: A Paris Jazz Story between the Great Wars* (Berkeley: University of California Press, 2001), 34.

24. Murphy, "Murphy by Murphy," 42–43.

25. David E. Shi, "Transatlantic Visions: The Impact of the American Cinema upon the French Avant-Garde, 1918–1924," *Journal of Popular Culture* 14, no. 4 (Spring 1981): 589–90. Vaché, a close friend of Breton's, died of a drug overdose in 1919. See Matthew Josephson, *Life among the Surrealists* (New York: Holt, Rinehart and Winston, 1962), 118.

26. Cited in Josephson, *Life among the Surrealists,* 123–24.

27. Though the *Coeur à barbe* program credits *Fumées de New-York* to Sheeler only, the film was made by Sheeler and Paul Strand. According to music scholar Mauro Piccinini, who is writing a biography of George Antheil, though the composer was on the bill he did not attend, being on vacation in Tunis at the time. E-mail correspondence with author, August 5, 2005.

28. Deke Dusinberre, "*Le retour à la raison:* Hidden Meanings," in *Unseen Cinema: Early American Avant-Garde Film 1893–1941,* ed. Bruce Posner (New York: Anthology Film Archives, 2001), 67.

29. See Josephson, *Life among the Surrealists,* 151–52; also Herbert R. Lottman, *Man Ray's Montparnasse* (New York: Harry N. Abrams, 2001), 93–94.

30. "Comments," by jh, *Little Review* 9, no. 3 (Spring 1923): 28–29.

31. Ibid., 27.

32. Unidentified newspaper clipping, presumably from a British film industry newspaper, with photo spread headlined "D. M. Pictures Present Novel Featurets," Murphy Family Collection. See also "A 'Featuret,'" *Daily Mirror,* London, July 28, 1923, 1.

33. Man Ray, *Self Portrait,* 218.

34. Lawder, *The Cubist Cinema,* 117.

35. See Moritz, "Americans in Paris," 126.

36. Lottman, *Man Ray's Montparnasse,* 126.

37. Moritz, "Americans in Paris," 126.

38. "Le *Ballet mécanique* connut incontestablement plusieurs phases de tournage, dont une première entre Murphy et Man Ray et une seconde entre Murphy et Léger." Jean-Michel Bouhours, "D'images mobiles en *ballets mécaniques,*" in *Fernand Léger* (Paris: Éditions Centre Pompidou, 1997), 161. All translations from the French are by Nadine Covert, unless otherwise noted.

39. See Freeman, "Bridging Purism and Surrealism," 43 n. 15; and Freeman, "Léger Reexamined," 353.

40. Man Ray, cited by Moritz, "Americans in Paris," 127. According to Julie Martin, coeditor of *Kiki's Memoirs,* this is essentially accurate. Though she had previously

modeled for several artists, once Kiki became involved with Man Ray she modeled for others only occasionally through 1928, and then only for personal friends. E-mail to author, March 13, 2005.

41. Murphy, "Murphy by Murphy," 45.

42. See Kiki [Alice Prin], *Kiki's Memoirs,* ed. Billy Klüver and Julie Martin (Hope-well, NJ: Ecco Press, 1996), 160. The art dealer Julien Levy apparently attempted a film with Kiki in the late 1920s, an adaptation of T. S. Eliot's *The Wasteland,* but did not get very far. Julien Levy, *Memoir of an Art Gallery* (New York: G. P. Putnam's Sons, 1977), 97.

43. See Moritz, "Americans in Paris," 126.

44. Murphy, "Murphy by Murphy," 42.

45. See Moritz, "Americans in Paris," 135 n. 28.

46. William Moritz, letter to Eric de Kuyper, deputy director of the Nederlands Filmmuseum, February 1988, 3, Dudley Murphy files, Moritz Collection at the Center for Visual Music, Los Angeles. The letter was later translated and published in the Dutch film journal *Versus* 2 (1988): 132–40.

47. Freeman, "Bridging Purism and Surrealism," 43 n. 10.

48. See Klüver and Martin, *Kiki's Paris,* 111.

49. Klüver and Martin, foreword to *Kiki's Memoirs,* 32. They noted that while the images were "more aesthetic than pornographic, they didn't pass the French censors in 1929 and are still too revealing to be printed in this edition of her *Memoirs.*"

50. Bruce Posner, telephone conversation with author, April 3, 2004. The version in question is in the collection of the Nederlands Filmmuseum in Amsterdam.

51. Moritz, "Americans in Paris," 129. Under the auspices of the Deutsches Filmmuseum, Moritz examined the existing prints of *Ballet mécanique,* then restored and reedited a 16mm version to conform more closely to his conception of the original cut. The Moritz version reorders key sequences and includes a brief glimpse of Kiki, shot from above and naked from the waist up, and subliminal erotic flashes—little more than blurred movement—intercut into the piston sequence. Carrying a release date of 1995, the Moritz restoration is currently distributed by Light Cone, a Paris film distribution company.

52. Freeman, "Bridging Purism and Surrealism," 43 n. 10.

53. Letter from Ezra Pound to his father, n.d., Ezra Pound Papers, Beinecke Rare Book and Manuscript Library, Yale University.

54. In the letter, Pound writes that "Leger's ballet negre opens Thursday." This is likely a reference to *La création du monde,* also known as *Ballet nègre.* Based on traditional African myths, it was produced by les Ballets suédois and premiered in Paris on October 25, 1923; the letter was presumably written a few days earlier. See Erickson, "Chronology," 268; and Freeman, "Léger Reexamined," 352.

In "Bridging Purism and Surrealism," Freeman cited an additional letter from Pound to his parents, dated September 12, 1923, from the Ezra Pound Papers, Beinecke Rare Book and Manuscript Library, Yale University. Freeman quoted the letter as mentioning a "Léger *projet*" that Pound and Antheil were working on at the time. As of April 2005, no letter from Pound to his parents bearing that date was on file at the Beinecke. According to Piccinini, it's unlikely that Antheil began working on the *Ballet mécanique* score before January 1924; in September 1923, he was writing two piano and violin sonatas commissioned by Pound for his mistress, violinist Olga Rudge. E-mail correspondence with author, August 5, 2005.

55. Letter from Dudley Murphy to Carlene Murphy, November 16, 1923, cited in Freeman, "Bridging Purism and Surrealism," 33. Freeman cites the letter as being sent to "Carlene Murphy Samoiloff." According to an obituary appearing in the *Boston Globe,* Carlene did not marry until 1928. See "Carlene Bowles Samoiloff, 85; Dancer, Active in Theater Arts," *Boston Globe,* November 9, 1985 (third edition), 14.

56. Letter from Dudley Murphy to Hermann Dudley Murphy, November 19, 1923, cited in Freeman, "Bridging Purism and Surrealism," 43 n. 13.

57. Letter from Ezra Pound to his father, dated January 29, 1924, Ezra Pound Papers, Beinecke Rare Book and Manuscript Library, Yale University.

58. See Noel Stock, *The Life of Ezra Pound,* expanded ed. (San Francisco: North Point Press, 1982), 255.

59. Léger, "Film by Fernand Léger," 43.

60. Man Ray, *Self Portrait,* 218. Cinematic lenses are made for specific camera models, so it's unlikely that the lenses used in *Ballet mécanique* were brought by Murphy from the United States. They were more likely purchased by him in Paris, either with the movie camera or sometime later.

61. Murphy credits Pound only with bringing him together with Léger and Antheil. See Murphy, "Murphy by Murphy," 41.

62. See Ezra Pound, "Paris Letter," *Dial* 74, March 1923.

63. Man Ray, *Self Portrait,* 150.

64. See George Antheil, *Bad Boy of Music* (Garden City, NY: Doubleday, Doran and Company, 1945), 137. See also letter from Ezra Pound to his father, November 22, 1923; and letter from George Antheil to Ezra Pound, n.d. [late 1925–26?], from 12 rue de l'Odéon, Paris; Ezra Pound Papers, Beinecke Rare Book and Manuscript Library, Yale University. Piccinini states that contrary to what Pound wrote, not all of Antheil's "Mechanisms" had been converted to player-piano rolls; at that point, only number 1, subtitled "Serpent mécanique," had been done. E-mail to author, August 5, 2005.

65. Antheil, *Bad Boy of Music,* 134–35.

66. See Freeman, "Léger Reexamined," 358 n. 35. According to Piccinini, neither Antheil nor Léger was fluent in the other's language, making it difficult to collaborate directly. Correspondence between them was conducted through Antheil's wife, Böski Markus Antheil, who did speak French. E-mail to author, April 13, 2005.

67. Paul D. Lehrman, "Music for *Ballet mécanique:* 90s Technology Realizes a 20s Vision," in *Unseen Cinema,* ed. Posner, 70–71. Lehrman states that the score called for two grand pianos and sixteen player pianos, but Piccinini questions this, suggesting that the extravagant number of player pianos was probably a jest on Antheil's part. E-mail from Mauro Piccinini to author, April 13, 2005.

68. "Antheil's Symphony Gets Mixed Reception," *New York Times,* June 20, 1926, 26. The American premiere of Antheil's "Ballet mécanique," presented at Carnegie Hall in 1927, was an unmitigated disaster from which his career never fully recovered. See Whitesitt, *The Life and Music of George Antheil,* 31–41. According to Freeman, the *Times'* account, which cites four player piano rolls for "Ballet mécanique," is incorrect; there were only three rolls. See Freeman, "Bridging Purism and Surrealism," 44 n. 23.

69. Freeman, "Bridging Purism and Surrealism," 34.

70. Ibid., 34.

71. See Fernand Léger, "The Esthetics of the Machine: Manufactured Objects Artisan and Artist," *Little Review* 9, no. 3 (Spring and Summer 1923): 44–49; and 9, no. 4 (Autumn and Winter 1923–24): 55–58.

72. Bowles was buried, as Caroline Bowles Murphy, in a family plot near Boston. Her father, Col. John Bowles, Murphy, and Murphy's sister, Carlene, are also interred in the plot, along with Carlene's husband and two more distant relatives. Murphy's father, Hermann, lies elsewhere.

73. "Indeed, there are several issues of authorship that have yet to be clarified in Léger scholarship. Questions of whose hands contributed to which painting are particularly relevant to Léger's large canvases." Judi Freeman, "Surveying Fernand Léger in Paris," exhibition review, *Apollo* 146 (October 1997): 42.

74. Freeman, "Léger Reexamined," 353.

75. See Christopher Green, *Léger and the Avant-Garde* (New Haven, CT: Yale University Press, 1976), 281. Erickson's "Chronology" states only that the film was completed by July (see 269). If editing on the film did continue beyond the completion of Léger's notes about the film, it would suggest an additional reason for Lawder's difficulty in reconciling Léger's structure for the film, as set forth in the notes, with the film itself. See Lawder, *The Cubist Cinema,* 131.

76. Léger pursued a film of Charlot Cubiste, a modified version of the animation he described to Epstein, for fifteen years. In 1935, he finally requested permission from Charlie Chaplin to use his "Little Tramp" character, known in France as "Charlot," in the film. Chaplin refused. See Erickson, "Chronology," 274.

77. Freeman, "Léger Reexamined," 353.

78. Ibid., 352.

79. Soundies were three-minute, 16mm films made to be played in coin-operated machines that resembled movie jukeboxes. See chapter 10.

80. For the *Neues 8 Uhr-Blatt* reference, see *A Tribute to Anthology Film Archives' Avant-Garde Film Preservation Program, an Evening Dedicated to Frederick Kiesler* (New York: Museum of Modern Art, 1977), fn. 4, excerpts from dissertation by Roger L. Held, "Endless Innovations: The Theories and Scenic Design of Frederick Kiesler."

81. In a letter to Hawley Murphy, written from France on Armistice Day, Murphy made reference to working on Ingram's film in its early stages. Murphy Family Collection.

82. Program booklet, International Theatre Exposition, 34, Kiesler Collection, Harvard Theatre Collection, Nathan Marsh Pusey Library, Harvard University.

83. "Projection Jottings," *New York Times,* March 14, 1926, sec. 8, 5.

84. Mordaunt Hall, "The Screen," *New York Times,* March 15, 1926, 18.

85. "Sub-titles," *New York Evening Post,* March 18, 1926, 12.

86. Richard Watts, Jr., "Apprehensive Glances at the Mechanization of the Screen," *New York Herald Tribune,* March 28, 1926, sec. 5, 3.

87. "November, 1975, Films Salvaged: Lillian Kiesler Finds Ballet Mecanique by Leger and Exelsior-Reifen by Ruttmann Stored in Her Home," *A Tribute to Anthology Film Archives.*

88. See Lawder, *The Cubist Cinema,* 185.

89. Murphy, "Murphy by Murphy," 48.

90. Symon Gould, "Round the Town," *New York Telegram,* June 8, 1926, 8.

91. Ibid. From this reference, it may be surmised that at least one screening was accompanied by an orchestra rather than a solo jazz drummer.

92. E-mail message to author, February 26, 2005.

93. See Lawder, *The Cubist Cinema,* 185.

94. In a letter to George Antheil, dated September 2, 1934, and written from London, Léger wrote that "Kisler [*sic*] et Dudley Murphy ont une copie du film—" (Kiesler and Murphy have a copy of the film). George Antheil Papers, Butler Library, Columbia University.

95. Program notes, London Film Society screening, March 14, 1926, British Film Institute National Film and Television Archives, London.

96. Helen Klumph, "'Black Pirate' Wins Plaudits," *Los Angeles Times,* March 14, 1926, 27. Now obscure, Santell was a well-regarded director at the time. Available credits for the film are slim, and Murphy's is not included. See entry for *The Dancer of Paris* in the AFI Catalog.

97. Reilly, "When Is It a Moving Picture?"

98. Klumph, "'Black Pirate' Wins Plaudits," 27. Interestingly, Klumph's article is datelined March 13, the day before *Ballet mécanique* premiered at the International Theatre Exposition and several days before it was first shown at the Cameo.

99. See Tony Guzman, "The Little Theatre Movement: The Institutionalization of the European Art Film in America," *Film History* 17, no. 2–3 (2005): 261–84.

100. Tamar Lane, "The Photoplay League Program," *Film Mercury* 4, no. 7 (July 16, 1926): 16.

101. Edwin Schallert, "League Show Offers Novelty," *Los Angeles Times,* July 14, 1926, sec. A, 9.

102. Murphy, "Murphy by Murphy," 48.

103. "Distribution Arranged," *Los Angeles Times,* May 6, 1928, sec. C, 12.

104. Taves, "Robert Florey and the Hollywood Avant-Garde," in *Lovers of Cinema,* ed. Horak, 99.

105. Levy was Murphy's assistant on the 1927 Gloria Swanson film, *The Love of Sunya,* for which Murphy created the special effects. Levy may have seen *Ballet mécanique* in one of its New York screenings or learned of it from Murphy when they worked together.

106. Levy, *Memoir of an Art Gallery,* 95–96.

107. See Erickson, "Chronology," 272.

108. See Glenn Myrent and Georges P. Langlois, *Henry Langlois, First Citizen of Cinema* (New York: Twayne, 1995), 34; also Mary Lea Bandy, "New York Friends Look at Documentary Film," in *Filming Robert Flaherty's "Louisiana Story": The Helen van Dongen Diary,* ed. Eva Orbanz (New York: Museum of Modern Art in collaboration with the Stiftung Deutsche Kinematek, Berlin, 1998), 13.

109. In 1935, Léger gave a lecture at MoMA in conjunction with an exhibition on his art; he would have brought the print with him then. See Eileen Bowser, program notes to accompany public screenings of *Ballet mécanique* at the Museum of Modern Art on December 3–4, 1979. Moritz, who studied this print in detail in 1977, noted

that one four-foot-long section included approximately fifty changes of color. See Moritz, letter to Eric de Kuyper, 8.

110. Moritz, letter to Eric de Kuyper, 2–3, 5–6.

111. In "Americans in Paris," 133, Moritz attributed the titling to Léger; in the de Kuyper letter, he attributed it to the Cinémathèque française: "When I spoke about [these titles] to Henri Langlois in the 1960s, he apologized and said he was particularly embarassed about them since he knew very well that Murphy played a major role in the creation, both artistic and practical, of the film. But, he sighed, we all know how important nationalism is to the 'fonctionnaires,' the civil servants who control budgets." Moritz, letter to Eric de Kuyper, 3.

112. Moritz, letter to Eric de Kuyper, 3.

113. According to Bruce Posner, different versions of the film and variant prints are located in the collections of the Nederlands Filmmuseum; Anthology Film Archives; the Museum of Modern Art, which holds two Synchro-Ciné-released prints (16mm hand-colored and 35mm black-and-white); the Cinémathèque française, which also holds two Synchro-Ciné-released prints; and the Musée Fernand Léger in Biot, France, which holds Léger's personal print at the time of his death. Telephone conversation with the author, April 3, 2004.

114. Freeman, "Bridging Purism and Surrealism," 38. According to James Cozart, quality assurance specialist at the Library of Congress Motion Picture Conservation Center, prints made for projection purposes in the 1920s often bore incidental splices, to insert tinted sequences, for instance, or to join together short reels. Frame-by-frame cutting of projection prints, however, was not common. Telephone conversation with the author, January 14, 2003. Moritz speculated that the Kiesler version might have been a work print, created expressly for editing purposes, rather than a projection print. Moritz, letter to Eric de Kuyper, 7.

115. Moritz, "Americans in Paris," 128. Moritz suggested that the idea of tinted and hand-colored footage probably originated with Murphy, who used them to dramatic effect in *Danse Macabre, Soul of the Cypress,* and other films. In a discussion of his inspection of the extant variant prints, he also concluded that "Léger himself hand-tinted at least two important [later] prints." Moritz, letter to Eric de Kuyper, 9. According to Posner, the two prints to which Moritz refers are the Nederlands Filmmuseum print, acquired in 1931, and the 16mm MoMA print. Conversation with the author, April 3, 2004.

116. Moritz, "Americans in Paris," 135 n. 28. Moritz states only that Murphy's print "burned in a nitrate fire," giving no further details. In a conversation a few months before his death, Murphy's son, Michael, denied that the print had been destroyed but did not know its whereabouts. Telephone conversation with the author, autumn 2004. According to Erin Murphy O'Hara, a house fire in 1982 probably destroyed whatever print or prints Michael himself might have held. E-mail to the author, September 15, 2005.

117. Moritz, "Americans in Paris," 129–30.

118. "Léger fut prolixe en anecdotes et détails pratiques sur le tournage, se faisant passer non sans complaisance pour un modeste mais zélé accessoiriste." Bouhours, "D'images mobiles en *ballets mécaniques*," 161.

119. In his lectures, Léger often presented *Ballet mécanique* with *Entr'acte,* the

René Clair film that premiered in late 1924, a few months after *Ballet mécanique*. See Erickson, "Chronology," 272–85.

120. Letter from George Antheil to Virgil Thomson, dated January 1, 1951, Virgil Thomson Papers, Irving S. Gilmore Music Library, Yale University. I am grateful to Mauro Piccinini for bringing the Antheil-Thomson correspondence to my attention.

121. Letter from George Antheil to Virgil Thomson, dated January 29, 1951, Virgil Thomson Papers, Irving S. Gilmore Music Library, Yale University.

122. Man Ray, *Self Portrait*, 218.

123. Freeman, "Bridging Purism and Surrealism," 28.

4. INTO THE MAINSTREAM

1. Liam O'Leary, *Rex Ingram: Master of the Silent Cinema*, new ed. (Pordenone, Italy: Le Giornate del Cinema Muto and the British Film Institute, 1993), 159.

2. Murphy, "Murphy by Murphy," 49.

3. Ibid., 49.

4. Letter from Dudley Murphy to Katharine Hawley Murphy, November 11 [1924], written on letterhead from the Carlton Hotel, Champs-Elysées, Paris, Murphy Family Collection.

5. Telephone conversation with the author, March 5, 2005.

6. "Credits on Ingram films are skimpy and vague. . . . We know for instance that Jean de Limur, Max de Vaucorbeil and many others worked on *Mare Nostrum* without a credit." O'Leary, *Rex Ingram*, 155–57. Lachman remained with Ingram for two more films, then moved on to a directing career in Hollywood.

7. See ibid., 129.

8. *Variety*, February 17, 1926, 40.

9. Murphy, "Murphy by Murphy," 51–52.

10. Bruce Kellner, *Carl Van Vechten and the Irrelevant Decades* (Norman: University of Oklahoma Press, 1968).

11. "Might-Have-Been Film Bears Inspiring Title," *New York Times*, June 6, 1926, sec. X, 2.

12. The French film about children may have been an English-language version of Jacques Feyder's *Visages d'enfants* (*Faces of Children*, 1925), which the International Film Arts Guild premiered at the Cameo on June 29, 1926. The program also included the American premiere of René Clair's 1924 film, *Paris qui dort*, known in the United States as *The Crazy Ray*. See Guzman, "The Little Theatre Movement."

13. Letter from Dudley Murphy to Hermann Dudley Murphy, June 11, 1926, Murphy Family Collection.

14. Letter from Dudley Murphy to Hermann Dudley Murphy, September 15, 1926, Murphy Family Collection.

15. Gloria Swanson, *Swanson on Swanson* (New York: Random House, 1980), 286.

16. See Levy, *Memoir of an Art Gallery*, 97.

17. Swanson, *Swanson on Swanson*, 286.

18. Norbert Lusk, "Roxy Theater Is Magnificent," *Los Angeles Times*, March 20, 1927, sec. C, 21.

19. Swanson, *Swanson on Swanson,* 401.

20. Matthew Josephson, "The Rise of the Little Cinema," *Motion Picture Classic* 24, no. 1 (September 1926); reprinted in George C. Pratt, *Spellbound in Darkness: A History of the Silent Film* (Greenwich, CT: New York Graphic Society, 1966), 486.

21. Murphy, "Murphy by Murphy," 53.

22. Ibid., 54.

23. Ayn Rand, "The Skyscraper," *Journals of Ayn Rand,* ed. David Harriman (New York: Penguin Putnam, 1997), 6.

24. With the closing of DeMille's studio in 1928, several members of the *Sky-scraper* team became contract regulars with Pathé, where they worked together on a number of films in the late 1920s. Director Howard Higgin, writer Tay Garnett, and title writer John Krafft teamed up with Boyd and Hale in the 1928 featurette *Power,* in which the two stars played characters resembling their *Skyscraper* roles. In 1929, Higgin, scenarist Elliott Clawson, and Boyd reunited for *High Voltage,* an early talkie about a busload of travelers marooned in a High Sierras snowstorm. Directed by Garnett, *The Flying Fool* (1929) starred Boyd in another early talkie with story by Clawson and script by Garnett and James Gleason. It's possible that Murphy was involved in staging the aerial scenes in these last two films, but he is not mentioned in the credits.

25. *Variety,* April 11, 1928, 12.

26. Mordaunt Hall, "The Screen," *New York Times,* April 7, 1928, 20.

27. Rand, "The Skyscraper," 6 and 15.

28. Emile Coué (1857–1926) was the author of the popular 1922 book *Self Mastery through Conscious Autosuggestion* and an influential advocate of the "power of positive thinking."

29. Murphy, "Murphy by Murphy," 55.

30. Letter from Dudley Murphy to Katharine Hawley Murphy (addressed to Katharine Hawley, Century Theatre), November 30, 1927, Murphy Family Collection.

31. See, for example, Myra Nye, "Society of Cinemaland" column, *Los Angeles Times,* January 16, 1927, sec. C, 30.

32. *Variety,* March 21, 1928, 22.

33. "The Screen," *New York Times,* May 1, 1928, 33.

34. "The Screen," *New York Times,* October 23, 1928, 33.

35. "This Is Good Show, It Seems, Except Mr. Green," *Chicago Daily Tribune,* September 10, 1928, 35.

5. THE BEGINNING OF THE AUDIBLE PERIOD

1. Mordaunt Hall, "Vitaphone Stirs as Talking Movie," *New York Times,* August 7, 1926, 6.

2. "First $3 Picture Show on Broadway; 'Don Juan' and Vitaphone Coupled," *Variety,* August 11, 1926, 5.

3. "Warner Bros. Stock Soars to 32 on 'Estimated Profits' Ahead," *Variety,* August 11, 1926, 9.

4. Donald Crafton, *The Talkies: American Cinema's Transition to Sound, 1926–1931,*

vol. 4 of *History of the American Cinema* (Berkeley: University of California Press, 1997), 82.

5. Scott Eyman, *The Speed of Sound: Hollywood and the Talkie Revolution, 1926–1930* (New York: Simon and Schuster, 1997), 145.

6. Crafton, *The Talkies,* 117.

7. *Variety,* July 11, 1928, 13.

8. See "Vitaphone Shorts," in *The Dawn of Sound,* ed. Mary Lea Bandy, American Moviemakers Series (New York: Museum of Modern Art, 1989), 44–48.

9. William C. deMille, *Hollywood Saga* (New York: E. P. Dutton and Company, 1939), 277. Apparently William C. deMille, his daughter Agnes de Mille, and brother Cecil B. DeMille all spelled their surname slightly differently. Agnes's name also frequently appears in print as "De Mille."

10. Crafton, *The Talkies,* 253.

11. One issue of *Variety*—October 13, 1928—devoted three major articles to these developments, two of them with page-spanning headlines: "Sarnoff's Talker Views," 3; "Radio and Keith Tie-Up," 5; and "Sarnoff-Kennedy Direction of Keith's Reorganization May Mean Many Changes," 29.

12. Crafton, *The Talkies,* 141.

13. Murphy, "Murphy by Murphy," 60.

14. Ibid., 60. A version of Connelly's script, as it was presented at the Dutch Treat Club, includes a second scene in which the traveler—who lives at 125th Street and normally takes the subway home—takes the train instead and is treated with absurd courtesy by the conductor and porter. See Marc Connelly, *The Traveler,* a Play in Two Scenes, the Marc Connelly Collection, Boston University Special Collections.

15. Connelly made at least one more short comedy with RKO independent of Murphy: *The Magnate* (1930), in which he played the nephew of a studio mogul who inherits his uncle's film companies. It was not a success; *Variety* characterized it as "Not so funny. . . . Ending is bound to disappoint." *Variety,* April 16, 1930, 21.

16. Osbert Sitwell, quoted in David Levering Lewis, *When Harlem Was in Vogue* (New York: Alfred A. Knopf, 1981; New York: Penguin Books, 1997), 183.

17. Lawrence Langner, quoted in Bruce Kellner, *Carl Van Vechten and the Irreverent Decades* (Norman: University of Oklahoma Press, 1968), 133.

18. Kellner, *Carl Van Vechten and the Irreverent Decades,* 200.

19. "Harlem—the Black Belt," *Variety,* January 4, 1928, 28.

20. "Small's Big Review," *Inter-state Tatler,* January 13, 1928, 7.

21. Thomas Cripps, *Slow Fade to Black: The Negro in American Film, 1900–1942,* reprint (1977; New York: Oxford University Press, 1993), 205.

22. Murphy, "Murphy by Murphy," 61–62.

23. Cited in Crafton, *The Talkies,* 402.

24. Harry Alan Potamkin, "The Aframerican Cinema," in *The Compound Cinema: The Film Writings of Harry Alan Potamkin,* ed. Lewis Jacobs (New York: Teachers College Press, Columbia University, 1977), 180.

25. See Eyman, *The Speed of Sound,* 195.

26. Frank Capra, "The Cinematographer's Place in the Motion Picture Industry," in *Cinematographic Annual,* vol. 2, 1931, ed. Hal Hall (New York: Arno Press and New York Times, 1972), 13.

27. See Charles Wolfe, "On the Track of the Vitaphone Short," in *The Dawn of Sound,* ed. Bandy.

28. Murphy, "Murphy by Murphy," 62.

29. Kellner, *Carl Van Vechten and the Irreverent Decades,* 208. Van Vechten went on to profile Smith in an article on women blues singers in the March 1926 issue of *Vanity Fair.*

30. By this time, RCA had built a state-of-the-art sound studio in a converted stable near Gramercy Park at 149 E. Twenty-fourth Street. See Murphy, letter to Eugene O'Neill, June 14, 1929, Papers of Eugene O'Neill, Clifton Waller Barrett Library of American Literature, Special Collections, University of Virginia Library, Charlottesville.

31. Most of the extras in the nightclub scene were members of the Hall Johnson Choir, who sang a background accompaniment to Smith's performance. See program notes, 1971 screening, Academy of Motion Picture Arts and Sciences, Los Angeles.

32. Murphy, "Murphy by Murphy," 62.

33. Ibid., 62.

34. See Crafton, *The Talkies,* 246.

35. Another such film that comes to mind is Rouben Mamoulian's *Applause* (1929), which makes inventive use of sound editing as part of its cross-cutting, montage structure. Shot in New York at Astoria Studios in Long Island City, the film premiered in October 1929, after *St. Louis Blues* but before *Black and Tan.*

36. Cited in Lewis, *When Harlem Was in Vogue,* 183.

37. Murphy, "Murphy by Murphy," 64.

38. "Talking Shorts," *Variety,* September 4, 1929, 13.

39. "The Screen," *New York Times,* August 26, 1929, 24.

40. "For an organisation like the National Association for the Advancement of Colored People, Bessie was the antithesis of their ideal. . . . A working-class, drunken, two-fisted, bisexual genius like Bessie was an anathema to them and, on the grounds of stereotyping, they tried to have her film, *St. Louis Blues,* destroyed." George Melly, "Black Divas," *Listener* 120, no. 3077 (August 25, 1988): 5.

41. "St. Louis Blues," *Chicago Defender,* June 29, 1929, 6. A spot search of African-American newspapers published during this period and a search of a major index yielded no other press mentions. See Charlene B. Regester, *Black Entertainers in African American Newspaper Articles* (Jefferson, NC: McFarland and Company, 2002).

42. Cited in entry for Dudley Murphy, *Film Daily Yearbook,* 1930, 190.

43. *New York Herald Tribune,* September 1, 1929, sec. 8, 4; September 8, 1929, sec. 7, 4; September 15, 1929, sec. 8, 5; September 22, 1929, sec. 8, 4.

44. *Variety,* September 4, 1929, 12.

45. Murphy, "Murphy by Murphy," 62–63.

46. Ibid., 63.

47. Jonathan Rosenbaum has identified the horn player as Arthur Whetsol. See Jonathan Rosenbaum, "Short Films: *Black and Tan,*" *Monthly Film Bulletin* 43, no. 510 (July 1976): 158.

48. Murphy enjoyed working with the same actors from one project to the next. The movers in *Black and Tan* are portrayed by actors who also appear in the crap-shooting scene that opens *St. Louis Blues;* they appear again a few years later in *The Emperor Jones.*

49. Rosenbaum, "Short Films," 158.

50. Murphy quoted by Matthew Josephson in Pratt, *Spellbound in Darkness,* 486.

51. "Black and Tan," *Film Daily,* November 17, 1929.

52. "Program Layouts," *Variety,* April 9, 1930, 22.

53. "'Black and Tan' a Vivid Musical," *New York Amsterdam News,* August 13, 1930, 9.

54. Amy H. Croughton, "Some Folks Say This—and Others That—Take Your Choice," *Rochester Times,* January 2, 1930.

55. See Crafton, *The Talkies,* 412–13.

56. Ibid., 410.

57. Cripps, *Slow Fade to Black,* 204; Lewis, *When Harlem Was in Vogue,* 99; Rogosin cited in Crafton, *The Talkies,* 402.

58. Lewis, *When Harlem Was in Vogue,* 99.

59. Carl Van Vechten, "The Negro in Art: How Shall He Be Portrayed?" published in the NAACP magazine *The Crisis;* cited in Kellner, *Carl Van Vechten and the Irreverent Decades,* 208. In 1925, Van Vechten took his own advice, coming out with *Nigger Heaven,* a novel of Harlem life that, by its title alone, ignited raging controversy in the black community and severely compromised his reputation among African Americans.

60. "At the Renaissance," *New York Amsterdam News,* May 22, 1929, 12.

61. "Critics Praise, Blame New Race Film" and "Preacher Lays His Bible Down, in 'Hallelujah,'" *Afro-American,* August 31, 1929, 8.

62. "Duke Ellington Starred," *Afro-American,* August 3, 1929, 8.

63. "Short Subject to Be Reissued," *Los Angeles Times,* November 6, 1934, 11.

64. Cripps, *Slow Fade to Black,* 203, 204.

65. Donald Bogle, *Toms, Coons, Mulattoes, Mammies, and Bucks: An Interpretive History of Blacks in American Films* (New York: Viking Press, 1973), 34.

66. Cripps, *Slow Fade to Black,* 205, 206.

6. NOT MURDER BUT MAYHEM: HOLLYWOOD AGAIN

1. "Once Cameraman, Now Film Director," *New York Journal American,* September 28, 1929.

2. According to David O. Selznick, sound production continued, at least for a while, at Paramount's Hollywood studio, with crews shooting on silent-film stages at night when external sound interference was minimal. David O. Selznick, *Memo from David O. Selznick,* ed. Rudy Behlmer, Modern Library: The Movies Series, ed. Martin Scorsese (New York: Modern Library, 2000), 18. Wanger had spent several years at Famous Players Lasky (which was folded into Paramount), moving to Columbia Pictures and then to MGM before becoming an independent producer. His production credits include *Stagecoach* (1939), *Foreign Correspondent* (1940), *Scarlet Street* (1945), and *Cleopatra* (1963). See Matthew Bernstein, *Walter Wanger, Hollywood Independent* (Berkeley: University of California Press, 1994).

3. Murphy, "Murphy by Murphy," 64.

4. Ibid., 65.

5. "Woman Found Dead in Film Man's Rooms," *New York Times,* January 16, 1930, 1.

6. Murphy compiled these clippings, many of them unnotated, in a personal scrapbook, which is the source for these citations. Murphy Family Collection.

7. "Broadway Films," *Lincoln, Nebraska Journal,* January 12, 1930; and "Walter Winchell on Broadway," *New York Daily Mirror,* January 4, 1930; Murphy Family Collection.

8. Murphy, "Murphy by Murphy," 66.

9. "Woman Found Dead in Film Man's Rooms," 1.

10. Although newspapers and trade publications carried numerous small notices about the film during production, research yielded no reviews or press coverage for *He Was Her Man* after January 1930.

11. "Mrs. Adler's Death Laid to Alcoholism," *New York Times,* January 17, 1930, 8.

12. Murphy, "Murphy by Murphy," 66.

13. See "Woman Found Dead, Choked by Pearls," *Washington Post,* January 16, 1930, 2; "Sift Death of Rich Divorcee in Man's Flat," *Chicago Daily Tribune,* January 16, 1930, 3; "Woman's Death Stirs Mystery," *Los Angeles Times,* January 16, 1930, 9.

14. Murphy shared the story credit on *Jazz Heaven* with Pauline Forney.

15. "Dud Murphy's Story," *Variety,* January 23, 1929, 10.

16. A brief item in the *New York Times* stated that novelist Louis Bromfield and Dudley Murphy, "according to Universal, will collaborate on the dialogue for the screen version of 'Dracula.'" "Talking Shadows in the Making," *New York Times,* August 24, 1930, sec. X, 5. Murphy worked on the second and fifth drafts of the script.

17. Grace Kingsley, "Dudley Murphy Writes Them," *Los Angeles Times,* December 31, 1930, sec. A, 6.

18. An entry for *A Lesson in Golf* is included in the *Film Superlist.* See Walter E. Hurst, *Film Superlist: Motion Pictures in the U.S. Public Domain 1894–1939,* vol. 1, ed. D. Richard Baer (Hollywood: Hollywood Film Archive, 1994), 466.

19. Grace Kingsley, "Dudley Murphy to Direct Films," *Los Angeles Times,* February 13, 1931, 13.

20. "Foster Signed for New Role," *Los Angeles Times,* March 15, 1931.

21. Selznick, *Memo from David O. Selznick,* 17.

22. Murphy, "Murphy by Murphy," 68–69.

23. Ibid., 69.

24. See William C. deMille, "20 Years in Hollywood," lecture notes, 33–34, Agnes De Mille Collection, Jerome Robbins Dance Division, New York Public Library for the Performing Arts.

25. Cited in Eyman, *The Speed of Sound,* 378.

26. Mordaunt Hall, "The Screen," *New York Times,* June 20, 1931, 20.

27. Crosby's first major role came the following year in *The Big Broadcast of 1932,* also for Paramount.

28. Thomas Schatz, *The Genius of the System: Hollywood Filmmaking in the Studio Era,* reprint (1989; Henry Holt and Company Metro Paperbacks, 1996), 159. As diversified corporations, the integrated majors were not only film producers but also distributors and exhibitors with chains of movie theaters. The other two integrated majors were MGM and Warner Bros.

29. Murphy, "Murphy by Murphy," 69.

30. Ibid., 70.

31. Ibid., 69. Eight years later, Murphy and Sidney collaborated again on *One Third of a Nation* (1939), which Murphy adapted and directed, again for Paramount.

32. Mordaunt Hall, "The Screen," *New York Times,* October 3, 1931, 20; *Variety,* October 6, 1931, 23.

33. Murphy, "Murphy by Murphy," 70–71.

34. Ibid., 72.

35. "Seeking Reno Divorces," *New York Times,* July 26, 1931, 23. It's unclear whether Hawley Murphy filed for divorce for her own reasons or at Murphy's behest. She remarried the following year. See "Other Weddings," *New York Times,* October 5, 1932, 25.

36. Murphy, "Murphy by Murphy," 72.

37. Ibid., 72–73.

38. *New York Daily News,* December 16, 1931.

39. Murphy, "Murphy by Murphy," 73.

40. Ibid., 74. According to Murphy's daughters, Hermann Dudley Murphy either bought the house for Murphy or put money toward its purchase. Interview with Poco Murphy and Erin Murphy O'Hara, April 17, 2001. See also "Corner Site Sale Brings Large Sum," *Los Angeles Times,* April 24, 1932, sec. D, 2.

41. The reorganization at MGM was prompted in part by the illness of Irving Thalberg, which required him to take an extended leave from the studio. See Schatz, *Genius of the System,* 122–24; and Bernstein, *Walter Wanger,* 81–82.

42. Schatz, *Genius of the System,* 79.

43. See Murphy, "Murphy by Murphy," 69–70.

44. Selznick's credit on the film is executive producer, a title that he claimed to have invented while at RKO. Selznick, *Memo from David O. Selznick,* 46.

45. Richard Barrios, *Screened Out: Playing Gay in Hollywood from Edison to Stonewall* (New York: Routledge, 2003), 76–77, 78.

46. Murphy, "Murphy by Murphy," 74.

47. Ibid., 74. The quip by scriptwriter Corey Ford made it into at least one West Coast gossip column. See Tip Poff, "That Certain Party," *Los Angeles Times,* September 11, 1932, sec. B, 15. Robert Benchley was credited for additional dialogue. In what may have been a Benchley touch, the film includes a scene in which Sandy, reporting a disastrous wipe-out in a high-speed car race, says, "It looks like Murphy." See AFI Catalog entry for *The Sport Parade.*

48. Mordaunt Hall, "Mr. McCrea as a Wrestler," *New York Times,* December 17, 1932, 22.

49. See Mark Spergel, *Reinventing Reality: The Art and Life of Rouben Mamoulian* (Metuchen, NJ: Scarecrow Press, 1993).

50. Capra, "The Cinematographer's Place in the Motion Picture Industry," 14.

51. In another reflection of the times, the actor who portrays Alex is not credited in the cast list.

52. Donald Bogle, *Dorothy Dandridge* (New York: Amistad Press, 1997), 94.

53. The Production Code Administration began rigorously censoring commercial films in 1934.

54. "Tsk, Tsk, Such Goings On," *Variety,* February 28, 1933, 2.

55. Barrios, *Screened Out,* 78. In the version of *The Sport Parade* currently aired on cable television, this scene has been edited out.

7. BETWEEN PICTURES

1. From the tables "Negro Population and Nativity of Foreign Born in Los Angeles, 1890–1930," and "Nonwhite Population as a Percentage of Total Population, Selected Cities, 1890–1930," in Fogelson, *The Fragmented Metropolis,* 76 and 82.

2. Selznick, *Memo from David O. Selznick,* 27–28.

3. Murphy did not mention Eisenstein in his memoir, but art historian Laurance Hurlburt has noted that Murphy was "a close friend of S. M. Eisenstein." Laurance P. Hurlburt, *The Mexican Muralists in the United States* (Albuquerque: University of New Mexico Press, 1989), 213. According to Eisenstein's biographer, Marie Seton, however, Murphy was among the director's many Hollywood acquaintances who did *not* sign a petition in support of his reentry into the United States on his way back from Mexico in 1932; the only one who did was Josef von Sternberg. Marie Seton, *Sergei M. Eisenstein,* rev. ed. (London: Dennis Dobson, 1978), 234.

4. Eisenstein apparently met Fernand Léger in Paris sometime in 1930. Léger gave him a small painting and dedicated his essay "À propos du cinéma" to Eisenstein. Presumably Léger also screened a version of *Ballet mécanique* for him. It's likely that Murphy also screened his print of the film for Eisenstein during his time in Los Angeles. See Erickson, "Chronology," 271. See also Marguerite Tazelaar, "Film Personalities: The Man Who Will Make 'Emperor Jones' for the Screen," *New York Herald Tribune,* April 2, 1933, sec. X, 3.

5. Murphy, "Murphy by Murphy," 76.

6. Grace Kingsley, "Tales of Hard Luck in Favor," *Los Angeles Times,* May 18, 1932, 11.

7. "Greta Nissen Sees Mate Swing Vainly at Escort," *Los Angeles Times,* October 15, 1932, sec. A, 2.

8. Grace Kingsley, "Young Star to Play Waitress," *Los Angeles Times,* November 9, 1932, 11.

9. Tip Poff, "That Certain Party," *Los Angeles Times,* November 27, 1932, sec. B, 13.

10. "Tables Turned on Menjou," *Los Angeles Times,* December 4, 1932, sec. B, 11.

11. According to Hurlburt, Siqueiros stated in an interview that he'd been invited to teach the course by the school's founder, Mrs. Nelbert M. Chouinard, while he was still in Mexico. See Hurlburt, *The Mexican Muralists,* 206. However, Shifra Goldman has written that Siqueiros was invited by painter Millard Sheets, a Chouinard instructor, after the muralist arrived in Los Angeles. See Shifra M. Goldman, "Siqueiros and Three Early Murals in Los Angeles," in *Dimensions of the Americas: Art and Social Change in Latin America and the United States* (Chicago: University of Chicago Press, 1994), 91.

12. Siqueiros and Eisenstein spent time together in Taxco in 1930–31, conversing about "the character of twentieth-century revolutionary esthetics." Hurlburt, *The Mexican Muralists,* 206.

13. From "América Tropical," undated manuscript by David Alfaro Siqueiros, cited in Hurlburt, *The Mexican Muralists,* 205.

14. As attested by Arthur Millier and artists Merrell Gage and Phil Paradise, cited in Goldman, "Siqueiros and Three Early Murals in Los Angeles," 92.

15. Cited ibid., 91.

16. Arthur Millier, "Power Unadorned Marks Olvera Street Mural," *Los Angeles Times,* October 16, 1932, sec. III, 16.

17. See Stephen Kinzer, "A New Life for Revolutionary Art," *New York Times,* October 29, 2002, sec. E, 1–2.

18. Hurlburt, *The Mexican Muralists,* 285 n. 49. Murphy makes no mention of Huston in his memoir, while St. Clair is discussed at some length.

19. In his memoir, Siqueiros "mentions meeting 'Charles Laughton, Charles Chaplin, Marlene Dietrich y otros artistas de menor renombre' [and other artists of lesser fame] at the Santa Monica home of film director Dudley Murphy. . . . Charles Laughton apparently became a lifelong patron of the artist—his 'mas grande Mecenas'—and one of the most ardent collectors of his more portable works." Peter Baxter, *Just Watch! Sternberg, Paramount and America* (London: British Film Institute, 1993), 182.

20. Murphy, "Murphy by Murphy," 75.

21. Cited in Hurlburt, *The Mexican Muralists,* 213.

22. Millier cited ibid., 214.

23. "Ousts Modernists as Art Committee," *New York Times,* September 8, 1928, 16.

24. Hurlburt has pointed out that "as realistic as the rest of the mural was in its depiction of the grave state of leftist opposition to Calles, the falsely positive aspect of this figure makes little sense since at this time there existed no visible leftist resistance to Calles in Mexico." Hurlburt, *The Mexican Muralists,* 215–16.

25. See ibid., 214–15.

26. Itala Schmelz, director of the Siqueiros Museum of Public Art in Mexico City, quoted in Kinzer, "A New Life for Revolutionary Art."

27. See Hurlburt, *The Mexican Muralists,* 285 n. 49.

28. Cited ibid., 214.

29. Murphy, "Murphy by Murphy," 75.

30. The mural, titled *Ejercicio plástico,* was painted for a wealthy Uruguayan-born businessman in his villa outside Buenos Aires. See Goldman, "Siqueiros and Three Early Murals in Los Angeles," 99–100 n. 37.

31. Murphy, "Murphy by Murphy," 76. Chávez was also a noted composer and music theorist.

32. See Susan Emerling, "A Wall on the Fly," *Los Angeles Times,* October 6, 2002, sec. F, 4; also Kinzer, "A New Life for Revolutionary Art."

8. STEPPING OUT OF THE SYSTEM: THE MAKING OF *THE EMPEROR JONES*

1. In a 1945 letter, O'Neill wrote that the play had been inspired by a story he'd heard about "President Sam of Haiti, from a man with Sells Circus who had traveled there. He gave me a President Sam coin as a pocket piece." Letter to Mr. Maxwell, May 8, 1945, in Travis Bogard and Jackson R. Bryer, eds., *Selected Letters of Eugene O'Neill* (New York: Limelight Editions, 1994), 570.

Haiti's seventh president in five years, the tyrannical Vilbrun Guillaume Sam was ousted in a particularly bloody revolt in July 1915, which ended with his being dragged out of the French legation and bodily dismembered. The event prompted the United States' occupation of Haiti until 1934. See John Edwin Fagg, *Cuba, Haiti, and the Dominican Republic,* The Modern Nations in Historical Perspective (Englewood Cliffs, NJ: Prentice-Hall, 1965), 129.

2. O'Neill had written a previous one-act play with a black protagonist, *The Dreamy Kid* (1918), which had brief Broadway runs in 1925 and 1928.

3. "Vidor's 'Hallelujah' Gives Real Impetus to Negro Dramas," *New York Herald Tribune,* August 25, 1929, sec. VII, 3.

4. Potamkin, "The Aframerican Cinema," 182–83.

5. In retaliation for the hostile response, the play's frustrated star, African-American actor Julius Bledsoe, literally thumbed his nose at the audience. See Theophilus Lewis, "Theatres," *Inter-state Tattler,* September 2, 1927, 4.

6. Letter to Eugene O'Neill, Jr., January 14, 1933; in Bogard and Bryer, eds., *Selected Letters of Eugene O'Neill,* 409.

7. Charles Musser has credited Gilpin's outstanding performance in *Jones* with hastening the demise of blackface as a practice in the American theater. See Charles Musser, "Troubled Relations: Robeson, Eugene O'Neill, and Oscar Micheaux," in *Paul Robeson: Artist and Citizen,* ed. Jeffrey C. Stewart (New Brunswick, NJ: Rutgers University Press, 1998), 81–103.

8. Letter to Mike Gold, May 1923, in Bogard and Bryer, eds., *Selected Letters of Eugene O'Neill,* 177.

9. Gilpin starred in the all-black film *Ten Nights in a Barroom* (1926), produced by the Colored Players of Philadelphia; the George Eastman House holds a 35mm print of the film. He was fired from the starring role in Universal's film version of *Uncle Tom's Cabin* (1926) for his "assertive" interpretation of the role; he was later dismissed from Fox's *Hearts in Dixie* (1929). See Cripps, *Slow Fade to Black,* 159–60, 162, 195–96, 237. See also Jennie Saxena, "Preserving African-American Cinema: The Case of *The Emperor Jones* (1933)," with contributions by Ken Weissman and James Cozart, *Moving Image* (Spring 2003): 57 n. 12.

10. Letter to Mike Gold, May 1923, in Bogard and Bryer, eds., *Selected Letters of Eugene O'Neill,* 177.

11. Despite Robeson's success, Charles Gilpin continued to appear in New York productions of *The Emperor Jones,* including a February 1926 revival at the Provincetown Playhouse in Greenwich Village and a November 1926 engagement at the Mayfair Theatre. "That role belongs to me," he remarked to one of O'Neill's friends. "That Irishman, he just wrote the play." Cited in Ross Wetzsteon, *Republic of Dreams: Greenwich Village: The American Bohemia, 1910–1960* (New York: Simon and Schuster, 2002), 150. Gilpin died in 1930 at the age of fifty-seven.

12. Potamkin, "The Aframerican Cinema," 183.

13. Letter from Dudley Murphy to Eugene O'Neill, June 14, 1929, Papers of Eugene O'Neill, Clifton Waller Barrett Library of American Literature, Special Collections, University of Virginia Library, Charlottesville.

14. In a letter to Carl Van Vechten written from France, September 30, 1929, O'Neill thanked him for the music he'd sent. "The records arrived—and they are

some camelias! . . . It is good to have Bessie around wahooing in the peaceful French evenings. She makes the ancestral portraits of the provincial noblesse shudder—or maybe it's shimmy!" Bogard and Bryer, eds., *Selected Letters of Eugene O'Neill,* 352.

15. Murphy, interdepartmental correspondence, RCA Photophone, Inc., April 20, 1929, Papers of Eugene O'Neill, Clifton Waller Barrett Library of American Literature, University of Virginia Library, Charlottesville.

16. Murphy, "Murphy by Murphy," 80.

17. *Porgy,* the 1927 play adapted from Heyward's novel, was directed by Rouben Mamoulian, who also directed *Porgy and Bess* in 1935. See Spergel, *Reinventing Reality,* 288–89, 292–93.

18. Lewis, *When Harlem Was in Vogue,* 234.

19. See John Krimsky, "The Emperor Jones—Robeson and O'Neill on Film," *Connecticut Review* 7, no. 2 (April 1974): 95; and Scott MacQueen, "Rise and Fall of *The Emperor Jones,* 1933," *American Cinematographer* 71, no. 2 (February 1990): 36.

20. Cited in MacQueen, "Rise and Fall of *The Emperor Jones,* 1933," 36.

21. Both Krimsky and MacQueen mention a clause in the contract stipulating that Robeson be cast as the lead. However, this agreement may have been verbal, as such a clause does not appear in the document. See "Agreement between Eugene O'Neill and John Krimsky and Gofford [*sic*] Cochran, Inc.," dated April 18, 1933, Eugene O'Neill Collection, Yale Collection of American Literature, Beinecke Rare Book and Manuscript Library, Yale University.

22. Dudley Murphy, treatment for *The Emperor Jones,* 1929, 1, Papers of Eugene O'Neill, Clifton Waller Barrett Library of American Literature, University of Virginia Library, Charlottesville.

23. In his essay, MacQueen includes Cochran on this trip, but Murphy's memoir mentions only Krimsky and Heyward. See MacQueen, "Rise and Fall of *The Emperor Jones,* 1933," 35–36; and Murphy, "Murphy by Murphy," 80.

24. Murphy, "Murphy by Murphy," 80–81.

25. Tazelaar, "Film Personalities."

26. Ibid.

27. Ibid.

28. Ibid.

29. "A Noble Experiment," *New York Times,* February 5, 1939, sec. 9, 4.

30. Eileen Creelman, "Picture Plays and Players: Dudley Murphy in Midst of Directing 'Emperor Jones' at Astoria Studio," *New York Sun,* July 5, 1933, 30.

31. See Swanson, *Swanson on Swanson,* 292–93.

32. Krimsky, "The Emperor Jones—Robeson and O'Neill on Film," 97.

33. Creelman, "Picture Plays and Players," 30.

34. Murphy, "Murphy by Murphy," 80.

35. "The Emperor Jones Is Back," *Chicago Defender,* May 6, 1933, 5.

36. "Robeson to Receive $5,000 for Film Role," *Afro-American,* week of March 11, 1933, 19; "Use Tall Men in 'Emperor Jones,'" *Afro-American,* July 1, 1933, 8.

37. Chappy Gardner, "Courier Critic Sees 'Emperor Jones' in Making," *Pittsburgh Courier,* June 24, 1933, sec. 2, 6.

38. MacQueen cites a figure of $290,000, but Krimsky cites $280,000, as does Martin Duberman in his biography of Robeson. See MacQueen, "Rise and Fall of

The Emperor Jones, 1933," 38; Krimsky, "The Emperor Jones—Robeson and O'Neill on Film," 97; and Martin Duberman, *Paul Robeson* (New York: New Press, 1996), 168.

39. This is MacQueen's figure. MacQueen, "Rise and Fall of *The Emperor Jones,* 1933," 38. According to Duberman, Robeson was paid fifteen thousand dollars for six weeks' work, plus travel expenses. Duberman, *Paul Robeson,* 167.

40. See MacQueen, "Rise and Fall of *The Emperor Jones,* 1933," 38. Haller later shot *Gone with the Wind* (1939), for which he won an Academy Award.

41. See Murphy, "Murphy by Murphy," 82. Unless this sequence was edited for the censors (which might have been the case), only one performer, a young boy in black tie and tails, could conceivably be a Nicholas Brother. If so, it was most likely Harold Nicholas, who would have been eleven or twelve at the time.

42. See, for instance, "The New Film . . . ," *New York Evening Post,* September 20, 1933; and *Film Art* 4 (Summer 1934): 65.

43. See Krimsky, "The Emperor Jones—Robeson and O'Neill on Film," 98. Originally related by Krimsky, this anecdote was repeated in Duberman, *Paul Robeson,* and MacQueen, "Rise and Fall of *The Emperor Jones,* 1933."

44. Tazelaar, "Film Personalities."

45. Cited in Duberman, *Paul Robeson,* 223.

46. "Vidor's 'Hallelujah' Gives Real Impetus to Negro Dramas," *New York Herald Tribune,* August 25, 1929, sec. VII, 3.

47. In a career that spanned 1914 to the 1930s, William C. deMille's output included more than fifty productions as director, producer, and screenwriter. His career peaked in the mid-1920s, dropping off dramatically after sound. DeMille's relationship with Hollywood was turbulent, especially in the latter part of his career. According to the AFI Catalog, *The Emperor Jones* was the last film on which he received screen credit, though the Web site allmovie.com lists him as working on two subsequent films: as associate director on *His Double Life* (1934) and as a screenwriter and dialogue director on *Captain Fury* (1939).

48. Whytock cut many of Rex Ingram's films, including *The Four Horsemen of the Apocalypse, The Prisoner of Zenda,* and *Mare Nostrum,* the project on which he and Murphy first met.

49. Letter from William C. deMille to Agnes De Mille, August 13, 1933, Agnes De Mille Collection, Jerome Robbins Dance Division, the New York Public Library for the Performing Arts.

50. MacQueen, "Rise and Fall of *The Emperor Jones,* 1933," 37.

51. Welford Beaton, "Murphy Makes Emperor Jones a Really Important Production," *Hollywood Spectator,* October 14, 1933, 6.

52. Krimsky, "The Emperor Jones—Robeson and O'Neill on Film," 97. According to David Shepard, in the early 1970s Krimsky told Shepard that he did fire Murphy from the project. The film credits and Krimsky's published account contradict this. E-mail from Shepard to author, July 29, 2005.

53. Krimsky and Cochran were scheduled to deliver the finished picture to United Artists on August 11, 1933, but requested a two-week extension, primarily to accommodate cutting required by censors. See MacQueen, "Rise and Fall of *The Emperor Jones,* 1933," 39.

54. Krimsky, "The Emperor Jones—Robeson and O'Neill on Film," 96.

55. The Hays Office was officially known as the Motion Picture Producers and Distributors of America. Will Hays, a well-connected Republican, was president of the organization from 1922 to 1945. As a self-censoring agency, the MPPDA was the film industry's attempt to ward off government censorship on state and local levels. Its Production Code Administration, under the leadership of Joseph Breen, began formally censoring films in 1934.

56. This scene was restored in the version released on video by Home Vision in the mid-1990s.

57. In addition to cuts required by the Hays Office, the distribution contract specified that United Artists was permitted to make additional cuts mandated by local censor boards in the United States and England. The two hallucinations were apparently cut before prints were made for general distribution. A studio print made at the time was splice-free in this part of the film. See Saxena, "Preserving African-American Cinema."

58. U.S. Bureau of the Census, "Estimated Net Black Migration for Ten Southern States by Decade, 1900–1930," 1975, cited in Stewart E. Tolnay and E. M. Beck, *A Festival of Violence: An Analysis of Southern Lynchings, 1882–1930* (Urbana: University of Illinois Press, 1995), 214; for percentage figures, see 241.

59. Leon F. Litwack, *Trouble in Mind: Black Southerners in the Age of Jim Crow* (New York: Alfred A. Knopf, 1998), 16.

60. "Lynching Oct. 8 Raises Total," *Afro-American*, October 14, 1933, 1.

61. "Mobs Burn Three Women, One Man; Four Bodies Found in Swamp," *Chicago Defender*, November 11, 1933, 2.

62. *Variety*, September 26, 1933, 15.

63. Murphy, "Murphy by Murphy," 82.

64. "Emperor Jones at Roosevelt," *New York Amsterdam News*, September 20, 1933, 7.

65. "Cinema: The New Pictures," review of *The Emperor Jones*, *Time*, September 25, 1933, 31; Mordaunt Hall, *New York Times*, September 20, 1933, 26, and September 24, 1933, sec. 9, 3. Hall later included the film among fifty runners-up to his top ten films of 1933. "The Outstanding Pictorial Features of 1933," *New York Times*, December 31, 1933, sec. 9, 5.

66. "A Standout Show Credit to Screen," *Hollywood Reporter*, September 15, 1933, 3.

67. *Variety*, September 26, 1933, 15.

68. *Time*, September 25, 1933, 31. *The Emperor Jones* was not Robeson's first film role. He had previously appeared in Oscar Micheaux's *Body and Soul* (1926), a silent film made for African-American audiences. A few years later, he and his wife, Eslanda (Essie) Goode Robeson, appeared in *Borderline* (1930), made in Switzerland by British director Kenneth Macpherson.

69. Regina Crewe, "Robeson Mighty in 'Emperor Jones,'" *New York American*, September 20, 1933, final edition, 11.

70. "Robeson Plays 'Jones'; Wins High Praise," *Chicago Daily Tribune*, November 17, 1933, 27.

71. *Variety*, September 26, 1933, 15.

72. Cited in a memorandum from Walter White, director of the NAACP, to NAACP staff member Roy Wilkins, dated September 21, 1933, detailing White's

phone conversation with Krimsky. NAACP Records, I:C-303, "Administrative File: Subject File: Films and plays: Emperor Jones," Library of Congress.

73. "Sister Aimee $5,000 Flop at Cap; 'Harmony' $60,000; M. H. $86,000; 'Jones' Wow 37G, 'Woman' 32G," *Variety,* September 26, 1933, 9.

74. "Emperor Jones at Roosevelt," *New York Amsterdam News,* September 20, 1933, 7.

75. See Thomas Cripps, "The Myth of the Southern Box Office: A Factor in Racial Stereotyping in American Movies, 1920–1940," *The Black Experience in America,* ed. James C. Curtis and Lester L. Gould (Austin: University of Texas Press, 1970), 116–44.

76. *Variety,* September 26, 1933, 15.

77. Krimsky, "The Emperor Jones—Robeson and O'Neill on Film," 97.

78. *Variety,* November 7, 1933, 8.

79. *Variety,* October 3, 1933, 10.

80. The film that succeeded *The Emperor Jones* at the Rivoli was *The Bowery.* It was produced by Samuel Goldwyn, who, after leaving MGM, eventually became one of United Artists' most successful early sound-film producers. See Crafton, *The Talkies,* 371.

81. Ralph Matthews, "Will 'The Emperor Jones' Restore Our Lost Place in the Movies?" *Afro-American,* September 23, 1933, 20.

82. "'Emperor Jones' as Film Better Than Stage Play," *Chicago Defender,* September 30, 1933, 5.

83. Rob Roy, "'Emperor Jones' Has More Than Paul Robeson's Acting," *Chicago Defender,* November 25, 1933, 5.

84. J. A. Rogers, "Takes a Poke at 'The Emperor Jones,'" "Ruminations" column, *New York Amsterdam News,* September 27, 1933, 6 and 9.

85. T. R. Poston, "Harlem Dislikes 'Nigger' in Emperor Jones but Flocks to See Picture at Uptown House," *New York Amsterdam News,* September 27, 1933, 9.

86. Rogers, "Takes a Poke at 'The Emperor Jones,'" 6.

87. "33 Insults Cut Out of Paul Robeson Film," *Afro-American,* October 7, 1933, 1.

88. "What to Do about the 'Emperor Jones,'" *Afro-American,* October 14, 1933, 16.

89. "33 Insults Cut Out of Paul Robeson Film"; "Attacked by Film Fans," *Chicago Defender,* November 11, 1933, 5.

90. Roy, "'Emperor Jones' Has More Than Paul Robeson's Acting."

91. Cited in Matthews, "Will 'The Emperor Jones' Restore Our Lost Place in the Movies?"

92. Rogers, "Takes a Poke at 'The Emperor Jones,'" 6.

93. William G. Nunn, "Private Preview at the Roosevelt Is Well Received," *Pittsburgh Courier,* October 21, 1933, sec. 2, 6.

94. See letter from Dudley Murphy to Walter White, dated October 6, 1933; letter from Walter White to Dudley Murphy, dated October 9, 1933; and memorandum from Walter White to Roy Wilkins, dated September 21, 1933; all in NAACP Records, I:C-303, "Administrative File: Subject File: Films and plays: Emperor Jones," Library of Congress.

95. For a thorough account of the restoration process, see Saxena, "Preserving African-American Cinema."

96. The restored Library of Congress version is currently available on DVD.

97. Krimsky, "The Emperor Jones—Robeson and O'Neill on Film," 97.

98. Murphy, "Murphy by Murphy," 83.

99. Matthews, *Afro-American,* September 23, 1933, 20.

100. Harold Bennison, "Director of Film 'Emperor Jones' Is the Son of Winchester Artist," *Boston Traveler,* September 23, 1933, 6.

101. Tazelaar, "Film Personalities."

9. AN EQUIVOCAL INDEPENDENCE

1. "Murphy to Vienna," *Los Angeles Times,* November 12, 1932, sec. A, 7.

2. See Grace Kingsley, "New Film Review; Studio Gossip Related," *Los Angeles Times,* June 16, 1933, sec. A, 9. The film, starring Jack Oakie and Jack Haley, was made and released in 1933, with Harry Joe Brown directing.

3. Murphy, "Murphy by Murphy," 83. Murphy doesn't refer to the agent by name.

4. Tazelaar, "Film Personalities."

5. "Murphy Takes Film Partner," *New York Morning Telegraph,* September 18, 1933, 1.

6. The NIRA was declared unconstitutional in 1935, but by that point the film industry had largely recovered.

7. Barrios, *Screened Out,* 138.

8. The other three MGM executives to head production units were Walter Wanger, Hunt Stromberg, and, nominally, Thalberg. See Schatz, *The Genius of the System,* 161–63.

9. Ibid., 253–54.

10. Murphy, "Murphy by Murphy," 84.

11. *The Night Is Young* was the last film Laye made in Hollywood. She continued her career on Broadway, in the London theater, and in British films, making her final screen appearance in a 1988 made-for-television movie, *The Woman He Loved.*

12. Cited in the AFI Catalog entry for *The Night Is Young.*

13. Capra, "The Cinematographer's Place in the Motion Picture Industry," 13.

14. Cited in the AFI Catalog entry for *The Night Is Young.* For more on Mamoulian and *Love Me Tonight,* see "Rouben Mamoulian, Director," in Evan William Cameron, ed., *Sound and the Cinema: The Coming of Sound to American Film* (Pleasantville, NY: Redgrave Publishing Company, 1980), 92.

15. *New York Times,* January 14, 1935, 11.

16. Murphy, "Murphy by Murphy," 85. The manuscript has Irving Thalberg's name as "Ben Thau." I am assuming an audio transcription error.

17. Ibid., 85.

18. deMille, *Hollywood Saga,* 298–99.

19. Edwin Schallert, "Virginia Weidler, First Real Rival of Shirley Temple, Loaned for 'Freckles,'" *Los Angeles Times,* May 17, 1935, 13; also Schallert, "Jeanette MacDonald Awarded New Contract and Picture Called 'San Francisco,'" *Los Angeles Times,* May 21, 1935, 13.

20. *New York Times,* March 2, 1936, 13.

21. *Variety,* March 4, 1936, 26–27.

22. "She Divorces 'Late' Husband," *Los Angeles Times,* July 14, 1934, sec. A, 3.

23. "Broadway by Ed Sullivan," *Washington Post,* March 26, 1935, 26; "Ann Harding Faces Jail for Contempt; Keeps Mum on Relations with Director," *Boston Traveler,* June 24, 1935.

24. "'Pol' Peabody to Wed Actor," *New York Daily Mirror,* September 2, 1935. Though the headline incorrectly identifies Murphy as an actor, the text refers to him as a director. In 1936, Jo-Jo married Twentieth Century-Fox director James Tinley, whose career spanned the 1920s through the early 1950s. See "Mrs. Murphy Married," *New York Times,* June 12, 1936, 20.

25. Murphy, "Murphy by Murphy," 86.

26. Ibid., 86.

27. "£675,000 on 15 films," *Today's Cinema,* September 4, 1936. *King for a Day,* elsewhere identified as *The King's Business,* may have been an adaptation of Hammett's 1928 story, "This King Business."

28. The article appears to be an abridged, syndicated version of a *New York American* column. The unnamed motion picture editor could be Regina Crewe.

29. Murphy, "Murphy by Murphy," 86–87.

30. "New Play to Be Produced by Dunning," *Los Angeles Times,* January 31, 1938, sec. A, 14; "Novel Dramatized," *Chicago Daily Tribune,* October 1, 1939, sec. E, 2.

31. The screenplay for *One Third of a Nation* is credited to Oliver H. P. Garrett.

32. Born in 1924, Lumet made his acting debut in 1928 alongside his father, Yiddish actor Baruch Lumet, in New York's Yiddish Art Theater. In 1935, he debuted on Broadway in *Dead End.* See Jay Boyer, *Sidney Lumet,* Twayne's Filmmakers Series (New York: Twayne Publishers, 1993).

33. Derek Owen, "1194 Dudley Murphy," *Film Dope* 46 (March 1991): 19.

34. Sidney Lumet's father, Baruch Lumet, has a small part in this scene as the dazed and bereaved tenant, Mr. Rosen.

35. *Variety,* February 15, 1939, 12.

36. *New York Times,* February 11, 1939, 13.

37. "Eastern-Made Cinema Received with Reserve," *Los Angeles Times,* February 20, 1939, 13.

38. "A Noble Experiment," *New York Times,* February 5, 1939, sec. 9, 4.

39. Leonard Lyons, "Broadway Chaff," *Washington Post,* April 2, 1939, sec. T, 3.

40. "Gossip of the Rialto," *New York Times,* December 3, 1939, 5.

41. Murphy, "Murphy by Murphy," 85.

42. Bosley Crowther, *New York Times,* November 9, 1939, 27.

43. *Variety,* November 8, 1939, 14.

44. deMille, *Hollywood Saga,* 299.

10. CHANGING DIRECTION

1. See "In Hollywood with Hedda Hopper," *Washington Post,* February 14, 1940, 8.

2. "Louella Parsons," *Washington Post,* August 18, 1940, sec. A, 1.

3. Murphy, "Murphy by Murphy," 87.

4. "Louella Parsons," *Washington Post,* August 22, 1940, 6.

5. "John Barrymore May Star in 'Hamlet' at El Capitan," *Los Angeles Times,* August 26, 1940, sec. A, 15.

6. Because of the mirrored rear-projection, soundies were originally reverse printed. In later repackaging for home film projection, they were reversed once again, to normal orientation. See Maurice Terenzio, Scott MacGillivray, and Ted Okuda, *The Soundies Distributing Corporation of America: A History and Filmography of Their "Jukebox" Musical Films of the 1940s* (Jefferson, NC: McFarland and Company, 1991), 17.

7. For comparative screen size estimates, see ibid., 2; and Leonard Maltin, "Soundies," *Film Fan Monthly* 142 (April 1973): 3.

8. Murphy, "Murphy by Murphy," 70. In 1943, Coslow returned to movie songwriting, continuing to work through the 1940s and 1950s.

9. Maltin, "Soundies," 4.

10. William Moritz attributes this soundie to Murphy, but Terenzio and his colleagues do not. No directing credit appears on the print held by the Library of Congress. See Dudley Murphy filmography in Horak, ed., *Lovers of Cinema,* 374.

11. Murphy is credited as codirector (with Joseph Berne) on *Yes, Indeed!*

12. "The 1940 United States Census reported that of the 2,426 actors in Los Angeles, only 51 were Black. Of the 910 male dancers, showmen, and athletes, a mere 33 were Black. Of the 1,271 experienced actors in Hollywood, 42 were Black. . . . [And] of the 743 actresses working in the film capital, only a paltry 15 were African American." Bogle, *Dorothy Dandridge,* 93–94.

13. Selznick, *Memo from David O. Selznick,* 162.

14. The group is identified as "The Five Spirits of Rhythm" on *Albany Bound* but is credited as "The Spirits of Rhythm" on *Yes, Indeed!*

15. The couple's first daughter, Christopher Caroline (Kit) Murphy, was born in December 1941. She died of cancer in 1977. Their second daughter, Erin, was born in 1951. Erin Murphy O'Hara interview with author, April 17, 2001.

16. The Library of Congress and Terenzio et al., *The Soundies Distributing Corporation of America,* list all Murphy's soundies as 1941. William Moritz dates *Mountain Dew, Yes, Indeed!* and *Merry-Go-Round* (identified by Terenzio et al. as *Merry-Go-Roundup*) as 1942. See Dudley Murphy filmography in Horak, ed., *Lovers of Cinema,* 374.

17. See Terenzio et al., *The Soundies Distributing Corporation of America,* 11–12.

18. See Sylvia Navarrete, *Miguel Covarrubias: Artista y explorador* (Coyoacán, Mexico: Consejo Nacional para la Cultura y las Artes, 1993), 63–67. Murphy's youngest daughter, Erin Murphy O'Hara, recalled visiting Covarrubias's widow, Rosa, in Mexico City on frequent family trips. Interview with the author, April 17, 2001.

19. "Al paracer, Reachi empezó a dirigir el mismo la película, pero acabó confiando su realización al norteamercano Dudley Murphy." Emilio García Riera, *Historia documental del cine mexicano,* vol. 2: *1938–1942* (Guadalajara, Jalisco, Mexico: Universidad de Guadalajara, 1993), 276. "Para que el toque cosmopolita del melodrama protagonizado por ella, *Yolanda,* fuera perceptible, Reachi cedió la responsabilidad de la dirección de la cinta al norteamericano Dudley Murphy." Emilio García Riera, *Historia documental del cine mexicano: Época sonora,* vol. 2, *1941–1944* (Guadalajara, Jalisco, Mexico: Ediciones Era, 1992), 87.

20. "El nombre de Murphy no figuró ni en los créditos ni en la publicidad de

la película, que pasó en México como no dirigida por nadie." García Riera, *Historia documental,* 2: *1938–1942,* 276. Translations from Spanish are mine, with help from Michelle Chase. García Riera also noted that when Reachi recut *Yolanda* for release in U.S. markets, the directing credit went to Armán Chelieu, who had beem credited as the author of the novel on which Reachi's film *El Cantante de Napoles* was based. It's plausible that "Armán Chelieu" was a near-anagramatic pseudonym for Manuel Reachi, who was a writer as well as a producer. He later wrote, under his own name, the novel from which Luis Buñuel's Mexican film *Susana* (1951) was adapted.

21. By the time García Riera's multivolume histories of Mexican film were published in the early 1990s, Murphy was again credited on the project.

22. According to Mexican film historian Gabriel Ramírez, the Ballet Theatre was an offshoot of the Ballets Russes, established in Mexico in 1938 with members of the Ballets Russes company and Leonid Massine as choreographer. In addition to its appearance in *Yolanda,* in the early 1940s the company appeared in the film *Los tres mosqueteros* (The Three Musketeers, 1942) and *Yo bailé con don Porfirio* (I Danced with don Porfirio, 1942). See Gabriel Ramírez, *Norman Foster y los otros directores norteamericanos en México* (Mexico City: Universidad Nacional Autónoma de México, 1992), 60 n. 33.

23. "La mentalidad de nuevo rico aconsejaba al cine mexicano inyecciones de cultura administradas conforme al gusto de las señoras gordas." García Riera, *Historia documental del cine mexicano: Época sonora,* 87. The film was released in the United States several years later as *Toast to Love.* In a brief review, the *New York Times* called it "a hackneyed hodge-podge of murky love troubles," adding that "the acting is presumptuous and dull." *New York Times,* November 7, 1951, 35.

24. "Film Man Accused of Cruelty in Divorce Complaint," unidentified news clipping (hand labeled "Herald"), dated March 20, 1943, Dudley Murphy file, Margaret Herrick Library, Academy of Motion Picture Arts and Sciences, Los Angeles.

25. Murphy, "Murphy by Murphy," 76; interview with Erin Murphy O'Hara, April 17, 2001. Barrymore's garden soliloquies may have coincided with the discussions about a possible production of *Hamlet* or may have inspired them. See note 5.

26. Virginia Bellondi Murphy died on October 8, 1979. See *Variety Obituaries, 1975–1979,* vol. 8 (New York: Garland Publishing, 1988).

27. *Tiempo* 7, no. 7 (1942), cited in Ramírez, *Norman Foster y los otros directores norteamericanos,* 59. *What Makes Sammy Run?* made Schulberg persona non grata in Hollywood for several years. He went on to write screenplays for two classic films of the 1950s, *On the Waterfront* (1951) and *A Face in the Crowd* (1957), but both were New York–based productions.

28. Murphy and Schulberg did collaborate on the screenplay for Murphy's second Mexican film, *Alma de bronce,* adapted from one of Schulberg's short stories. *El mexicano* reached the screen in 1944 as the debut film of Mexican director Agustín P. Delgado; in 1952, Elia Kazan made *Viva Zapata!* from a script by John Steinbeck. See Ramírez, *Norman Foster y los otros directores norteamericanos,* 60 n. 34.

29. Tom Dardis, *Some Time in the Sun* (New York: Charles Scribner's Sons, 1976), 127.

30. Thomas M. Pryor, "Hands across the Border," *New York Times,* November 21, 1943, sec. X, 3.

31. Ramírez characterized the film as having "un héroe de opereta (Armendáriz),

un villano de zarzuela (Andrés Soler), y una mujer tango (Gloria Marín)." Ramírez, *Norman Foster y los otros directores norteamericanos,* 61.

32. The article is by Virginia Wright, who in the 1940s wrote on film for the Los Angeles *Daily News.* It's likely that the clipping came from that paper. Given that the interview occurs after *Alma de bronce* was completed but before its Mexican release, it presumably took place in summer or early fall of 1944.

33. Ibid.

34. "Si Foster habia logrado hacer cintas lo suficientemente buenas para taparles la boca a algunos xenófobos, Murphy fue objeto de toda suerte de sarcasmos y criticas." García Riera, *Historia documental del cine mexicano: Época sonora,* 232.

35. "una magnífica película para turistas, realizada también por un turista." *Cine mexicano* 2, no. 12 (1944), cited in Ramírez, *Norman Foster y los otros directores norteamericanos,* 61.

36. "Decididamente los elementos norteamericanos que trabajan en nuestro cine sienten una marcada preferencia por una tema que nosotros, los mexicanos, quisiéramos olvidar: el de nuestra ya remota guerra intestina que dio pretexto a la intervención francesa. Aquí, en *Alma de bronce,* como ya va siendo costubre, el 'liberal' es un muchacho apuesto, simpático, francote y noble, en tanto que el 'conservador' es un viejo avaro, hipócrita y perverso. ¡Admirable sistema de hacer historia!" Cited in García Riera, *Historia documental del cine mexicano: Época sonora,* 232.

37. "'Soul of the Bell' Patriotic Mexican Saga," *Los Angeles Times,* November 15, 1945, 19.

38. Ethel McCall Head, "Diamond in the Rough," *Los Angeles Times,* April 6, 1947, sec. F, 4.

39. "'Pol' Peabody to Wed Actor," *New York Daily Mirror,* September 2, 1935.

40. The house was later owned by Ayn Rand. During World War II, its shiplike appearance made it a favorite mock-bombing target of the Air Corps, which strafed it repeatedly. See Thomas S. Hines, *Richard Neutra and the Search for Modern Architecture* (New York: Oxford University Press, 1982), 138.

41. See Esther McCoy, *Richard Neutra* (New York: George Braziller, 1960), 119.

42. Aline B. Louchheim, "New Design Proves Worth in Hotels," *New York Times,* June 11, 1950, sec. X, 3.

43. According to Erin Murphy O'Hara, one writer who wintered there was hoping to write a series of children's books about her: Erin of Holiday House, much like Eloise at the Plaza Hotel. E-mail correspondence with author, August 18, 2005.

44. "Kit Wit Captures Autumn Sail Series," *Los Angeles Times,* November 30, 1948, sec. C, 4; Bob Ruskauff, "Small Boats Race at Three Ports Today," *Los Angeles Times,* March 13, 1949, 29.

45. "Neutra Designs a Small, Simple, but Deluxe Hotel with a Grandstand View of Ocean Beach," *Architectural Forum,* July 1949, 104–5.

46. William Saroyan, "Take Her to Vegas," *Saturday Evening Post,* September 23, 1961, 48–53.

47. Man Ray, *Self Portrait,* 218.

48. Edwin Schallert, "New Murder Thriller Will Vie with Classic," *Los Angeles Times,* July 23, 1948, 15; Edwin Schallert, "Clift Reported Warming on Remake of 'Tragedy'; Sarnoff May Join MGM," *Los Angeles Times,* April 21, 1949.

49. Walter Ames, "Notre Dame Grid Games to Be Telecast Locally; Video Credited with Jalopy Aid," *Los Angeles Times,* August 25, 1950, 18.

50. Edwin Schallert, "Drama," *Los Angeles Times,* March 3, 1951, 9; Walter Ames, "Television, Radio, News and Programs," *Los Angeles Times,* May 18, 1951, 26.

51. "Un momentito . . . with Pepe Romero," *Mexico City News,* December 16, 1960.

52. Letter from George Antheil to Virgil Thomson, dated January 1, 1951, Estate of George Antheil, Virgil Thomson Papers, Irving S. Gilmore Music Library, Yale University.

53. Murphy, "Murphy by Murphy," 48.

54. Dave Sheehan, "Lamplighter" column, *West L.A. Independent,* January 28, 1965.

55. More than one obituary gave Murphy's age at his death as seventy-two. But his date of birth (July 10, 1897) and date of death (February 22, 1968) indicate that he was seventy.

FILMOGRAPHY OF
DUDLEY MURPHY

1920

Soul of the Cypress (director, producer, scenarist). Musically inspired short film featuring Chase Herendeen Murphy, set to Debussy's *Prelude to the Afternoon of a Faun.*

Aphrodite (director, producer, scenarist). Musically inspired short film featuring Katharine Hawley as the Greek goddess.

Anywhere out of the World (director, producer, scenarist). Musically inspired short film featuring Chase Herendeen Murphy, based on the Baudelaire poem of the same title.

The Way of Love, aka *The Romance of the White Chrysanthemum* (director, producer, scenarist). Musically inspired short film about a young Japanese woman and her lover.

1922

Danse Macabre, aka *Dance of Death, Death and the Maiden* (director, producer). Adaptation of an Adolph Bolm ballet starring Bolm and Ruth Page.

1923

High Speed Lee (director). Feature-length romantic comedy adapted from the J. P. Marquand story "Only a Few of Us Left," starring Reed Howes and Rosalind Fuller. Produced by Atlantic Film Company released by Arrow Film Company.

The Syren (director, producer, scenarist). Musically inspired short film loosely based on classical mythology, starring Katharine Hawley and set to the song "O Sole Mio." Produced by D. M. Films.

1924

Ballet mécanique (codirector). Experimental short film made in collaboration with Fernand Léger with contributions by Man Ray and Ezra Pound. Music composed by George Antheil. Premiered September 1924 at the Internationale Ausstellung neuer Theatertechnik (International Exposition for New Theater Techniques), Vienna.

1926

Mare Nostrum (uncredited assistant director to Rex Ingram). Produced by MGM.

Finding His Job (director). Script by Mrs. James S. Metcalf. Produced by the Bedford Garden Club of Bedford, New York.

1927

The Love of Sunya (consultant on crystal sequence). Directed by Albert Parker. Produced by Swanson Producing Corp., released by United Artists.

1928

Alex the Great (director, scriptwriter). Feature comedy starring Richard "Skeets" Gallagher. Produced by FBO.

Skyscraper (original story). Romantic drama starring William Boyd and Alan Hale. Produced by the Cinema Corporation of America, released by Pathé.

Stocks and Blondes (director, scriptwriter). Wall Street romance starring Albert Conti, Richard "Skeets" Gallagher, and Gertrude Astor. Produced by FBO.

1929

The Traveler (director). Short sound-film comedy based on a sketch by Marc Connelly. Produced by RKO Pictures.

The Burglar (director). Short sound-film comedy based on a sketch by Marc Connelly, starring Connelly. Produced by RKO Pictures.

Jazz Heaven (cowriter, original story). Romantic comedy feature starring John Mack Brown and Sally O'Neil. Produced by RKO Pictures.

St. Louis Blues (director, scriptwriter). Short musical drama starring Bessie Smith and Jimmy Mordecai with Isabel Washington. Produced by RKO Pictures.

Black and Tan (director, scriptwriter). Short musical drama starring Duke Ellington and Fredi Washington. Produced by RKO Pictures.

1930

He Was Her Man (director, scriptwriter). Short musical drama based on the popular song "Frankie and Johnny," starring Gilda Gray. Produced by Paramount Pictures.

1931

Dracula (additional dialogue). Horror feature starring Bela Lugosi, directed by Tod Browning. Produced by Universal Pictures Corp.

Confessions of a Co-ed (codirector). Campus melodrama codirected with David Burton, starring Sylvia Sidney, Norman Foster, Phillips Holmes, and Claudia Dell. Produced by Paramount Publix Corp.

Twenty-four Hours (associate director). Drama directed by Marion Gehring, starring Clive Brook, Kay Francis, and Miriam Hopkins. Produced by Paramount Publix Corp.

1932
A Lesson in Golf (director). Sports short produced by MGM as part of its Sport Champion Reel series.
The Sport Parade (director). Romantic drama starring Joel McCrea, William Gargan, Marian Marsh, and Robert Benchley. Produced by RKO Radio Pictures, Inc.

1933
The Emperor Jones (director). Screen adaptation of the Eugene O'Neill play, starring Paul Robeson. Produced by John Krimsky and Gifford Cochran, Inc., released by United Artists.

1935
The Night Is Young (director). Operetta-style musical set in Vienna, starring Ramon Novarro and Evelyn Laye. Produced by MGM.

1936
Don't Gamble with Love (director). Romantic drama about a professional gambler and his family, starring Ann Sothern and Bruce Cabot. Produced by Columbia Pictures Corp.

1939
One Third of a Nation (director, coproducer). Romantic drama about slum life, adapted from a WPA play of the same name, starring Leif Erikson, Sylvia Sidney, and Sidney Lumet. Produced by Paramount Pictures, Inc.
Main Street Lawyer (director). Legal drama starring Edward Ellis and Anita Louise. Produced by Republic Pictures Corp.

1941
I Don't Want to Set the World on Fire (director). Soundie with Johnny Downs, Bonnie Kildare; music by Lud Gluskin.
Lazybones (director). Soundie with Hoagy Carmichael, Dorothy Dandridge, Floyd O'Brian, Peter Ray; music by Bob Crosby and His Orchestra.
Merry-Go-Roundup (director). Soundie with Gale Storm, the Dorn Brothers and Mary, the Palladium Handicap Girls; music by Bob Crosby and His Bobcats.
Yes, Indeed! (codirector with Josef Berne). Soundie with Dorothy Dandridge, the Spirits of Rhythm.

Additional Soundies
Abercrombie Had a Zombie. With Lee Murray, Liz Tilton; music by Bob Crosby and His Orchestra.
Alabamy Bound. With Jackie Greene, the Five Spirits of Rhythm.
Easy Street. With Dorothy Dandridge.
Jazzy Joe. With the Dorn Brothers and Mary; music by Bob Crosby and His Orchestra.
Jim, aka *Carrying the Torch for Jim.* With Judy Carroll.
Mountain Dew. With Mabel Todd, the Pickards.

1942

Yolanda, aka *Brindis de amor* (*Toast to Love*) (director). Romantic drama starring Irina Baranova, David Silva, and Miguel Arenas. Produced by Promesa Films. Released in the United States in 1951 as *Toast to Love.*

1944

Alma de bronce (Soul of Bronze), aka *La campana de mi pueblo* (director). Adaptation of "The Bell of Tarchova," a short story by Budd Schulberg, starring Pedro Armendáriz, Gloria Marín, and Andrés Soler. Produced by Artistas Asociados.

SELECTED BIBLIOGRAPHY

Anderson, Susan. "Journey into the Sun: California Artists and Surrealism." In *On the Edge of America: California Modernist Art, 1900–1950*, ed. Paul J. Karlstrom, 181–209. Berkeley: University of California Press in association with the Archives of American Art, Smithsonian Institution, and the Fine Arts Museums of San Francisco, 1996.

Antheil, George. *Bad Boy of Music*. Garden City, NY: Doubleday, Doran and Company, 1945.

Archer-Straw, Petrine. *Negrophilia: Avant-Garde Paris and Black Culture in the 1920s*. New York: Thames and Hudson, 2000.

Baker, James T. *Ayn Rand*. Twayne's United States Authors Series, ed. Warren French. Boston: Twayne Publishers, 1987.

Bandy, Mary Lea, ed. *The Dawn of Sound*. American Moviemakers Series. New York: Museum of Modern Art, 1989.

———. "New York Friends Look at Documentary Film." In *Filming Robert Flaherty's "Louisiana Story": The Helen van Dongen Diary*, ed. Eva Orbanz, 11–20. New York: Museum of Modern Art in collaboration with the Stiftung Deutsche Kinematek, Berlin, 1998.

Barrios, Richard. *Screened Out: Playing Gay in Hollywood from Edison to Stonewall*. New York: Routledge, 2003.

Barron, Stephanie, Sheri Bernstein, and Ilene Susan Fort. *Reading California: Art, Image, and Identity, 1900–2000*. Berkeley: Los Angeles County Museum of Art and University of California Press, 2000.

Baum, Timothy. *Man Ray's Paris Portraits, 1921–39*. Washington, DC: Middendorf Gallery, 1989.

Baxter, Peter. *Just Watch! Sternberg, Paramount and America*. London: British Film Institute, 1993.

Bernstein, Matthew. *Walter Wanger, Hollywood Independent*. Berkeley: University of California Press, 1994.

Bogard, Travis, and Jackson R. Bryer, eds. *Selected Letters of Eugene O'Neill.* New York: Limelight Editions, 1994.

Bogle, Donald. *Dorothy Dandridge.* New York: Amistad Press, 1997.

———. *Toms, Coons, Mulattoes, Mammies, and Bucks: An Interpretive History of Blacks in American Films.* New York: Viking Press, 1973.

Bouhours, Jean-Michel. "D'images mobiles en *ballets mécaniques.*" In *Fernand Léger,* 158–163. Paris: Éditions Centre Pompidou, 1997.

Bowser, Eileen. Program notes to accompany public screenings of *Ballet mécanique* at the Museum of Modern Art, December 3–4, 1979.

Boyer, Jay. *Sidney Lumet.* Twayne's Filmmakers Series. New York: Twayne Publishers, 1993.

Brougher, Kerry, et al., eds. *Visual Music: Synesthesia in Art and Music since 1900.* New York: Thames and Hudson, 2005.

Brownlow, Kevin. *The Parade's Gone By . . .* Berkeley: University of California Press, 1968.

Burian, Hermann M., M.D. "The History of the Dartmouth Eye Institute." *Archives of Ophthalmology* 40 (August 1948).

Cameron, Evan William, ed. *Sound and the Cinema: The Coming of Sound to American Film.* Pleasantville, NY: Redgrave Publishing Company, 1980.

Capra, Frank. "The Cinematographer's Place in the Motion Picture Industry." In *Cinematographic Annual,* vol. 2, 1931, ed. Hal Hall, 13–14. New York: Arno Press and New York Times, 1972.

Crafton, Donald. *The Talkies: American Cinema's Transition to Sound, 1926–1931.* Vol. 4 of *History of the American Cinema.* New York: Charles Scribner's Sons, 1997.

Creelman, Eileen. "Picture Plays and Players: Dudley Murphy in Midst of Directing 'Emperor Jones' at Astoria Studio," *New York Sun,* July 5, 1933, 30.

Cripps, Thomas. *Hollywood's High Noon.* Baltimore: Johns Hopkins University Press, 1997.

———. "The Myth of the Southern Box Office: A Factor in Racial Stereotyping in the American Movies, 1920–1940." In *The Black Experience in America: Selected Essays,* ed. James C. Curtis and Lester L. Gould, 116–44. Austin: University of Texas Press, 1970.

———. "Paul Robeson and Black Identity in American Movies." *Massachusetts Review* 11, no. 3 (Summer 1970): 468–85.

———. *Slow Fade to Black: The Negro in American Film, 1900–1942.* 1977; reprint, New York: Oxford University Press, 1993.

Dardis, Tom. *Some Time in the Sun.* New York: Charles Scribner's Sons, 1976.

de Francia, Peter. *Fernand Léger.* New Haven, CT: Yale University Press, 1983.

deMille, William C. *Hollywood Saga.* New York: E. P. Dutton and Company, 1939.

Douglas, Ann. *Terrible Honesty: Mongrel Manhattan in the 1920s.* New York: Farrar, Straus and Giroux, 1995.

Duberman, Martin. *Paul Robeson.* New York: New Press, 1996.

Dusinberre, Deke. "*Le retour à la raison:* Hidden Meanings." In *Unseen Cinema: Early American Avant-Garde Film 1893–1941,* ed. Bruce Posner, 64–69. New York: Anthology Film Archives, 2001.

Ehrens, Susan. *A Poetic Vision: The Photographs of Anne Brigman.* Santa Barbara, CA: Santa Barbara Museum of Art, 1995.

Emerling, Susan. "A Wall on the Fly." *Los Angeles Times,* October 6, 2002, sec. F, 4.

Enyeart, James. *Bruguière: His Photographs and His Life.* New York: Alfred A. Knopf, 1977.

Erikson, Kristen. "Chronology." In Carolyn Lanchner, *Fernand Léger.* New York: Museum of Modern Art, 1998.

Eyman, Scott. *The Speed of Sound: Hollywood and the Talkie Revolution, 1926–1930.* New York: Simon and Schuster, 1997.

Fagg, John Edwin. *Cuba, Haiti, and the Dominican Republic.* The Modern Nations in Historical Perspective Series, ed. Robin W. Winks. Englewood Cliffs, NJ: Prentice-Hall, 1965.

Fairbrother, Trevor J. *The Bostonians: Painters of an Elegant Age, 1870–1930.* Boston: Museum of Fine Arts, Boston, 1986.

Fernett, Gene. *American Film Studios: An Historical Encyclopedia.* Jefferson, NC: McFarland and Company, 1988.

Fogelson, Robert M. *The Fragmented Metropolis: Los Angeles, 1850–1930.* Classics in Urban History. Berkeley: University of California Press, 1993.

Foresta, Merry, et al. *Perpetual Motif: The Art of Man Ray.* New York: Abbeville Press, 1988.

Fort, Ilene Susan. "Altered State(s): California Art and the Inner World." In *Reading California: Art, Image, and Identity, 1900–2000,* ed. Stephanie Barron, Sheri Bernstein, and Ilene Susan Fort, 31–49. Berkeley: University of California Press, 2000.

Freeman, Judi. "Bridging Purism and Surrealism: The Origins and Production of Fernand Léger's *Ballet mécanique.*" In *Dada and Surrealist Film,* ed. Rudolf E. Kuenzli, 28–45. New York: Willis Locker and Owens, 1987.

———. "Fernand Léger and the Ballets Russes: An Unconsummated Collaboration." In *The Ballets Russes and Its World,* ed. Lyn Garafola and Nancy Van Norman Baer, 135–51. New Haven, CT: Yale University Press, 1999.

———. "Léger and the People: The Figure-Object Paintings and the Emergence of a Cinematic Vision." In *Fernand Léger 1911–1924: The Rhythm of Modern Life,* ed. Dorothy Kosinski, 230–37. Munich: Prestel, 1994.

———. "Léger Reexamined." Book review. *Art History* 7, no. 3 (September 1984): 349–59.

———. "Surveying Fernand Léger in Paris." Exhibition review. *Apollo* 146 (October 1997): 40–43.

Gammell, R. H. Ives. *The Boston Painters 1900–1930.* Orleans, MA: Parnassus Imprints, 1986.

García Riera, Emilio. *Historia documental del cine mexicano: Época sonora.* Vol. 2: *1941–1944.* Guadalajara, Jalisco, Mexico: Ediciones Era, 1992.

———. *Historia documental del cine mexicano.* Vol. 2: *1938–1942.* Guadalajara, Jalisco, Mexico: Universidad de Guadalajara, 1993.

Goldman, Shifra M. *Dimensions of the Americas: Art and Social Change in Latin America and the United States.* Chicago: University of Chicago Press, 1994.

Green, Christopher. *Léger and the Avant-Garde.* New Haven, CT: Yale University Press, 1976.

Guzman, Tony. "The Little Theatre Movement: The Institutionalization of the European Art Film in America." *Film History* 17, no. 2–3 (2005): 261–84.

Haskell, Barbara. *The American Century: Art and Culture 1900–1950*. New York: Whitney Museum of American Art in association with W. W. Norton, 1999.

Heyman, Therese. *Picturing California: A Century of Photographic Genius*. San Francisco: Chronicle Books, 1989.

Hines, Thomas. *Richard Neutra and the Search for Modern Architecture*. New York: Oxford University Press, 1982.

Horak, Jan-Christopher. "The First American Film Avant-Garde, 1919–1945." In *Lovers of Cinema: The First American Film Avant-Garde 1919–1945*, ed. Jan-Christopher Horak, 14–66. Wisconsin Studies in Film. Madison: University of Wisconsin Press, 1995.

———. "Introduction." In *Lovers of Cinema: The First American Film Avant-Garde 1919–1945*, ed. Jan-Christopher Horak, 3–13. Wisconsin Studies in Film. Madison: University of Wisconsin Press, 1995.

———, ed. *Lovers of Cinema: The First American Film Avant-Garde 1919–1945*. Wisconsin Studies in Film. Madison: University of Wisconsin Press, 1995.

Hurlburt, Laurance P. *The Mexican Muralists in the United States*. Albuquerque: University of New Mexico Press, 1989.

Hurst, Walter E. *Film Superlist: Motion Pictures in the U.S. Public Domain 1894–1939*, vol. 1, ed. D. Richard Baer. Hollywood: Hollywood Film Archive, 1994.

James, David E. *The Most Typical Avant-Garde: History and Geography of Minor Cinemas in Los Angeles*. Berkeley: University of California Press, 2005.

———. "*Soul of the Cypress:* The First Postmodernist Film?" *Film Quarterly* 56, no. 3 (Spring 2003): 25–31.

Josephson, Matthew. *Life among the Surrealists*. New York: Holt, Rinehart and Winston, 1962.

———. "The Rise of the Little Cinema." *Motion Picture Classic* 24, no. 1 (September 1926): 34–35, 69, 82. Reprinted in George C. Pratt, *Spellbound in Darkness: A History of the Silent Film,* 483–88. Greenwich, CT: New York Graphic Society, 1973.

Karlstrom, Paul J., ed. *On the Edge of America: California Modernist Art, 1900–1950*. Berkeley: University of California Press in association with the Archives of American Art, Smithsonian Institution, and the Fine Arts Museums of San Francisco, 1996.

Kellner, Bruce. *Carl Van Vechten and the Irreverent Decades*. Norman: University of Oklahoma Press, 1968.

Kiesler, Lillian, et al. *A Tribute to Anthology Film Archives' Avantgarde Film Preservation Program: An Evening Dedicated to Frederick Kiesler; Leger—Murphy—Ruttmann—Cornell—Deren—Leslie*. Museum of Modern Art, New York, October 19, 1977; American Film Institute, John F. Kennedy Center, Washington D.C., November 10, 1977.

Kiki [Alice Prin]. *Kiki's Memoirs*. Trans. Samuel Putnam, ed. and annotated Billy Klüver and Julie Martin. Hopewell, NJ: Ecco Press, 1996.

Kimmelman, Michael. "With Music for the Eye and Colors for the Ear." *New York Times,* July 1, 2005, sec. E, 33.

Kinzer, Stephen. "A New Life for Revolutionary Art." *New York Times,* October 29, 2002, sec. E, 1–2.

Klüver, Billy, and Julie Martin. *Kiki's Paris: Artists and Lovers 1900–1930*. 1989; reprint, New York: Harry N. Abrams, 2002.

Koszarski, Richard. *An Evening's Entertainment: The Age of the Silent Feature Picture, 1915–1928*. Vol. 3 of *History of the American Cinema*. New York: Charles Scribner's Sons, 1990.

Krimsky, John. "The Emperor Jones—Robeson and O'Neill on Film." *Connecticut Review* 7, no. 2 (April 1974): 94–99.

Lanchner, Carolyn. *Fernand Léger*. New York: Museum of Modern Art, 1998.

Lawder, Standish D. *The Cubist Cinema*. New York: New York University Press, 1975.

Léger, Fernand. "The Esthetics of the Machine: Manufactured Objects Artisan and Artist." *Little Review* 9, no. 3 (Spring and Summer 1923): 44–49; and 9, no. 4 (Autumn and Winter 1923–24): 55–58.

———. Notes on *Ballet mécanique*. *L'esprit nouveau* 28 (n.d. [most likely November or December 1924]).

———. "Film by Fernand Léger and Dudley Murphy, Musical Synchronism by George Antheil." *Little Review* (Autumn 1924–Winter 1925): 42–44.

Lehrman, Paul D. "Music for *Ballet mécanique*: 90s Technology Realizes a 20s Vision." In *Unseen Cinema: Early American Avant-Garde Film 1893–1941*, ed. Bruce Posner, 70–74. New York: Black Thistle Press/Anthology Film Archives, 2001.

Levy, Julien. *Memoir of an Art Gallery*. New York: G. P. Putnam's Sons, 1977.

Lewis, David Levering. *When Harlem Was in Vogue*. New York: Alfred A. Knopf, 1981; New York: Penguin Books, 1997.

Litwak, Leon F. *Trouble in Mind: Black Southerners in the Age of Jim Crow*. New York: Alfred A. Knopf, 1998.

Lottman, Herbert R. *Man Ray's Montparnasse*. New York: Harry N. Abrams, 2001.

Louchheim, Aline B. "New Design Proves Worth in Hotels." *New York Times,* June 11, 1950, sec. X, 3.

MacQueen, Scott. "Rise and Fall of *The Emperor Jones,* 1933." *American Cinematographer* 71, no. 2 (February 1990): 34–40.

Maltin, Leonard. "Soundies." *Film Fan Monthly* 142 (April 1973): 3–9.

Mann, William J. *Behind the Screen: How Gays and Lesbians Shaped Hollywood 1910–1969*. New York: Viking, 2001.

Man Ray. *Self Portrait*. Reprint. 1963; Boston: Little, Brown and Company, 1988.

McCoy, Esther. *Richard Neutra*. New York: George Braziller, 1960.

McGilligan, Patrick. *Fritz Lang: The Nature of the Beast*. New York: St. Martin's Press, 1997.

McWilliams, Carey. *Southern California Country: An Island on the Land*. American Folkways Series. New York: Duell, Sloan and Pearce, 1946.

Melly, George. "Black Divas." *Listener* 120, no. 3077 (August 25, 1988): 4–5.

Moritz, William. "Americans in Paris: Man Ray and Dudley Murphy." In *Lovers of Cinema: The First American Film Avant-Garde 1919–1945*, ed. Jan-Christopher Horak, 118–36. Wisconsin Studies in Film. Madison: University of Wisconsin Press, 1995.

———. "The Dream of Color Music, and Machines That Made It Possible." *Animation World* 2, no. 1 (April 1997): 1–5. Also at www.awn.com/mag/issue2.1/articles/moritz2.1.html.

———. "Visual Music and Film-as-an-Art before 1950." In *On the Edge of America: California Modernist Art, 1900–1950,* ed. Paul J. Karlstrom, 211–41. Berkeley: University of California Press in association with the Archives of American Art, Smithsonian Institution, and the Fine Arts Museums of San Francisco, 1996.

Musser, Charles. "Troubled Relations: Robeson, Eugene O'Neill, and Oscar Micheaux." In *Paul Robeson: Artist and Citizen,* ed. Jeffrey C. Stewart, 81–103. New Brunswick, NJ: Rutgers University Press, 1998.

Myrent, Glenn, and Georges P. Langlois. *Henry Langlois, First Citizen of Cinema.* New York: Twayne, 1995.

Navarrete, Sylvia. *Miguel Covarrubias: Artista y explorador.* Coyoacán, Mexico: Consejo Nacional para la Cultura y las Artes, 1993.

"Neutra Designs a Small, Simple, but Deluxe Hotel with a Grandstand View of Ocean Beach." *Architectural Forum,* July 1949, 104–5.

O'Leary, Liam. *Rex Ingram: Master of the Silent Cinema,* new ed. Pordenone, Italy: Le Giornate del Cinema Muto and the British Film Institute, 1993.

O'Neill, Eugene. *Complete Plays 1913–1920.* New York: Library of America, 1988.

———. *The Emperor Jones: "Anna Christie": The Hairy Ape.* New York: Vintage International Books, 1995.

Ott, John. "Landscapes of Consumption: Auto Tourism and Visual Culture in California, 1920–1940." In *Reading California: Art, Image, and Identity, 1900–2000,* ed. Stephanie Barron, Sheri Bernstein, and Ilene Susan Fort, 51–67. Berkeley: University of California Press, 2000.

Owen, Derek. "1194 Dudley Murphy." *Film Dope* 46 (March 1991): 18–19.

Posner, Bruce, ed. *Unseen Cinema: Early American Avant-Garde Film 1893–1941.* New York: Anthology Film Archives, 2001.

Potamkin, Harry Alan. "The Aframerican Cinema." In *The Compound Cinema: The Film Writings of Harry Alan Potamkin.* Edited by Lewis Jacobs. New York: Teachers College Press, Columbia University, 1977.

Pound, Ezra. "Paris Letter." *Dial* 74 (March 1923): 273–75.

Pratt, George C. *Spellbound in Darkness: A History of the Silent Film.* Greenwich, CT: New York Graphic Society, 1966.

Pryor, Thomas M. "Hands across the Border." *New York Times,* November 21, 1943, sec. X, 3.

Ramírez, Gabriel. *Norman Foster y los otros directores Norteamericanos en México.* Mexico City: Universidad Nacional Autónoma de México, 1992.

Rand, Ayn. *Journals of Ayn Rand.* Edited by David Harriman. New York: Penguin Putnam, 1997.

Regester, Charlene B. *Black Entertainers in African American Newspaper Articles.* Jefferson, NC: McFarland and Company, 2002.

Rosenbaum, Jonathan. "Short Films: *Black and Tan.*" *Monthly Film Bulletin* 43, no. 510 (July 1976): 158.

Saroyan, William. "Take Her to Vegas." *Saturday Evening Post,* September 23, 1961, 48–53.

Saxena, Jennie. "Preserving African-American Cinema: The Case of *The Emperor Jones* (1933)." With contributions by Ken Weissman and James Cozart. *Moving Image* (Spring 2003): 42–58.

Schaefer, Eric. *"Bold! Daring! Shocking! True!" A History of Exploitation Films, 1919–1959.* Durham, NC: Duke University Press, 1999.

Schatz, Thomas. *The Genius of the System: Hollywood Filmmaking in the Studio Era.* Reprint. 1989; Henry Holt and Company Metro Paperbacks, 1996.

Selznick, David O. *Memo from David O. Selznick.* Edited by Rudy Behlmer. Modern Library: The Movies Series, ed. Martin Scorsese. New York: Modern Library, 2000.

Seton, Marie. *Sergei M. Eisenstein.* Rev. ed. London: Dennis Dobson, 1978.

Shack, William A. *Harlem in Montmartre: A Paris Jazz Story between the Great Wars.* Berkeley: University of California Press, 2001.

Sheehan, Perley Poore. *Hollywood as a World Center.* Hollywood, CA: Hollywood Citizen Press, 1924.

Shi, David E. "Transatlantic Visions: The Impact of the American Cinema upon the French Avant-Garde, 1918–1924." *Journal of Popular Culture* 14, no. 4 (Spring 1981): 583–96.

Sims, Patterson. *Whitney Museum of American Art: Selected Works from the Permanent Collection.* New York: Whitney Museum of American Art in association with W. W. Norton, 1985.

Sitney, P. Adams. *Visionary Film: The American Avant-Garde.* New York: Oxford University Press, 1979.

Smeaton, Suzanne. "American Picture Frames of the Arts and Crafts Period, 1870–1920." *Magazine Antiques* 136 (November 1989): 1124–37.

Spergel, Mark. *Reinventing Reality: The Art and Life of Rouben Mamoulian.* Metuchen, NJ: Scarecrow Press, 1993.

Starr, Kevin. "Carey McWilliams's California: The Light and the Dark." In *Reading California: Art, Image, and Identity, 1900–2000,* ed. Stephanie Barron, Sheri Bernstein, and Ilene Susan Fort, 13–29. Berkeley: Los Angeles County Museum of Art and University of California Press, 2000.

———. "Los Angeles 1900–1930: The Great Gatsby of American Cities." In Sarah Vure, *Circles of Influence: Impressionism to Modernism in Southern California Art 1910–1930,* 9–24. Newport Beach, CA: Orange County Museum of Art, 2000.

———. *Material Dreams: Southern California through the 1920s.* New York: Oxford University Press, 1990.

Sternberg, Josef von. *Fun in a Chinese Laundry.* San Francisco: Mercury House, 1965.

Stewart, Jeffrey C., ed. *Paul Robeson: Artist and Citizen.* New Brunswick, NJ: Rutgers University Press, 1998.

Stock, Noel. *The Life of Ezra Pound.* Expanded ed. San Francisco: North Point Press, 1982.

Stovall, Tyler. *Paris Noir: African Americans in the City of Light.* Boston: Houghton Mifflin Company, 1996.

Swanson, Gloria. *Swanson on Swanson.* New York: Random House, 1980.

Tate Gallery. *Pound's Artists: Ezra Pound and the Visual Arts in London, Paris, and Italy.* London: Tate Gallery, 1985.

Taves, Brian. "Robert Florey and the Hollywood Avant-Garde." In *Lovers of Cinema: The First American Film Avant-Garde 1919–1945,* ed. Jan-Christopher Horak, 94–117. Wisconsin Studies in Film. Madison: University of Wisconsin Press, 1995.

Tazelaar, Marguerite. "Film Personalities: The Man Who Will Make 'Emperor Jones' for the Screen." *New York Herald Tribune,* April 2, 1933, sec. X, 3.

Terenzio, Maurice, Scott MacGillivray, and Ted Okuda. *The Soundies Distributing Corporation of America: A History and Filmography of Their "Jukebox" Musical Films of the 1940s.* Jefferson, NC: McFarland and Company, 1991.

Tolnay, Stewart E., and E. M. Beck. *A Festival of Violence: An Analysis of Southern Lynchings, 1882–1930.* Urbana: University of Illinois Press, 1995.

Torrence, Bruce T. *Hollywood: The First Hundred Years.* New York: New York Zoetrope, 1982.

Variety Obituaries, 1975–1979. Vol. 8. New York: Garland Publishing, 1988.

Vieira, Mark A. *Sin in Soft Focus: Pre-Code Hollywood.* New York: Harry N. Abrams, 1999.

Vure, Sarah. *Circles of Influence: Impressionism to Modernism in Southern California Art 1910–1930.* Newport Beach, CA: Orange County Museum of Art, 2000.

Weisberg, Gabriel P., and Jane R. Becker. *Overcoming All Obstacles: The Women of the Académie Julian.* New York and New Brunswick: Dahesh Museum and Rutgers University Press, 1999.

Weiss, Andrea. *Paris Was a Woman: Portraits from the Left Bank.* London: Harper-Collins Publishers, 1995.

Wetzsteon, Ross. *Republic of Dreams: Greenwich Village: The American Bohemia, 1910–1960.* New York: Simon and Schuster, 2002.

Whitesitt, Linda. *The Life and Music of George Antheil 1900–1959.* Studies in Musicology no. 70. Ann Arbor, MI: UMI Research Press, 1981.

Young, Stark. "The Color Organ." *Theatre Arts Magazine* 6 (January 1922): 20–32.

Zilczer, Judith. "Music for the Eyes: Abstract Painting and Light in Art." In *Visual Music: Synesthesia in Art and Music since 1900,* ed. Kerry Brougher et al., 24–85. New York: Thames and Hudson, 2005.

INTERNET RESOURCES

American Film Institute Catalog Online. www.afi.chadwyck.com.

Center for the Advancement of Objectivism. www.aynrand.org.

Haïti progrès. www.haitiprogres.com.

National Film Preservation Foundation. www.filmpreservation.org.

Oklahoma Historical Society Honeysprings Battlefield Site: The Battle of Honey Springs, Indian Territory. http://checotah.lakewebs.net/honeysprings/LHF-bhs.htm.

The Vitaphone Project. www.vitaphoneproject.com.

INDEX

Waller, Fats, xii, 101, 115, 169
Walpole, Hugh, 160
Wanger, Walter, 100, 102, 103, 109, 132, 211n.2
Ward, Lester, 7
Warner, Harry, 109, 160, 161
Warner, Jack, 10
Warner Bros., 82, 83, 84, 109, 158, 159, 160, 164
wartime support, 167–68
Washington, Fredi, 93, 94, 112, 139, 141
Washington, Isabel, 89
Watts, Richard, Jr., 60, 91
Way of Love, The. See Japanese film
Welles, Orson, 175
Wendt, Julia Bracken, 7
West Coast Murphys, 5
Western Electric, 85, 132
What a Widow!, 75
Whistler, James McNeill, 3
White, Alice, 159
White, Pearl, 46
White, Walter, 87, 147
Whitney, Cornelius Vanderbilt, 185

Whitney, James, 51, 65
Whitney, Jock, 115
Whytock, Grant, 70, 138, 218n.48
Wilfred, Thomas, 34, 198n.73
Wilkins, Roy, 147
Wilshire, Gaylord, 11, 20
Wilshire, Mary, 11, 13, 20
Wilson, Frank, 141, 144
Winchell, Walter, 102
Wolcott, Alexander, 86
Woodard, Gordon Keith, 168
Works Project Administration (WPA), 161–62
Wright, Frank Lloyd, 10
Wright, Lloyd, 10, 12, 193n.26
Wright, Virginia, 179–80, 225n.32

Yates, Herbert, 164
Yes, Indeed!, 170
Yolanda, 175–77; press response, 177

Zanuck, Darryl F., 106, 109
Zeitlin, Jake, 12, 117, 182, 193n.26
Zukor, Adolph, 76, 129

Susan Delson is a writer and film historian living in New York City. She is working on a book about the 1940s music films known as soundies.